Time

A Philosophical
Introduction

ALSO AVAILABLE FROM BLOOMSBURY

Time

A Philosophical Introduction

James Harrington

Bloomsbury Academic
An imprint of Bloomsbury Publishing Plc

B L O O M S B U R Y
LONDON · NEW DELHI · NEW YORK · SYDNEY

Bloomsbury Academic

An imprint of Bloomsbury Publishing Plc

50 Bedford Square	1385 Broadway
London	New York
WC1B 3DP	NY 10018
UK	USA

www.bloomsbury.com

BLOOMSBURY and the Diana logo are trademarks of Bloomsbury Publishing Plc

First published 2015

British Library Cataloguing-in-Publication Data
A catalogue record for this book is available from the British Library.

ISBN: PB: 978-1-4725-0647-4
HB: 978-1-4725-0557-6
ePDF: 978-1-4725-1337-3
ePub: 978-1-4725-0864-5

Library of Congress Cataloging-in-Publication Data
Harrington, James (Senior Lecturer in Philosophy)
Time: a philosophical introduction/James Harrington. – 1st [edition].
pages cm
Includes bibliographical references and index.
ISBN 978-1-4725-0647-4 (pb) – ISBN 978-1-4725-0557-6 (hb) – ISBN 978-1-4725-0864-5
(epub) – ISBN 978-1-4725-1337-3 (epdf) 1. Time. 2. Ontology. I. Title.
BD638.H2765 2015 115–dc23
2015010320

Typeset by Deanta Global Publishing Services, Chennai, India
Printed and bound in Great Britain

Contents

List of Figures

List of Historical-Biographical Notes

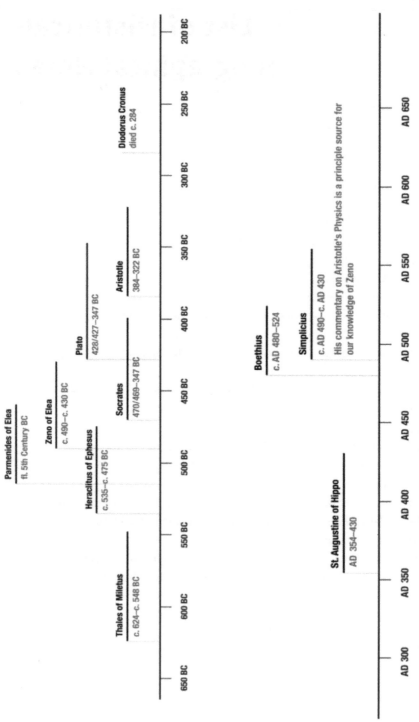

Figure 1 Classical Greek, Hellenistic, and Early Medieval philosophy of time.

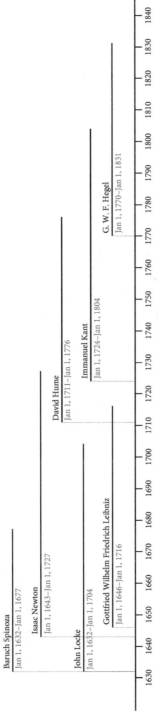

Figure 2 Selected figures in seventeenth- and eighteenth-century philosophy of time.

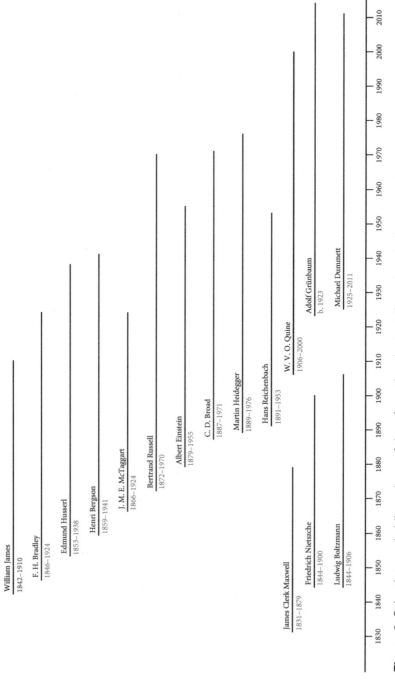

Figure 3 Scientists and philosophers of time from the nineteenth century to the present.

List of Technical Asides

Acknowledgments

A large number of friends, colleagues, and students contributed to this project. I would like to especially thank my family and all of the friends who encouraged me when the energy lagged. My colleagues at Loyola, especially Paul Moser and Mark Waymack, my two department chairs, make it a wonderful place to teach and do philosophy. Mark Waymack also helped arrange funding for a professional index. Many students have been subjected to various versions of this material, but I would like to especially thank the students who took Issues in Metaphysics, a course I taught in Spring 2014 and Spring 2015, in which most of this material was first "tried out." Several anonymous reviewers made extremely valuable contributions; I would like to especially thank the reader who caught and helped to repair some serious problems in Chapter 2 late in the production process. My editor at Bloomsbury, Colleen Coalter, encouraged the original proposal and has shepherded the project throughout. Abdus Salam's patient copyediting has made this a much better book than it would have been otherwise, while Anita Singh of Deanta Global patiently managed the production process for Bloomsbury. Finally, this book is dedicated to my parents without whose constant support it would never have existed.

All line drawings were prepared using iDraw for the Mac, except the timelines which were prepared in Beedocs Timeline 3D.

How to read this book

The book is intended to be accessible to the interested reader with no philosophical or scientific background, but it does presuppose a willingness to work though some quite difficult material. While every author hopes that their book will be popular, this is not a popularizing book. A careful reader of the book, even one with no prior background, will be prepared to dip into the specialist literature on all of these topics by the time they're finished.

All chapters are designed with the beginning reader in mind and try not to presuppose any particular philosophical, mathematical, or scientific background. However, some readers are likely to find the language and the proposed frameworks of various chapters more familiar than others. Readers whose background and interests are more philosophically oriented may want to begin with the discussion of various classical metaphysical problems of time in Chapters 2–5. Except for the Technical Interlude in Chapter 2 and a brief digression on non-standard systems of logic in Chapter 4, these chapters are organized around standard philosophical problems and figures likely to be familiar to anyone with an exposure to the history of philosophy.

Chapters 6–9, however, all involve debates and problems in contemporary physics—especially relativity theory, thermodynamics, and cosmology. Readers comfortable with contemporary physics might choose to begin with the second half of the book and later revisit the early chapters to place those issues into a broader philosophical context. Such readers are strongly encouraged to at least skim the early sections of Chapters 2 and 3 where some important terminology and concepts are introduced that are appealed to in the later chapters.

A note on some of the special features of the book. In addition to the usual selection of discussion questions and suggested reading, there are other distinctive features to the book. The four technical interludes, in Chapters 2, 3, 6, and 9, can all be skipped on a first reading. The basic philosophical morals of those chapters don't depend on them, although they are necessary to see why those morals hold. In addition, the Technical Interludes in Chapters 2, 6, and 9 do depend on each other to construct a general, if somewhat incomplete, account of the mathematical representation of time in physics. There are also two different collections of boxed material. The Historical Notes both provide useful historical background to the individual debates and can be assembled into a general account of the history of the philosophy of time. The Technical Asides are just that, interesting bits that some readers might find intriguing. Finally, the study exercises after Chapters 2, 4, and 5 are simply thought-provoking, related puzzles somewhat outside the general scope of the book.

1

Introduction:
Being and Becoming

What defines the philosophy of time? Two central problems—one ancient and one modern. The ancient problem is the tension between being and becoming. Is *being*—existence—the fundamental truth of the universe? Or is it more accurate to say that the universe *happens*, continuously renewing itself? Both positions have problematic consequences. The modern problem is the apparent lack of coherence between contemporary physics, particularly Einstein's theory of relativity, and our conception of a universe evolving in time.

At first appearance, it might seem odd that there could be a philosophy of time. Time, the becoming of the world, seems to be either too basic or too mysterious to pose the kinds of puzzles that concern philosophers. We all know the feeling of the opportunity missed, running away from us into the past—of that perfect sunrise over a shore made more perfect precisely because it is so fleeting. We know in our bones that nothing lasts—that everything in the future, whether the dreaded exam or the anticipated birth of our child, will be then and gone from us forever. That our past, whether a first love or first death, runs away from us into the past, captured only in our fading memories.

Now stop for a moment and notice two puzzles. First, who is this "I" that mourned, that writes, that waits? Not everything seems to be in flux; there is a fixed point from which this flux appears or to whom it happens. Second, whence are these past and future people and things? On the one hand, my grandparents are no more; on the other hand, they seem just as real as they ever did. By this I don't mean anything metaphorical or spiritual, merely that my memories and beliefs about them are just as true or false as they ever were. I know that my grandfathers both worked for the US Post Office, and that one grandmother was a social worker. Since these are true, there must be some facts that make them true. Unfortunately, none of these people any longer exist in a way relevant to their employment, so that no facts about the present seem to be sufficient to make these beliefs true.

This is the first fundamental mystery about time. Any attempt to describe becoming seems to presuppose its opposite—something that simply is rather than becomes. Any description of the fleeting nature of existence seems to demand a perspective outside of the flow; any attempt to describe the rushing away of the past seems to presuppose that the past is in some sense real enough to make true statements about.

In fact there is a plausible version of the history of philosophy in which this is the fundamental philosophical mystery—the one from which all philosophy begins. Our story begins with two pre-Socratic philosophers from the fifth century BC, Parmenides and Heraclitus.[1] Both of them seem to have recognized how basic the experience of becoming is to our human experience of the world and how apparently paradoxical it also is. In the face of this mess both of them seem to have thrown up their hands in disgust. Parmenides seems to have decided that if our human representation of the world as becoming is self-contradictory, then so much the worse for becoming. Heraclitus, about whom we know less than Parmenides, seems to have decided that if talking about becoming generates contradictions, then so much the worse for talking; becoming is real nonetheless! Here we already have the fundamental tension between philosophies of being and the philosophy of becoming.

The philosophy of being

Come now, I will tell thee—and do thou hearken to my saying and carry it away—the only two ways of search that can be thought of. The first, namely, that It is, and that it is impossible for anything not to be, is the way of conviction,

for truth is its companion. The other, namely, that It is not, and that something must needs not be,—that, I tell thee, is a wholly untrustworthy path. For you cannot know what is not—that is impossible—nor utter it.

Parmenides of Elea, fifth century BC

Space, time, extension, and motion are not things but well-founded modes of our consideration.

Extension, motion, and bodies themselves, insofar as they consist in extension and motion alone, are not substances but true phenomena, like rainbows and sun dogs.

Gottfried Wilhelm Leibniz, 1646–1715

Parmenides and Heraclitus represent the extreme versions of positions that we will encounter in many different forms. We know Parmenides of Elea primarily as the author of a difficult metaphysical poem in which he seems to argue that all change and becoming is fundamentally illusory. Parmenides claims that nothing ever either comes into existence or passes out of existence because the conception of such becoming is self-contradictory.

Historical Note 1: Parmenides of Elea

Parmenides of Elea (fl. fifth century BC) formulates a radical perspective on reality—only the entire world, conceived of as a single permanent substance. Parmenides is known to us both through the remaining fragment of a poem defending radical metaphysical monism and through his portrayal in Plato's dialogues, especially *Parmenides*. Parmenides's core doctrine seems to have been "metaphysical monism" linked with an associated idealism about the ordinary world. As a monist, Parmenides taught that reality consists of a single, eternal, unchanging substance. Accordingly, the ordinary world, which appears to consist of a multiplicity of distinct things interacting with each other and changing, must actually be mere appearance. As such, ordinary middle-sized dry goods are ideas or appearances within our minds with no corresponding objects.

Parmenides believed that he discovered this and demonstrated it to others by revealing the self-contradictory nature of appearance. For example, change seems to require that something both be the same thing and not the same thing. Parmenides's use of such arguments means that he may well deserve to be considered the founder of metaphysics as a distinct discipline dedicated to discovering the fundamental nature of reality via pure intellect, rather than as an outcome of the combination of empirical investigation and rational theorizing characteristic of other early Greek philosopher-scientists. cf. Historical Note 4.

Parmenides reasons as follows. Suppose I claim that "John no longer exists." In order for the name "John" to be meaningful, it must refer to something. The thing I'm talking about must be real in order for me to talk about it; but then I'm saying that something that exists no longer exists. And, that seems incoherent. Parmenides concludes from this that reality must be single, unchanging, and hidden from us behind a veil of appearance.

Parmenides and his immediate followers, the Eleatic school, are the paradigmatic examples of philosophers of being. For the Eleatics, becoming is an illusion; things merely seem to change. Intuitively, there are three kinds of possible change:

1 Something that does not exist, begins to exist.
2 Something that does exist, ceases to exist.
3 The same thing either begins to possess features that it previously lacked, or loses features that it previously possessed.

According to Parmenides and his followers none of these three kinds of events can actually occur. Instead, they merely appear to us without actually occurring in the world. As odd as it might seem to claim that nothing ever changes, this Eleatic strand in the philosophy of being remains an important influence on various forms of philosophical idealism. Idealists about some aspect of reality claim that some apparent feature of the world is merely present in our consciousness of the world, not present in the world independently of our minds. Examples of Eleatic idealism include the monism of Baruch Spinoza, Gottfried Leibniz's monadology, Kant's "transcendental idealism," and the nineteenth-century absolute idealism of F.H. Bradley. Despite vast differences among them, all Eleatic idealists claim that the appearance of things in time is the product of our mental apparatus, that we experience things in time because we are, to use a contemporary metaphor, "hard-wired" to experience them in that way and no other. In addition, they all claim that to the extent that there is anything real beyond mere appearance it must be fundamentally atemporal. Finally, all of these philosophical projects take as their fundamental task the identification of the permanent reality hidden from us by transitory illusions.

There is a more moderate version of the philosophy of being. According to the Platonic reductive versions of the philosophy of being, the ordinary transitory world of becoming is not illusory, but merely of secondary reality and importance. The ancient Greek philosopher Plato (429–347 BC) introduced a metaphysical picture according to which individual objects in the world are products of another eternal and unchanging world of forms.

In general, the Platonic tradition presents the ordinary world of becoming as the product of the activity of a more basic atemporal reality. As with the Eleatic strand, the primary task of philosophy is to identify this more basic reality. This philosophy of being, grounded in the impulse to discount transitory experience, has two sources.

One of them is straightforward; becoming and change are notorious sources of paradox. The most famous of these are the ancient paradoxes of Zeno, a direct disciple of Parmenides, and the modern paradox proposed by J. M. E. McTaggart. In Chapters 2 and 3 respectively, we will examine these in detail, but a taste will help us get started. One of Zeno's paradoxes, called "the dichotomy," attempts to prove that motion is impossible by proving that it takes, or should take, an infinite time to run any finite distance. Loosely speaking,[2] in order to move one mile, I must first move to the halfway point which will take some finite time. However, before I can do that I must move halfway to the half-mile point, to the quarter-mile point. But, that also takes some finite time. I can keep dividing the distance infinitely many times, and I therefore have to carry out an infinite number of tasks, each of which takes a finite amount of time before I can get to the end of the original track. But, adding an infinitely long sequence of finite values would seem destined to give an infinite value.

Something has apparently gone wrong; how to respond to this puzzle? The Eleatic idealists take this, and similar arguments, as fundamental evidence that becoming and temporality are not an aspect of fundamental reality. At best my experience of the runner on the track must be a confused representation of some unchanging underlying reality. The Platonic reductionists instead explain the paradox as the result of the failure to describe the underlying reality of the racetrack in the proper mathematical terms. Once we adopt the proper mathematical representation, we discover that not every sum of an infinite number of finite terms is infinite. Infinite sums, and other infinities, have very odd properties which mathematicians and philosophers only really started to understand in the nineteenth century as they developed tools that allowed them to abstract from the concrete processes in time.

This illustrates the classic Platonic reductive move. When paradox appears, assume that the apparently paradoxical phenomena must be the product of some intrinsically comprehensible underlying reality. In this case, many philosophers, including some who would not describe themselves as Platonists, treat becoming as produced from a sequence of more ontologically basic states of being. This broad relationship indicates one of the deep, if often implicit, sources for the philosophy of being as anchored in the meaning of philosophical and scientific understanding. To understand some occurrence is to grasp the conditions that produce that occurrence and no other. Those conditions must be, in some sense, more permanent or more real than the occurrence to be explained. Otherwise I don't seem to have made any progress; I might have shifted the discussion to a new topic, but the demand for understanding remains. Thus, the very possibility of a scientific or philosophical understanding of the world seems to drive us toward a metaphysics of being that treats becoming either as a problem to be solved or as an illusion to be overcome.

The philosophy of becoming

We step and do not step in to the same rivers; we are and are not.
Heraclitus, fifth century BC

But though, by straining itself to the point of giddiness, it may end by giving itself the illusion of mobility, its operation has not advanced it a step, since it remains as far as ever from its goal. In order to advance with the moving reality, you must replace yourself within it. Install yourself within change, and you will grasp at once both change itself and the successive state in which it might at any instant be immobilized.
Henri Bergson, *Creative Evolution*, 1911

There is a third option, beyond idealism and reductionism, call it *Heraclitean* realism. Heraclitus, a near contemporary of Parmenides, seems to be the father of this attitude toward becoming. The Heraclitean philosophers of becoming believe that the paradox arises not in becoming itself, but in the attempt to grasp becoming in language. Unlike Parmenides, all we have of Heraclitus's own words are a few brief and enigmatic sayings. We also have various reports from his opponents; for example, Plato reports in his dialogue *Theaetetus* that Heraclitus's followers so distrust language that they communicate only in grunts and nonsense syllables. However, all of the sources seem to agree that Heraclitus endorsed a doctrine of radical flux. For Heraclitus, everything is radically new and different at every moment, including the self. From this we can see why the Heracliteans might have been suspicious of language. Language and the possibility of communication rests essentially on the *permanence* of meaning, and thus for Heraclitus it cannot help but misrepresent a world without permanence.

Historical Note 2: Heraclitus of Ephesus

Heraclitus flourished at Ephesus in Asia Minor, modern Turkey, around the late sixth century BC. Heraclitus seems to have concluded that there is no material principle of identity; there is only flux and becoming. He does recognize a *logos,* a word or principle, governing such transformations. However, there is substantial interpretive controversy over the nature of this *logos.* Some fragments seem to indicate that the *logos* should be treated as a metaphysical principle, something like what we would call a law of nature. Other fragments lend themselves to an interpretation according to which the *logos* is merely a word in the literal sense; we apply words and names to the world and fool ourselves into thinking that there is permanence there.

Because of this emphasis on flux, Heraclitus comes to represent the fundamental opposition to any metaphysical system founded on a commitment to stable existence and the identification of a fundamental reality.

On the one hand, this seems to commit philosophers of becoming to a kind of *mysterianism* about the universe. If the nature of explanation requires that I understand some phenomenon in terms of some other more basic and permanent fact, then a world in which flux is basic cannot be understood. If the nature of systems of representation and communication require that we grab snapshots of the universe and abandon becoming in favor of false being, then I seem to be incapable of even describing the experience of becoming to others. It seems as though the only thing that a philosopher of becoming can accomplish is to cultivate the intuition of becoming in their audience through a kind of *via negativa.* In theology, the *via negativa,* or negative theology, is the attempt to wean a student from reliance on theology by demonstrating to them how inadequate every attempt to describe or understand God is doomed to be. Philosophers of becoming demonstrate how every attempt to explain the world in philosophical or scientific theorizing fundamentally must do so by ignoring certain crucial facts of becoming.

However, things are not quite so bad as to reduce us to Heraclitean silence. Many philosophers have suggested that history, the historical sciences like biology, and even literature provide us with models of understanding that deal with novelty and complexity in more respectful ways than idealism or reductionism. In history, it often seems to be the case that every account of an event is merely a perspective on the event; that human events fundamentally outrun every attempt to explain them. Hegel and his idealist successors often seem to be suggesting that there are things in the human social world that flow from a source of creative productivity that we can at best appreciate but not understand. In the nineteenth century, Darwin's theory of evolution inspired philosophers such as Henri Bergson to invoke a creative impulse within the universe that throws up new forms and new species beyond the social world. In twentieth-century physics, the discovery of radical randomness in the quantum theory of radioactive decay seemed to point us toward a universe doomed to permanently outrun our ability to reduce events to their causes and understand them in terms of it. The modern philosophers of becoming may not be advocating Heraclitean silence, but they do at least seek to remind us that a universe constantly creating itself anew out of creative flux dooms us to a permanent game of catch-up.

Einstein, time, and the fourth dimension

Henceforth space by itself, and time by itself, are doomed to fade away into mere shadows, and only a kind of union of the two will preserve an independent reality.

Hermann Minkowski, 1909

I conclude that the problem of the reality and the determinateness of future events is now solved. Moreover, it is solved by physics and not by philosophy.... Indeed, I do not believe that there are any longer any philosophical problems about Time; there is only the physical problem of determining the exact physical geometry of the four-dimensional continuum that we inhabit.

Hilary Putnam, 1967

Unfortunately for the philosophy of becoming, the history of twentieth-century physics mostly points toward the triumph of being.[3] The relativistic revolution in physics that opened with Albert Einstein's introduction of special relativity in 1905 has had consequences in philosophy that are still being worked through. Since his special theory and his general theory of relativity, the second of which was proposed in 1915, are theories of the structure of space-time, many of those consequences should inform the philosophy of time.[4] And, we will examine many of those in the second half of this book. Here, I draw your attention to just one of them—according to relativity, time can no longer be universal.

Prior to Einstein, there was a general agreement that "becoming," whether it was to be embraced, eliminated, or ignored, was a universal phenomenon in at least three senses. On the traditional views, time must be

1 universally ordered.
2 universally paced.
3 universally directed.

First, time was taken to be universally ordered in that for any two events no matter where they were located, either those events occurred at the same time or one of them was earlier than the other. Those relationships between the events were an objective fact about those events independent of any other facts about the universe. Secondly, time was taken to be universally paced in that it passed at the same rate for every entity in the universe. For any two events, the elapsed duration between those events was a fact about those events. Thirdly, time was universally directed in that once an event happened, the same event could not either happen again or "un-happen."[5]

The time of modern physics is not universal in any of these senses. Einstein's derivation of the relativity of simultaneity demonstrates that the time order of spatially separated events depends on the relative speed of the observers. Second, time is not universally paced; there can be no single cosmic clock that determines the elapsed duration of any process. This is manifest in many features of the physical universe. According to special relativistic time dilation, moving clocks run slow and the elapsed duration of various processes depends on the relative speeds of the clocks used to measure that duration. In addition, general relativity demonstrates that powerful gravitational fields have the same effect. To an individual in orbit near a black hole, mere seconds will have passed while the sun grows old and dies.[6] Finally, general relativity provides many theoretically allowable systems that would make events seem to "un-happen" for particular things or people within the universe. Less tendentiously, general relativity seems to allow for the possibility that the same event could be both in the past and in the future for some particular observers within the universe. Whether these are space-times with large-scale violations of time order like those discovered by the mathematician Kurt Gödel or various local "causality violating devices," as

Historical Note 3: Albert Einstein

Albert Einstein (1879–1955), born in Germany to a well-off Jewish family and largely educated in Switzerland, is generally acclaimed as the most important physicist since Isaac Newton. In 1905 while working as a patent examiner in Switzerland, he published three revolutionary scientific papers. He used statistical techniques of the type pioneered by Maxwell and Boltzmann (cf. Historical Note 20) to explain Brownian motion, thus providing what is generally understood as the ultimate proof of the atomic nature of matter. He showed how to use the early quantum theory to resolve certain apparent inconsistencies in our understanding of the photoelectric effect. He is therefore taken to have shown that the energy carried by electromagnetic waves such as light must come in discrete particle-like packets now called photons. Finally, he revolutionized our physical understanding of space and time with the theory of relativity (see Chapter 6 ff.).

Then, in 1915, Einstein published his general theory of relativity in which he claims that the structure of space and time is not merely different from that of classical physics and common sense, but is also contingent and dependent on the distribution of matter in the universe. The attempt to identify the structure of space-time compatible with the distribution of matter in the actual universe led George Lemaître (1894–1966) and others to the big bang cosmology. This ultimately resulted in the modern discipline of physical cosmology (Chapter 8).

The general theory results in at least one further radical break with classical thought about time. Beginning with Kurt Gödel's (1906–1978) discovery, in 1949, of a consistent cosmological solution containing closed time-like curves, time travel becomes a matter of serious physical study. This is particularly the case, with the discovery beginning in the 1970s, of other solutions not so obviously inconsistent with the observed structure of our universe. See the second half of Chapter 9 for a more detailed discussion.

they're called, such as wormholes, the modern physics of space and time allows different mechanisms that can be plausibly construed as producing time travel. Whatever our ultimate metaphysical decision about such cases, they seem to demand a substantial revision in our very concepts of the past and the future.[7]

To the idealist or reductionist philosopher of being, the locality and relativity of time pose no particular philosophical challenges. These phenomena merely reinforce such philosophers' prior conviction that time is a manifestation of an atemporal structure of being, in this case the four-dimensional space-time of physics. However, it seems to strike a devastating blow against any metaphysical system that takes becoming as its basic principle. Consider, for example, the famous "twin paradox" of special relativity. Formally, there is nothing paradoxical about this phenomenon. According to special relativity, the elapsed time between events depends on the path taken by the clocks used to measure that elapsed time. Consider two identical twins. The astronaut-twin, Jill, travels round-trip to the sun's nearest stellar neighbor Alpha Centauri, while her twin, Kathy, waits for her at home on Earth. Assuming that Jill's average speed, as measured from Earth, is about 86.6 percent of the speed of light, Kathy will wait about 10.28 years to see her sister. However, relativistic time dilation implies that Jill would only wait about 5.14 years to see Kathy! If the becoming of the universe manifests itself in the evolving lives of the two twins, how is it possible that it does so in such radically different ways? How is it possible that two lives, originating literally at the same moment, can come to be temporally out of sync?

This is a profound challenge that philosophers of becoming have yet to entirely meet. However, it also poses a profound, if different, challenge to philosophers of being. The austere desert landscapes of Eleatic metaphysics might have a certain aesthetic appeal, but they are uncomfortable landscapes for human beings to actually occupy. Our experience of ourselves as agents—as beings who act so as to bring about our own futures—is absolutely central to our own self-awareness. If nothing ever happens, then it is difficult to see how human choices, human creativity, or human actions can ever bring anything about. If, as the Eleatics believe, my future was simply there waiting for me, how can it be the product of my choices and actions? While most of the rest of this book focuses on a series of particular puzzles and problems about time, this tension between the logical clarity of being and the more comfortable world of becoming unifies these various problems.

The structure of the book

While we will return to the general questions of being and becoming at moments throughout the book, we focus more closely on particular issues from here on out. Loosely speaking, the book can be divided into three sections on, respectively, the logic of time, the epistemology of time, and the physics and metaphysics of time. In Chapters 2 and 3, I defend standard resolutions of some of the most famous paradoxes raised by thinking about time. Chapter 2 presents Zeno's paradoxes of motion and defends the standard resolution in terms of modern mathematical theories of continuity and infinity. Chapter 3 presents McTaggart's paradox of tense and defends the analogy between spatial and temporal indexicals, for example, between "here" and "now."

The next three chapters, on the epistemology of time, focus on the relationship between our experiences and our knowledge of time. Chapter 4 focuses on our experience of ourselves as agents and whether that gives us good reasons to believe that the future is either unreal or undetermined. Chapter 5 focuses on what seems to be our most distinctive experience of time itself—the presentness of our experience and our experience of flow.

We will also discuss how to accommodate those experiences within the physical arguments in favor of the reality of the future. Finally, Chapter 6 explores the role of measurement and our experience of ordinary material objects in our knowledge of time, largely under the heading of the absolute versus relational debates about the nature of space, time, and space-time. These debates will also provide us with an opportunity to discuss special relativity in some detail.

The final three chapters focus on particular problems about the structure of time at the boundaries of philosophy and physics. We'll examine the problem(s) of the direction of time in Chapter 7. What facts about the universe or the arrangement of things in the universe determine which direction in time is the past and which is the future? Chapter 8 discusses the shape of time. These questions largely take two forms. First, we will explore the relationship between philosophical accounts of the beginning or ending of time and modern physical cosmology which claims that the universe originated in a "big bang" some thirteen to fourteen billion years ago. Second, we'll look at the claim that time might be cyclical, rather than linear. Could the universe, as whole, actually reset itself and repeat? Finally, the book concludes with a discussion of time travel. Can we return to the past? Could I build a machine that would allow me to go back and correct my mistakes? And we'll discover that there is a deep tension between what seem to be good philosophical reasons for thinking that this should be impossible and the fact that physicists seem to think that they can describe how to build such a device. Hopefully by this point, the reader won't be too surprised to leave the book with a better understanding of the problems, even though she might have less confidence in her answers.

Further reading

On the pre-Socratics:

Diels, H. and Kranz, W. (2004), *Die Fragmente der Vorsokratiker: griechisch und deutsch*, Hildesheim: Weidmann.

The standard collection of pre-Socratic fragments.

Curd, P. and McKirahan, R. D. (1996), *A Presocratics Reader*, Indianapolis, IN: Hackett Publishing Company.

A nice collection of English translations from DK.

Barnes, J. (1982), *The Presocratic Philosophers*, Routledge: The Arguments of the Philosophers; London: Kegan & Paul.

A very nice introduction to the pre-Socratics focused on the tension between being and becoming. There are many editions and translations of Plato's dialogues, including those available online. He discusses and criticizes the Heraclitean doctrine of flux in Theaetetus. *His account of the spatiotemporal world of becoming produced by the world of being is in his* Timaeus.

Other introductions to the philosophy of time:

Callender, C. and Edney, R. (2010), *Introducing Time*, London: Icon; Lanham, MD, USA: Totem Books; Distributed to the trade in the USA by National Book Network.

Dainton, B. (2001), *Time and Space*, Montreal: McGill-Queens University Press.

Dowden, B. (2009), *The Metaphysics of Time: A Dialogue*, Lanham: Rowman & Littlefield.

Le Poidevin, R. (2003), *Travels in Four Dimensions: The Enigmas of Space and Time*, Oxford, New York: Oxford University Press.

Some Useful Anthologies

Westphal, J. and Levenson, C. A. (1993), *Time*. Hackett Pub. Co., Indianapolis.

A collection of foundational texts in the philosophy of time from Plato through the mid-Twentieth century.

Le Poidevin, R. and MacBeath, M. (1993), *The Philosophy of time*. Oxford University Press, Oxford.

The standard collection of foundational contemporary texts.

Callender, C. (2011), *The Oxford Handbook of Philosophy of Time*. Oxford, New York: Oxford University Press.

A major collection of papers covering all significant aspects of and questions within the philosophy of time.

Oaklander, L. N. (2014), *Debates in the metaphysics of time*. London, New York: Bloomsbury.

A useful collection of newly commissioned papers on many areas of the philosophy of time.

Pop science books on time and modern physics:

Stephen Hawking's book *A Brief History of Time* published in 1988 triggered a cottage industry in books about time by physicists for a popular audience. Among the most interesting are:

Davies, P. (1995), *About Time: Einstein's Unfinished Revolution*, New York: Simon & Schuster.

Kaku, M. (1995), *Hyperspace: A Scientific Odyssey Through Parallel Universes, Time Warps, and the Tenth Dimension*, New York: Anchor Books.

Thorne, K. S. (1994), *Black Holes and Time Warps: Einstein's Outrageous Legacy*, New York: The Commonwealth Fund Book Program. W. W. Norton.

Penrose, R. (2007), *The Road to Reality: A Complete Guide to the Laws of the Universe*, New York: Vintage Books, 1st vintage books edition.

In this deeply challenging work, prominent mathematician and physicist Roger Penrose attempts to lay out all of the necessary mathematics necessary to explain real modern physics to a lay audience. He comes closer than any one had any right to expect. This is the place to turn for those who want to really understand the physics discussed in Chapters 6–9 without going back to school for several years.

Discussion questions

1 Explain why our ability to make statements about the past and the future creates a philosophical problem of time.

2 Explain the distinction between realist, idealist, and reductionist theories of time.
3 Can you explain two reasons for adopting a metaphysics of being? Of becoming?
4 In general terms, why does special relativity seem to undermine any metaphysics of becoming?

Notes

1. The pre-Socratics are the Greek philosophers before Socrates. Socrates created a break with previous Greek traditions by effectively criticizing his predecessors' focus on "big" metaphysical questions and their alleged neglect of more human-focused problems of ethics, morality, and social life.
2. See Chapter 2, p. 34 for a detailed discussion of the dichotomy and proposed solutions.
3. Unfortunately, it's hard to take much philosophical solace in quantum theory. Even those who developed it and turned it into one of the most phenomenally successful predictive tools in science didn't claim that they understood it. Except for a brief discussion of quantum gravity at the end of the book, we'll largely ignore it. See the Further Reading section for some starting points for the interpretive problems of quantum theory.
4. Roughly the special theory of relativity describes the space-time structure of the world as compatible with modern theories of electricity and magnetism, but only for worlds without gravity. General relativity provides a theory of gravity compatible with special relativity. See Chapter 6 for further discussion.
5. Here it's important to remember that "same" means numerically identical. What cannot happen, on common-sense accounts of time, is that I can go back and re-experience my arrival in France last May, even if I could experience another event as similar as you like to that previous arrival.
6. Technically any human being attempting that close an approach to a standard black hole would be torn apart by tidal forces, even in their own rest frame, before this could happen. As part of the derivation of the "twin paradox" in Chapter 6, we will explore rigorous treatments of the relativity of simultaneity and of time dilation.
7. We'll look at several of these in Chapter 9.

2

Zeno's Paradoxes and the Nature of Change

What is time and how is it related to change more generally? We begin with an explanation of the difficulty of the question and five suggested starting points for thinking about it, along with a brief history of the problem of change in ancient Greek philosophy. We move on to Zeno's four paradoxes and his attempt to demonstrate that change is impossible. We consider the traditional responses, before introducing modern mathematics and its application to Zeno's paradoxes. We conclude with some reasons to be skeptical of the mathematical resolution, and consider some remaining questions.

Introduction: What is time?

So what is becoming? What would it be for the world to become in time and how would that be different from a world of pure Eleatic being? Unfortunately, we have no good definition of time; probably because we are too close to it. Good philosophical definitions offer necessary and sufficient conditions for the application of the concept. Such definitions set up boxes into which we put only some of the things that we find in the world. What kinds of things don't go in the box marked "time?"

For example, a definition of dogs allows us to pick out all and only the dogs. Analogously, we might think of time, becoming in the language of the previous chapter, as something that happens to other things. The goal would be to explain what it is to become rather than not to do so. Unfortunately, the only reasonably plausible candidates for existing without being in time, for example God or abstract objects like numbers, pose massive philosophical problems in their own right. Alternatively, we might try to identify time as a distinct element of reality in its own right. This creates a similar problem; one wants to say what it is to be "time" rather than what? Any such definition will depend on a quite general metaphysical picture of reality and all of the philosophical work is being done by the general metaphysics. The ubiquitous and fundamental presence of time simply makes it hard to "pick out" from the general background. It seems to be worries like these that lead St. Augustine to lament in his *Confessions*

> What is this time? If no one asks me, I know; if I want to explain it to a questioner, I do not know.

Instead of a definition, what we will do is identify five basic phenomena or aspects of experience deeply associated with time. Each of these has been plausibly identified as the essential temporal phenomenon.

Material becoming Ordinary material change and motion.
The transient now or pure becoming That there is a fundamental distinction between the present and all other times, and that the content of the present is constantly changing.
The unreality of the future That unlike the present, and perhaps the past, the future does not exist and will be brought into existence.
The sense of flow That we can *feel* the ongoing flow of the present into the future, as opposed to merely having a succession of distinct experiences.
Physical time The fundamental parameter of science and the quantity measured by clocks.

The boundaries between these phenomena are a bit arbitrary, and as we might expect, one's attitude toward one of them is likely to shape one's attitude toward others. For example, certain theories of material change seem to depend on the reality of pure becoming. If a material object only undergoes change when a new fact about that object becomes present, then pure becoming present must be a real feature of the world. What each of these do have in common is the existence of distinct arguments against their reality or metaphysical significance. We will therefore consider the metaphysical significance of each of these phenomena separately.

We will begin with some of the oldest extant arguments against the reality of change and time: those attributed to Zeno of Elea, friend and student of Parmenides. As reported by Aristotle, Zeno presented four arguments intended to demonstrate that there is no logically coherent description of the motion of an object from one place to another. The soundness of these arguments, collectively referred to as Zeno's paradoxes, would seem to confirm the Eleatic belief that the world of ordinary changing material objects is an illusion.

In addition to their intrinsic historical and philosophical significance, Zeno's paradoxes illustrate two other important philosophical lessons. First, they illustrate the general role of paradox in philosophical reasoning. Second, they illustrate the way in which the resolution of philosophical puzzles can depend on an adequate appreciation of technical issues in other disciplines, in this case mathematics. As we will see, Zeno's arguments hinge on certain ideas about continuity and infinity. Resolving them will require us to learn at least a bit about the theory of these concepts in contemporary mathematics, which we will do on pp. 35–52. Before we can dive into Zeno's actual arguments, we need a better picture of the relationship between change and time as well as the evolution of those concepts in early Greek philosophy.

Time and change from Parmenides to Aristotle

The problem of change might be the founding problem of philosophy. We have little direct information about the deep origins of Greek philosophy, traditionally attributed to Thales (c. 620 BC–c. 546 BC). However, even he seems to have been concerned with the nature of change since he seems to have believed that the fundamental substance of water transforms itself into all of the other things which we see in the world.

As we saw in the introduction, this is really a version of a more general problem: how can something be both the same and different? To recap, in order for some *thing* to undergo change it must be the same *thing*, but change requires it to be different. Different from what? The obvious answer is that it is different from itself, but that's not even really grammatical let alone true.

Historical Note 4: Thales and Early Greek Natural Philosophy

Thales of Miletus, who seems to have flourished in the late seventh and early sixth century BC, is one of the Seven Sages of Ancient Greece and is traditionally considered the founder of philosophy. Thales is given this honor as the first person traditionally understood to have attempted to explain the entire world as the product of a single underlying principle. Thales seems to have suggested that everything in the world is the product of various transformations of water. Before dismissing Thales, remember that water is the only substance routinely available in all three states of matter—solid, liquid, and gas. By identifying the problem of change, Thales also seems to have set the agenda for his successors; what is going on with all of these things changing into other things around us, if they're not just water under different guises?

The fragmentary evidence available indicates that most of Thales successors in the Greek world remained focused on the identification of some fundamental principle of stability and change. This seems to have culminated in the four-element cosmology—earth, air, fire, and water—proposed by Empedocles (c. 490 BC–c. 430 BC) that became standard for more than 1,000 years. We can also reconstruct a progressive articulation of the distinction between material principles of constitution and formal principles of change culminating in the extreme positions of Heraclitus and Parmenides.

A difference seems as though it must always be a difference between two things, not one thing. The obvious solution here is that change occurs when the same thing has different properties *at different times*.

This seems to solve the problem. To claim that something is in Chicago but will be in Paris is clearly not as absurd as claiming that something is both in Chicago and in Paris. Not really though! What is the *it* that is moving around? And what are these times that seem to have the ability to overcome contradiction? Although our primary concern is obviously with the second question, we need to take a moment to look at the answers to the first question.

As we saw in the introduction, there are two extreme answers to the problem of identifying the "it" underlying change. The Eleatic response, following Parmenides, is that there is only one thing, the world itself, and it is always the same. Any appearance of change or movement among its parts is merely an illusion; everything is what it is and nothing else. Alternatively, the Heraclitean solution is to deny that there is any change because there is no underlying continuity. Each event occurs followed by other events, but without any continuity. They don't happen to anything; they simply happen. At best it might be possible to identify certain patterns, the *logos*, within the flux.[1]

There is an intermediate strategy. Beginning historically with the immediate response to Parmenides, philosophers attempt to identify some fixed background *substance* whose *nature* or *essence* does not change, but whose accidental properties can change. For example, on the classical four element theory, the fundamental properties of the elemental substances of earth, air, fire, and water do not change; there are changes merely to the proportions in which they are mixed in various regions of the world. This is not an entirely unfamiliar way of thinking; it's roughly the way we treat chemical elements in introductory chemistry. We have a collection of different kinds of stuff, many more than four of course, and some rules governing the proportions in which they can or cannot combine with each other.[2]

As Plato recognized, these kinds of material accounts of unity don't do a very good job explaining the most interesting cases, especially those of living things. Even if living organisms are mixtures of different substances, they are not merely *mixtures* of such substances. Their parts interact with each other and they interact with their environments according to functional principles that create a different kind of unity. Plato suggests that each distinctive thing in the world copies or manifests an Ideal Form to a greater or lesser extent. Each of the things in the world is like a bad photocopy of an ideal form that exists in a distinct abstract realm or heaven. This seems to be basically the point of his famous Allegory of the Cave. Those features that the things in the material world inherit from their Ideal Forms constitute a stable core of identity. It is precisely those other imperfections resulting from poor copying which change.

Plato's student, and later competitor, Aristotle offers a very similar, but more down to earth account. Metaphorically, we might think of Plato's Ideal Forms as molds or stamps imposed on the world from the outside. Aristotle's forms are more like seeds present within the world manifesting their essential properties by drawing the world into a particular state. These are merely metaphors and contentious ones at that, and any adequate treatment of the

Historical Note 5: Plato

Plato (428/427 BC–347 BC) is, with Aristotle, one of the two most significant philosophers of ancient Greece. Plato was a disciple of Socrates (470/469 BC–399 BC) although he was also profoundly influenced by Parmenides and the Eleatics. Plato was born to a wealthy and aristocratic family in Athens which allowed him to travel widely and dedicate himself to the composition of many philosophical dialogues. Most of Plato's public work seems to have survived although there are hints of esoteric doctrines only passed on orally within his school, the famous Academy.

Plato's principle literary form was the philosophical dialogue featuring fictional or fictionalized conversations about philosophical problems, often featuring characters named after real people in Plato's social milieu. Socrates is the central character in most, but not all, of Plato's work. One of the central interpretive puzzles in Platonic scholarship is identifying Plato's actual doctrine and distinguishing it from that of the characters in his dialogues. This is especially pressing given the role of Socrates both in the dialogues and in Plato's life.

Two of Plato's core doctrines are particularly important for later speculation regarding time. The doctrine of forms, most fully developed in *The Republic,* states that each thing in the world is merely a reflection or copy of a perfect version of itself that exists in some separate metaphysical realm (cf. Chapter 2). In his *Timaeus,* Plato explains the ordinary material world as the product of a god-like *demiurge* or craftsman constructing the world based on those models. There, the patterns of change characteristic of the passage of time for Plato are literally "the moving image of eternity" (cf. Chapter 6).

problem of substance and substantial form would take us far beyond both an introductory text and our concern with the problem of time. It does, however, provide enough background to see how from Parmenides to Aristotle and beyond the concrete problem of change evolves into the more abstract problem of time while never completely leaving its roots behind. That's what we will turn to now.

The passage of time is closely related to this problem of variation in unity. Time passes as the same candle becomes shorter; the same sand that was in the top of an hourglass is now in the bottom of the same hourglass, or the same sun appears at different locations in the sky over the course of the day or the year. However, time itself seems to be distinct from these particular concrete processes. If time were simply another way of describing the evolution of each of these processes, then each of them would seem to have their own time. This possibility is realized by Albert Einstein's theory of relativity in a sense to be explored in Chapter 6, but the occurrence of time dilation in special relativity does not inform the more common-sense conception of time at work here.

Instead, time seems to be something within which or relative to which these processes become. It is not merely that candle A burns and candle B burns; I can compare the rate at which they are consumed relative to certain amounts of time. There is one time that binds together the becoming of all of the material processes within the universe. Perhaps then there is a "master process" that generates the temporal structure of all of the subprocesses within the universe.

This is the suggestion pursued by Plato in his great cosmological dialogue *Timaeus*. According to Plato, the motions of the heavenly bodies, the sun, the moon, and the stars, are a "moving image of eternity." While not eternal in the sense of a pure Eleatic being or Platonic form, the heavenly bodies are locked into an eternal and mathematically precise pattern of motion. As such, for Plato, they serve both as the master clock and as the engine of becoming within the material world.

There are various reasons why this can't be right. The most obvious is that our conception of the actual motions of the heavenly bodies is radically different from Plato's. [See Chapter 6, pp. 154–159 for a description of how the modern worldview undermines the universal clock.] There are, also, philosophical reasons to believe that Plato still makes the connection between some particular processes and the passage of time too intimate. Imagine, for example, a world in which the progress of the heavenly bodies comes to a halt, but all the ordinary terrestrial processes of growth and change continue. We have no reason to believe that such a world simply steps outside of time.

Concerns such as these seem to be what drove Aristotle to describe time as the "measure or number of change" in Book IV, chapter 10 of his *Physics*. The precise details of Aristotle's theory are more than a bit contentious, but the general idea is clear enough and largely accepted by all succeeding Western philosophers. Just as geometry is the study of the abstract structure of space separately from the location of any particular objects and

Historical Note 6: Aristotle

Aristotle (384 BC–322 BC), himself a student of Plato, is Plato's only competitor for the title of the most influential philosopher of Greek antiquity. Aristotle was born in Stagira, in what was then Macedonia. His father was court physician to Philip of Macedon, and Aristotle himself was tutor to the young Alexander the Great. Aristotle was trained as a physician and did important empirical and theoretical work in biology. Aristotle's surviving writings touch on almost every major subject of intellectual endeavor. In logic, his theory of the syllogism provides the first systematic account of valid arguments. His theory of the four causes, perhaps better characterized as four modes of explanation, remains an important influence on modern debates about scientific method.

Like Plato, Aristotle teaches that things in the world become what they are *via* some more fundamental level of being. Unlike Plato, Aristotle teaches that the forms of things are immanent rather than transcendent. Aristotle sees the world as a collection of substances resulting from the immanent forms shaping unformed matter into structured active beings. It is precisely our ability to compare, order, and measure these processes of growth, decay, and change, along with motion in space, that makes time a meaningful category for Aristotle. For Aristotle, time conceived as "the measure or number of change" is a real, but not a fundamental, aspect of the world.

As such Aristotle can truthfully be described as the first "philosopher of time." Aristotle considers almost all of the important problems in the philosophy of time that do not depend critically on modern physics. He is our primary source for Zeno's paradoxes and articulates a subtle and underrated account of the difference between moments of time and intervals of time in response, as discussed in Chapter 2. He seems to have been the first thinker to clearly formulate the problem of future contingents and of logical fatalism (Chapter 4). In his *Physics,* he considers a version of the absolute versus relational debate (Chapter 6). In his work on astronomy, *On the Heavens,* he argues that the world cannot have a beginning, and in *Physics* again, he argues that every time must be preceded by more time, cf. Chapter 8.

arithmetic studies the structure of counting, there must be an abstract order "time" within which all processes of change and becoming are arranged. Once we accept that the temporal structure of change is at least conceptually distinct from all particular changes, we can really begin to engage all of the questions listed in the introduction to this chapter. How do the various locations within the structure depend on each other? Do certain locations within the structure confer a metaphysical distinction on the events that occupy that location? What is the structure of the structure; is it continuous or discrete?

The one thing that has only rarely been in question is that time is the structure of *change*, and that if change itself is illusory, we have no reason to believe in time either. Although this assumption has been challenged—see Chapter 6, pp. 159–162 for a brief discussion of Sidney Shoemaker's argument for time without change—it seems that if nothing in the world really changes, then nothing in the world is in time or possesses a temporal structure. It's this line of attack which is taken by Zeno of Elea.

Zeno's paradoxes: Ancient sources and modern formulations

Zeno of Elea appears as a character in Plato's *Parmenides*, as the author of a book defending his friend and mentor Parmenides. Unfortunately, Zeno's book, allegedly containing forty arguments designed to demonstrate that common-sense ideas of plurality, motion, and becoming are as problematic as the radical monism of the Eleatics, has not survived. Thus, our primary sources for Zeno's life and works are his opponent's reports. Our primary source for the arguments regarding motion is Aristotle's *Physics* and a commentary on it by Simplicius.

Although our lack of access to Zeno's original presentation creates some room for scholarly dispute about his intentions, the philosophical significance of his arguments is fairly clear. We saw earlier in this chapter that we can think of time as the structure of change; we can think of it as an ordered collection of temporal locations, analogous to the points on a line, at which changes can or do occur. This should immediately lead us to wonder about the structure of the structure. Is it smooth or continuous the way we normally think of an interval of space or a geometrical curve? Or is it discrete, like the sequence of integers or counting numbers?

Historical Note 7: Zeno of Elea

Parmenides's most direct influence on all future philosophy of time is through his most famous disciple, Zeno (c. 490 BC–c. 430 BC). Zeno's dates are a traditional reconstruction based on his apparent age difference with Socrates in Plato's *Parmenides,* one of our two most significant sources regarding him. Since many contemporaries understandably found Parmenides's monism implausible, *Parmenides* reports that Zeno composed a book with forty arguments attempting to demonstrate that alternative conceptions of the world involving change and multiplicity are equally so.

Although the actual work seems to have been in circulation well into Roman times, our only sources for its contents are the arguments regarding motion attributed to Zeno in Aristotle's *Physics* and a commentary on *Physics* by Simplicius (c. 490 AD–c. 560 AD).

Taken together, Zeno's arguments seem to show that neither of these can be correct. If his arguments were sound, then his arguments known as "the dichotomy" and "Achilles and the tortoise," jointly known as the paradoxes of divisibility, would demonstrate that any continuous process takes an infinite amount of time. On the other hand, "the arrow" and "the stadium," the paradoxes of velocity, seem to demonstrate that the concept of discontinuous change is equally paradoxical. Aristotle seems to think that all four of these arguments are trivial, in some cases foolish, sophisms. As we will see below, major philosophers of both Eleatic and Heraclitean bent have long been suspicious of the Aristotelian resolutions.

While acknowledging these alternative responses to Zeno, in the remainder of this chapter we are going to follow Bertrand Russell in treating the paradoxes as deep or difficult sophisms. Zeno's arguments are invalid, but they can be shown as such only when we apply a quite sophisticated contemporary mathematical theory of continuity and infinity. In the rest of this section, we familiarize ourselves with the classical form of the paradoxes and with Aristotle's classical responses. We then step away from the metaphysics of time, in order to examine some important results from modern mathematics regarding continuity, infinity, and the concept of a limit. We will then return to the problems posed by Zeno's paradoxes, and I will argue that, armed with these new results, none of the radical interpretations need be endorsed.

The paradoxes of divisibility: The dichotomy and "Achilles and the Tortoise"

The paradoxes of divisibility seem to demonstrate that there must be some lower limit on the duration of the stages of any process. According to Aristotle,

> The first [The Dichotomy] asserts the non-existence of motion on the ground that that which is in locomotion must arrive at the half-way stage before it arrives at the goal. This we have discussed above.

> The second is the so-called "Achilles," and it amounts to this, that in a race the quickest runner can never overtake the slowest, since the pursuer must first reach the point whence the pursued started, so that the slower must always hold a lead. (Aristotle, *Physics* 239b11 ff.).

Begin by considering the dichotomy. Why would the need to arrive at the halfway stage, or at the previous location of the lead runner in the Achilles, constitute grounds for the nonexistence of motion? Assume that both space and time are continuous. That means that for any two times, no matter how short the interval between them is, there is at least one time between them. Similarly for locations in space.

That means that in order to complete the race I must, as Aristotle attributes to Zeno, first run half of the race. However, in order to run half of the race, I must run a quarter of the race. This can be continued literally to infinity. For any proportion of the race, $1/n$, there is at least one shorter race that must be completed first. Therefore, completing any finite race requires one to first complete an infinite number of finitely long sub-races. It would therefore seem to require an infinitely long time to complete any race—which is absurd, so motion is impossible.

As Aristotle realized, the Achilles is really a version of the dichotomy with a moving finish line. It depends on precisely the same crucial assumption of infinite divisibility resulting from the continuity of space and time. In a modern version assume that I have to race Usain Bolt in the 100-meter dash. I would insist on at least a 25-meter head start. Obviously, by the time Bolt runs the first 25 meters of the course, I'll no longer just be standing there: I'll have run some distance, say 10 meters. By the time he runs those 10 meters, I will have run another 4 meters. Again, literally ad infinitum. No matter where he runs to, I will have already left there. Worse, the Achilles seems to generate an actual contradiction. Bolt gets to the end before me, in about ten seconds, compared to my twenty-five seconds. However, the previous arguments seem to prove that he does so without ever catching up to me. He therefore both does and does not pass me.

Aristotle believed that both of these puzzles are straightforward sophisms; they are merely instances of the fallacy of equivocation. According to Aristotle, there are two senses in which any magnitude can be infinite: they can be either (a) infinitely large or (b) infinitely divisible. Zeno's arguments demonstrate that the assumption that spatial and temporal intervals are continuous requires that the race be infinitely divisible. The runner must, in some sense, occupy an infinite number of distinct geometrical points in the course of the race. This leads to a paradox if Zeno can show that this requires either that the runner actually complete an infinite number of distinct tasks or complete an infinitely long race. According to Aristotle, this Zeno cannot do; the length of the racecourse is the sum of intervals making up the course not the points. Or, as Aristotle puts it, the points themselves are not constituent parts of the racecourse. This is most obvious when we remember that the geometrical points and instants, by definition, have zero length or duration. One cannot, therefore, construct any nonzero magnitude by collecting them; an infinite number of zero duration instants laid "end to end" so-to-speak is still a zero duration "interval."

Instead, Aristotle seems to suggest that we think of the instants as merely potential. There are an infinite number of places the runners could have stopped; an infinite number of shorter races contained within the larger race that they could have run. They do not, however, run any of these races. To say that the race is continuous is merely to claim that there are no limits on how finely it is possible to divide the race, not to complete the division into infinite races.

Aristotle resolves the paradox by insisting on a distinction between the actual finite duration intervals that constitute the time of the race and the merely potential infinity of moments related to the potentially infinite division of the interval. This solution remained standard until sometime in the nineteenth century. However, there always remained a subtext of discontent with the Aristotelian resolution, especially within the idealist tradition in philosophy. Most significantly, Aristotle's resolution of Zeno's paradoxes of divisibility as confusing actual and potential infinity seems to conflict with the concept of being at a place at a time. In order to complete the race there must be some time when I am at the halfway point of the race;

I complete the race by occupying all of the locations on the racecourse sequentially in time.

How can I sequentially occupy a series of places that only potentially exist? This is particularly puzzling since this form of an "at-at" theory of motion is central to Aristotle's own resolution of Zeno's "arrow" paradox to which we now turn.

The paradoxes of velocity: The arrow and the stadium

Aristotle also reports two arguments from Zeno that seem to be directed against the possibility of discrete time. As with the paradoxes of divisibility, the precise nature of Zeno's original intention is subject to debate. However, both of these arguments seem to imply that a conception of motion as a sequence of states at consecutive times leads to contradictory conclusions. These arguments are reported by Aristotle immediately following the previous two.

> The third is that already given above, to the effect that the flying arrow is at rest, which result follows from the assumption that time is composed of moments: if this assumption is not granted, the conclusion will not follow.

What Aristotle seems to be referring to here is the very beginning of book V, chapter 9:

> Zeno's reasoning, however, is fallacious, when he says that if everything when it occupies an equal space is at rest, and if that which is in locomotion is always in a now, the flying arrow is therefore motionless. This is false; for time is not composed of indivisible nows anymore than any other magnitude is composed of indivisibles.

Before we examine Aristotle's reasoning, we should try to make sense of what Zeno might have been after in this argument. One of the things that we seem to require from motion is that the arrow occupy each of the places between the bow and its target on the way to its target. In fact it must occupy each of those locations at or in some particular time. But to occupy a place at a time seems to be just what it means to be at rest in that place. We seem to have uncovered another contradiction in motion; motion is just rest!

Here's a slightly different interpretation of Zeno's argument that seems to lead to the same conclusion. It depends on a certain natural way of describing motion. When the arrow is shot, it arrives, sequentially, at each place along its path to the target. It occupies each of those places before moving on to the next one. In this description, the arrow seems to move through its path by being at rest at each place along its path, and this seems to be a contradiction. Something cannot move by being at rest.

Rejecting Zeno's conclusion seems to require one of two possible moves. Either the relationship between the path of the arrow and the motion of the arrow has been incorrectly described, or there is some other fact about the moving arrow that distinguishes it from the arrow at rest. The second solution, often called *impetus theories of motion* have been popular at some periods in history, but the dominant theories have been *at-at theories of motion*, according to which the arrow moves merely by occupying different places at different times; according to at-at theories there is no additional fact about the arrow, its state of motion, that exists over and above its path through space at various times.

Aristotle's response seems to be dependent on his discussion of motion and rest earlier in the same book of *Physics*. There he endorses a particular conception of the at-at theory. Aristotle enforces a crucial distinction between being in a particular place at a particular time such that "at any now it is always over against something" and being in that place over some time. Aristotle seems to want to distinguish two ways in which we might be tempted to describe motion. On one description, which Aristotle clearly thinks is mistaken, we think of motion through a point as a kind of three-stage process. The arrow moves by first, arriving at the location, being at that location for some possibly zero length of time, then leaving there to move to the next location. It should be clear why such a description seems to collapse motion into rest; it characterizes motion as a sequence of states of rest and builds in a kind of implicit "jerkiness."

Part of Aristotle's objection is that this treats moments of time and geometrical points in space as completely analogous to longer temporal intervals, or larger regions of space. Think of the arrow after it is at rest in the target; the time when it is at rest in the target has moments as boundaries, the moment when it arrives and when it is removed. However, at what moment does it arrive at each of the points between the bow and the target? The moment when it occupies each of those places is a boundary of various intervals, but those moments don't themselves *have* any boundaries. The arrow doesn't arrive there, be there, then leave there; instead arrival, presence, and departure collapse into a single action distinct from any of those states as they involve being at rest. In something closer to colloquial English than

Aristotle's terminology, the arrow is merely "passing through" each of the points.

Unfortunately, there are two serious problems with Aristotle's resolution of the arrow paradox. First, modern mathematical treatments of the continuum do treat intervals of time as collections of moments just as they treat lines in space as collections of points. This threatens the coherence of Aristotle's solution as follows. If every interval of time is merely a collection of moments of time, then being at a place over some interval of time is merely to be there at all of the moments that make up the interval. However, a set consisting of exactly one moment is still a set of moments making for an interval of zero length. Now Aristotle's attempt to distinguish being at a place over an interval and being there at a time seems to break down.

Thus, Aristotle's claim that there is a fundamental distinction between being at a place at a time and being at a place over some time seems incompatible with our ability to represent motion using modern calculus. As we will see in the next section, our ability to represent time using contemporary mathematics depends on our ability to place the moments of time in an interval into correspondence with the numbers in some interval of the real numbers. And, pretty much all of the physics that we know how to do depends on this correspondence.

Second, there also seems to be a deeper problem lurking in the arrow than Aristotle recognizes. If the state of an object is merely its location at each time, then there doesn't seem to be anything about the object at any time which could cause it to be at a different location at a later time. A snapshot of the arrow at any instant is indistinguishable from a snapshot of an unmoving arrow taken at the same instant. However, we will see that this very description of the arrow as moving by jumping from one place to another over a sequence of times commits us to the existence of a smallest indivisible time. There might be an idealized sense in which the resting and the flying arrow are indistinguishable at each truly duration-less moment. However, if time is continuous, then they can be distinguished during every interval around that moment, even an infinitesimally small one. We will revisit this point in the Technical Interlude.

In Chapter 2, p. 50 we will see in some detail how the contemporary solution works mathematically, but conceptually it relies on clarifying what we mean by motion. It's tempting to characterize motion by describing the object as being in a particular place and then later being in some other place. Instead, think of the arrow being in motion at some point along its trajectory because although it is at that place at some time, it is not at that place at *any other time*. This might seem odd; it seems to make the state of the arrow at a particular time depend on where it is not at other times. However, the theory of limits and derivatives sketched below will allow us to see how to relate the overall path of the arrow to its state of motion at each time in a way that seems to confirm the "at-at" theory of motion.

Zeno's fourth argument is, by far, the most obscure. Here's what Aristotle says:

> The fourth argument is that concerning equal bodies which move alongside equal bodies in the Stadium from opposite directions—the ones from the end of the stadium, the others from the middle—at equal speeds, in which he thinks it follows that half the time is equal to its double.

Aristotle seems to think that Zeno has in mind a situation somewhat like the depiction in Figure 2.1.

Obviously, the distance between the two moving objects changes by two spatial units for every tick of the clock, despite the fact that each of them moves relative to the stadium only one unit per tick. Aristotle seems to believe that this is at the heart of the stadium paradox. Consider object A. In Figure 2.1(a) it is four spaces from object B, but in Figure 2.1(b) it is adjacent. This despite moving only two spaces relative to the stadium markers 1–6. If it is moving at both one unit per tick and two units per tick, then the time it takes to cover two units is both double the time it takes to cover one unit and twice that.

As Aristotle points out, this is a trivial fallacy confusing relative and absolute motion:

> The fallacy consists in requiring that a body traveling at an equal speed travels for an equal time past a moving body and body of the same size at rest.

Here it's tempting to think that Aristotle has misread Zeno, especially since there is another reading of the argument which is not foolish. Even by Aristotle's standards, the other three arguments might be fallacious but they are not entirely trivial. In Figure 2.1(c) A and B have passed each. However, there is no time between T_2 and T_3 at which they pass each other. If time is discrete, then the chariots pass each other without ever being next to each other. This is odd to say the least.

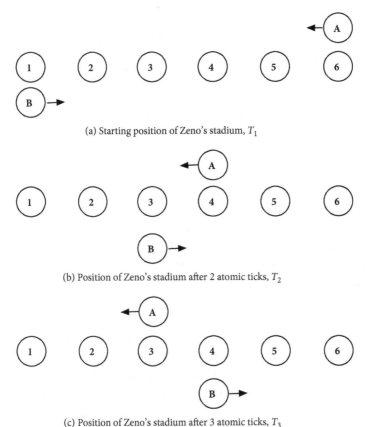

(a) Starting position of Zeno's stadium, T_1

(b) Position of Zeno's stadium after 2 atomic ticks, T_2

(c) Position of Zeno's stadium after 3 atomic ticks, T_3

Figure 2.1 Zeno's stadium.

Whatever Zeno intended—and Aristotle's access to Zeno's original makes it hard to challenge him on this score—this seems to be what Zeno should have intended to prove with the stadium setup. Just what a serious problem this poses for ordinary conceptions of change and motion can be brought out even more clearly with a slightly different version of the stadium. Instead of chariots moving antiparallel to each other, consider two chariots starting equal distances from a common intersection and moving perpendicular to each other. Contrary to every expectation, discrete time and space allows them to move through the intersection without colliding. Remember that since both time and space are discrete, there is literally no time at which A and B are between 3 and 4. While this is not a straightforward contradiction, it certainly seems a paradoxical consequence of any discrete theory of space and time. As with the arrow paradox, the stadium seems to provide a good reason to try to salvage the continuity of motion.

Let us summarize before we proceed to examine more recent reactions to Zeno's arguments. First, the stadium and to a lesser extent the arrow paradoxes create serious problems for any conception of time and of change as consisting of discrete stages. Together they are widely, but not universally, considered to demonstrate that time, space, and change must be continuous. Unfortunately, the dichotomy and the Achilles seem to demonstrate that every finite continuous process involves problematic infinite quantities. As we saw on p. 28 above, Aristotle's response is to argue that they involve only potentially infinite quantities and not a metaphysically problematic realized or actually infinite quantity.

As mentioned, there has long been an undercurrent of dissatisfaction with the Aristotelian insistence that geometrical points of space and moments of time have merely potential reality. The most obvious objection is that the various racers and projectiles must, in some sense, occupy all of the places along their path as they complete that trajectory. It is simply not clear what it means to say that a racer passes through the distance from the starting line to the finish line over the course of the race, without ever strictly speaking arriving at the points between. This becomes even more puzzling when one considers Aristotle's at-at resolution of the arrow paradox. If those instantaneous times have merely potential existence, how can the motion of the arrow be explained in terms of the presence of the arrow at a sequence of different locations at distinct times? Finally, as indicated above, the contemporary mathematical conception of the continuity of time relies on the correspondence between intervals of time and intervals of the real numbers; intervals which are themselves actually infinite collections of numbers.

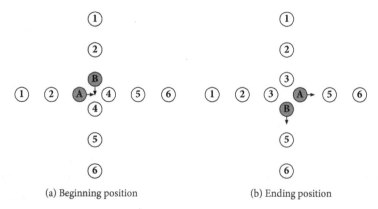

(a) Beginning position   (b) Ending position

Figure 2.2 Perpendicular stadium.

From here, reactions to the paradoxes divide into two basic families. Metaphysical reactions to the paradoxes treat them as having revealed serious metaphysical problems with our ordinary conception of motion. Those who accept that the paradoxes reveal deep metaphysical problems offer either Eleatic or Heraclitean reactions. Some, like Zeno himself, apparently, take them as demonstrating the fundamental incoherence of time and change and the need to adopt a purified metaphysics of being. Others, like the French philosopher Henri Bergson, offer Heraclitean supplements to the ordinary conception of time and motion. We will return to these in the section following the Technical Interlude. First, we will examine the mathematical solution of the paradoxes; the demonstration that the standard model of time as continuous can be restated in terms of the modern mathematical theory of the continuum and shown to be free of contradiction.

Technical interlude #1: Limits, continuity, and infinity in modern mathematics

Our goal in this section is to show that the standard model of time and space as continuous magnitudes is free of any obvious paradox or contradiction. More precisely, I will argue that the standard model is free of contradiction as long as the standard contemporary account of the real numbers and of calculus is so. While the foundational status of the mathematics discussed in this section is not entirely uncontroversial, it is both an important part of *the* standard foundations of modern mathematics and fundamental to our ability to use calculus in physics.

Prelude

Before the nineteenth-century revolutions in the foundations of mathematics, the continuity of space and time were understood directly or intuitively by analogy with our direct awareness of continuous processes. Thus, a curve was understood to be continuous just in case it could be drawn on paper in a single action without gaps on the page or the need to start and stop. The continuity of the real numbers and other abstract mathematical structures was understood as gapless in an analogous way. The role of such vague and intuitive notions in the calculus as originally developed in the eighteenth century generated serious mathematical and philosophical concerns regarding the status of the calculus. The nineteenth-century development of rigorous foundations for calculus led to the realization that the formal continuity of the real numbers makes a better foundation than such vague intuitions. The continuity of space, time, and continuous processes can be represented by the use of formally continuous structures like the real numbers.

Today we say that time and space are continuous in the sense that they can be represented by the real numbers as described below. This requires that each interval of time be placed into a proper correspondence with an interval of the real numbers; for each interval of time we can define a correspondence that assigns each and every moment of that period to a number from the interval in the real numbers, with no numbers left over. Such correspondences between two sets, for example the set of moments in an interval of time and the set of real numbers in some interval of the reals, can be represented as a *map* or *mathematical function*. We say that there is a function τ *from* time, the set of all instants T, *into* the real numbers, $\mathbb{R} - \tau : T \to \mathbb{R} : t \to \tau(t)$. When such a function is one-to-one, associating each object in both sets with a unique object in the other set, we call such a map a *bijection*.

Not just any such correspondence will do to represent time, of course. We want our representation of time by the real numbers to also represent the structure of time, of the set of moments that makes up each interval. Most importantly for our purposes here are two aspects of that structure.[3] Every moment of time is either earlier or later than every other distinct moment. We will say that the set of moments is *totally ordered* by both the "earlier-than" and "later-than" relationships. Any reasonable representation of time by the real numbers should *respect* that structure; I should be able to tell by "looking at" the numbers assigned to two moments of time which of them is earlier. The obvious way to do this is to make sure that the earlier-than relation between moments of time matches up with the less-than relation between the numerical stand-ins.

The second crucial fact is that every pair of moments of time marks the end of an interval of determinate length or duration. Our ordinary conception of time involves a distance or *metric* structure in addition to the *order structure* described above. For reasons that will become clear later, we don't want to assume that we know the temporal distance between any two moments, but one of those reasons is that such distances are plausibly taken as empirical facts subject to measurement. Instead we can characterize more generally what it means to say that temporal distance is a well-defined quality. We can write the distance between any two moments of time, a and b as $\ell(a,b)$. In order to qualify as distance, the quantities given by ℓ need to satisfy three conditions. First, the distance from a to b must be the same as the distance from b to a, $\ell(a,b) = \ell(b,a)$; we say that such relations are symmetric. We also require such a distance to be *non-singular*; the only moment zero distance from a given moment is itself.[4]

$$\ell(a,b) = 0 \text{ if and only if } a = b$$

Finally, we want the distances to "add up" properly. Consider any three moments, a, b, and c. If b is later than a but earlier than c, we require that

$$\ell(a,b) + \ell(b,c) = \ell(a,c)$$

We can match this up with the numerical stand-ins for the moments if we require that the absolute value of the difference between the numbers assigned to the moments be proportional to the distance between the moments. Let's say that any two moments, a and b, are assigned temporal coordinates $\tau(a)$ and $\tau(b)$, using the Greek letter "tau" for time. Then, we require that the distance from a to b be proportional to the absolute value of the difference between their coordinate, or in symbols:

$$\ell(a,b) \; \alpha \; |\tau(a) - \tau(b)|$$

This is just what clocks do for us. We select some material process; label the various stages of the process with numbers, or some other kind of names; we then use the clock to assign "times" to other events and processes. A good clock can simply be defined as one that allows us to properly track the order of events and that assigns numbers to events in such a way that the length of time separating them is accurately represented by the difference between their labels.

Mathematicians call such a one-to-one correspondence in which aspects of the "target set," or *range*, preserve or represent structural aspects of the original set, or *domain*, an *isomorphism*. Such isomorphisms are useful because they allow us to use results that we can derive regarding relatively well-understood structures such as the real numbers instead of attempting to directly comprehend more obscure structures such as time. In this case we want to use the isomorphism between time and the real numbers to derive three facts about time necessary to resolve Zeno's paradoxes.

First, we need to understand how it is possible for each interval of the real numbers to contain an infinity of numbers without being infinitely long. Since the argument in the next section relies only on those aspects of the real numbers that represent aspects of temporal structure, we can then apply the reasoning directly to time. We'll fill in some details in the next section, but the basic reasoning mirrors Aristotle's in important respects. Aristotle claimed to have identified an equivocation between two senses of size for an interval—an equivocation that he explicates in terms of a distinction between the actual length of the interval and its potential locations of divisibility. The contemporary mathematical solution also identifies an equivocation between two conceptions of the size of interval, but it identifies the two conceptions of size directly instead of in terms of a distinction between the actual and the potential. In the next section we will explain the basic reasoning that indicates why the length of a continuous interval and the number of points it contains, called its *cardinality*, are independent of each other. Since every interval contains the same number of points, or instantaneous moments, the length of the intervals and the size of the associated set of points must be logically distinct from each other. Thus the next section will demonstrate the following:

> **The Continuity of Time and the Cardinality of the Continuum** Time is continuous just in case it is *isomorphic* to, shares a structure with, the real numbers. Since every interval of real numbers contains precisely the same number of real numbers as the total set of real numbers, the same is true for continuous time. This number, the cardinality of the continuum, is strictly larger than the number of integers or rational numbers, $\aleph_0$.

Second, even if we can show that intervals of finite duration can consist of an infinite collection of moments, we still have the problem that each interval can be divided up into an infinite number of individually finite durations. How is it possible to add together an infinite number of finite intervals such that they add up to a finite value? This requires the mathematical concept of the limit of an infinite series. Consider a simple infinite sum such as we get by adding together $1/2^n$ for all values of n greater than or equal to 1. Symbolically, we can write this[5]:

$$\sum_{n=1}^{\infty} \frac{1}{2^n} = 1/2 + 1/4 + 1/8 + 1/16 \cdots$$

Notice that, as I add additional terms, each sum gets closer and closer to 1 without ever going over. Thus, the first four terms above add to 15/16, while with the fifth term, 1/32, the total becomes 31/32. No matter how many terms we have listed we can tell that adding an additional term will take us to a value closer to 1 but always less than it. We say that 1 is *the limit of the series as n goes to infinity.* It should be relatively clear that there must be some relationship between the value of the infinite sum and limit approached by the sequence of partial sums; the limit is what we are "approaching" but never "reaching" because there are still terms to be added in. What else could it mean to "add in" all of the remaining infinite terms except to reach the limit? Later in this section, we will look at a more rigorous definition of the limit and be able to provide a bit more justification for this claim. We can define the sum of an infinite series as follows:

Infinite Sums The sum of an infinite series of terms is the limit of the sequence of partial sums as the number of terms in the sequence approaches infinity.

$$L = \sum_{n=1}^{\infty} a_n \Leftrightarrow L = \lim_{k \to \infty} \{S_k\}$$

where
$\{S_k\}$ = the sequence of partial sums associated with infinite summation.

Finally, we need some way to express the difference between a moving object and a resting arrow *at each point in the arrow's path.* In physics, since Newton we have represented the *instantaneous velocity* of an object as the instantaneous rate of change of its position at a time given by the *derivative* of its path. It is easier to put discussion of this off entirely until p. 50, but we can define the instantaneous velocity rigorously:

Instantaneous Velocity The instantaneous velocity of a moving object is the value of the derivative of its position relative to time.

$$v = \frac{dx}{dt}$$

where
$x(t)$ is the position of the object at time t.

Continuity and infinity in modern mathematics

Our goal is to explicate the conception of time as a continuous magnitude such that every interval of time consists of an infinite collection of duration-less moments. Let's begin with a pretty familiar collection with an infinite number of members: the set of all of the ordinary counting numbers, {0, 1, 2, 3, …}. The first thing to notice is the "curly braces" which mathematicians use to indicate that they are talking about the collection, or *set*, of things they contain, not about each of them separately. I hope everyone can recognize that this set goes on "forever"; I can't ever list all of the counting numbers. Mathematicians call these *the natural numbers* and use the symbol $\mathbb{N}$ as a name for the complete set of them.

However, these are far from all of the numbers with which we know how to work. Notice that while addition and multiplication are well defined for them, neither subtraction nor division is. I can pick any two numbers and either add or multiply them to get another natural number. But, I can't subtract a greater number from lesser nor can I divide a number by any number of which it is not a whole multiple; that is, I haven't yet defined either negative numbers or fractions. If I define a new set of numbers as all of those that I can get by adding, *subtracting*, or multiplying whole numbers, I get *the integers*, {… −2, −1, 0, 1, 2, …} generally referred to as $\mathbb{Z}$. If I then define *division* and include the results, I get the *rational numbers* or $\mathbb{Q}$, which are more traditionally, but equivalently, defined as all of the numbers that can be expressed as a fraction of integers, a/b.

These are also not all of the numbers. Since at least the ancient Greeks, we have known that there are *irrational* numbers that cannot be expressed as a fraction of whole numbers; the numbers we call π and $\sqrt{2}$ seem to have been some of the first to be identified.[6] Mathematicians call the set consisting of the rational numbers plus all of the irrational numbers, the *real numbers* or $\mathbb{R}$. How might we be able to tell when we have identified all of these numbers?

Let's reflect for a moment on how we identify $\sqrt{2}$ as an irrational number. We know that there must be some number that gives the length of the diagonal of a square in terms of the length of its side; from the basic Pythagorean theorem a square of side a must have diagonal length $\sqrt{2 \times a^2} = a \times \sqrt{2}$ (cf. Figure 2.3). We can also determine that this number, $\sqrt{2}$, is between 1.41 and 1.42, but that there is no precise fractional or decimal number between those numbers that it is. The square root of 2 "lives in" an identified gap in the rational numbers; it is the location in our system of numbers where there should be a number, but doesn't seem to be one.

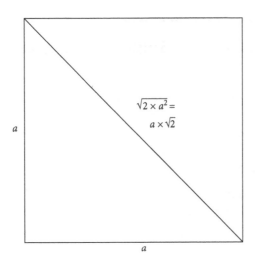

Figure 2.3 Identifying an irrational number.

Is there a general way to characterize such "gaps" in the rational numbers? It turns out that there is; the best known and simplest to describe is the method of Dedekind cuts. Consider all sequences of rational numbers; that is all lists of rational numbers with each list arranged in order from the least to the greatest. Include infinitely long sequences such as all rational numbers greater than zero or all even positive integers or all rational numbers less than 2. Some of these sequences have *an upper bound*; it's possible to specify some rational number such that every member of the sequence is less than that number. Of the examples given above, only the third, all rational numbers less than 2, has an upper bound. In addition, some bounded sequences also have a *least upper bound*; the smallest rational number greater than the greatest member of the sequence; 2 is clearly the least upper bound of the sequence of all rational numbers less than 2.

Now consider the sequence of all rational numbers less than $\sqrt{2}$. There clearly are rational numbers that are an upper bound for that sequence, 1.42 and 1.416 are examples. But there is no rational number that is the least upper bound of that sequence. This is, in a sense, what it means to say that $\sqrt{2}$ is irrational; one can always find another fractional approximation closer to it than what one has available, but can never find one that matches it precisely.

We can use this to define the real numbers relative to the rational numbers. Unlike the rational numbers, real numbers are *[Dedekind] complete*; every

Technical Note 1: Some Ordering Relations on Sets

The various systems of numbers have various *ordering relations*. The natural numbers are *well-ordered*, meaning that every collection of natural numbers has a least element. As a consequence of being well-ordered, $\mathbb{N}$ has three additional properties; well-ordered sets are *totally ordered*, *discrete*, and *complete*.

Total Ordering A set is *totally ordered*, by a given order relation, by $\leq$ just in case, for all a and b, $a < b$ or $b < a$, or $a = b$.

Discrete A set is *discrete* just in case every element has a unique successor.

[Dedekind] Complete A set is *complete* just in case every subset with an upper bound has a least upper bound.

Based on these definitions it should be easy to see that the integers are not well-ordered, but otherwise satisfy all of these conditions. $\mathbb{Z}$ is totally ordered, discrete, and complete but, for example, the set of all negative integers has no least member. It's worth noting that for discretely, totally ordered sets, completeness is fundamentally trivial; if I have a subset all of whose members are less than some value, the least number than which they are less is simply the successor of the greatest element of the subset.

Things get more interesting when we look at the rationals. They are certainly totally ordered, but they are neither discrete nor complete. Instead, the rationals are *dense*:

Denseness A set is *densely ordered* just in case, for any two elements of the set, there is always a third element between those two.

sequence of real numbers with an upper bound has a least upper bound. Technically, the real numbers $\mathbb{R}$ is the totally ordered [Dedekind] complete field.

So all four sets of numbers have an infinite number of elements, but are they all the same size? To begin we need a conception of comparative size for infinite sets. We begin with the conception of a map or function connecting the elements of one set with that in another set. For pairs of finite sets we can specify such maps directly simply by listing the relevant pairs. For example,

Technical Note 2: Axioms for a Field and Subsidiary Mathematical Structures

Technically, a *field* is any collection with two operations, traditionally called addition and multiplication satisfying the following axioms or rules:

Commutativity Both addition and multiplication are commutative. $a + b = b + a$ and $a * b = b * a$.

Associativity Both addition and multiplication are associative. $(a + b) + c = a + (b + c)$ and $(a * b) * c = a * (b * c)$

Additive Inverse For every number, a, there is another number, b, such that $a + b = 0$. Intuitively, this is simply $-a$ and is the same as defining subtraction.

Multiplicative Inverse For every number, a, there is another number, b, such that $a * b = 1$. Intuitively, this is simply $1/a$ and is the same as defining division.

Existence of Identity Elements Both addition, for 0, and multiplication, for 1, possess identity elements. $a + 0 = a$ and $a * 1 = a$.

Distribution of Multiplication over Addition $a * (b + c) = (a * b) + (a * c)$

No "divide by zero" For any a and b, if $a * b = 0$, either $a = 0$ or $b = 0$.

Notice that the natural numbers, $\mathbb{N}$, has multiplication and addition with commutativity, associativity, and distribution of multiplication over addition, but no inverses. The integers, $\mathbb{Z}$, with an additive inverse but no multiplicative inverse, are an example of a structure called a *ring*. The rationals, $\mathbb{Q}$, and the reals, $\mathbb{R}$, are both fields.

if I have four apples and three oranges on my kitchen counter, I can define a "function" from apples to oranges simply by listing pairs of apples and oranges that go together. However, for infinite sets we need to specify a rule that tells us for a given element, a, of the set A, called *the domain* how to select the corresponding element b from set B, called *the range*. For example, the function, $f(n) = 2n$ from the natural numbers back into the natural numbers associates every number with its double.

Given this understanding of functions, what does it mean to say that two sets are the same size? For finite sets it just means that there's a way to pair up the elements of the two sets one-to-one; I have the same number of apples and oranges when I can match each apple to an orange with no leftovers. To transfer this to infinite sets, we define a special kind of function called a *bijection*; a rule that associates every element of the domain with exactly one element of the range. Our doubling function above is obviously a bijection; it pairs every natural number with an even natural number and every even natural number with a natural number. Therefore, there are precisely as many even natural numbers as there are total natural numbers. Mathematicians say that the sets have the same *cardinality*. For obvious reasons any such function mapping a set into the natural numbers is called an *enumeration* of the set; such sets are also said to be *countable* or *countably infinite* or *denumerable*.

It turns out that both the integers and the rational numbers are countable in this sense. Here is an example of an enumeration for the integers:

$$\phi(x) = \begin{cases} 2x - 1 & x > 0 \\ -2x & x \leq 0 \end{cases}$$

A little reflection allows us to see that this is an enumeration of the integers in the following order $\{0, 1, -1, 2, -2, 3, -3, \ldots\}$.

Constructing this for the rational numbers is a bit trickier, and the simplest version relies on some basic facts about prime numbers, especially the *fundamental theorem of arithmetic* according to which every integer greater than one is either prime or has a unique prime factorization. Since it requires a bit more calculation, we'll reserve it for a Technical Note. No such enumeration can be constructed for the real numbers. Here's a simple, but not entirely rigorous argument that no such enumeration exists. Begin by demonstrating that there are more infinitely long sequences of natural numbers than there are natural numbers. The proof proceeds by reductio ad absurdum; assume that there is an enumeration of all sequences of natural numbers, call it S (See Figure 2.4.) Define the sequence S_0 such that the kth digit of S_0, $s_{0k} = d_{kk} + 1$ where d_{kk} is the kth element of the kth sequence in S. In words, add 1 to each of the circled diagonal elements of the array of series. The first five digits of S_0 based on the partial enumeration in Figure 2.4 are $\langle 4, 8, 9, 8, 7 \rangle$. S_0 is not included in S since by construction it differs from every sequence included in S in at least one place. Therefore, contrary to our initial hypothesis S does not enumerate every sequence of natural numbers, so no enumeration exists and the cardinality of the set of sequences is strictly larger than the natural numbers.

Technical Note 3: Enumerating the Rational Numbers

The fundamental theorem of arithmetic states that for any positive integer x, there is a sequence of prime numbers, p_n, such that $x = \Pi_{i=1...n} p_i^{a_i}$. For those unfamiliar with the notation, Π is the product operator and simply says to multiply together all of the terms. For example, $504 = 2^3 * 3^2 * 7$.

Now consider the set of all positive rational numbers as defined above. From basic arithmetic and the fundamental theorem, we can see that any such fraction, a/b, has an equivalent representation, q/r, such that q and r are mutually prime, that is, they share no prime factors except 1. To see this, assume that a and b are not mutually prime; simply divide the numerator and denominator by the common factors until you are left with a fraction with mutually prime numerator and denominator, q/r, which will be equivalent to the initial fraction.

Now consider the prime factorizations of q and r, $q = \Pi_{q_n} q_n^{a_n}$ and $r = \Pi_{r_m} r_m^{b_m}$, where all of the q_n and r_m are prime numbers. To uniquely associate each such fraction with a positive integer, form the following product:

$$x\left(\frac{q}{r}\right) = \prod q_n^{2a_n} \times \prod_m r_m^{2b_m - 1}$$

This obviously associates a positive integer with each such fraction and therefore by the argument given above with each positive rational number. To find the rational associated with a positive integer, x, simply consider its prime factorization, for example $2{,}940 = 2^2 \times 3 \times 5 \times 7^2$. Using the formula above, divide the even exponents by 2 to get the prime factorization of the numerator for the associated rational number; for the denominator, add 1 to the odd exponents and then divide by 2. In this case, you get 14/15.

Simply assign $x(0) = 0$ and for negative rationals simply use the negative of the positive integer associated with the absolute value. Then enumerate the integers themselves using the rule given above and you have an enumeration of the rationals.

This is called Cantor's diagonal construction, for obvious reasons, and was first published by Georg Cantor in 1891. Both the proof itself and the general strategy for comparing the cardinality of sets used in the diagonal construction are central to modern set theory and number theory.

$$
\begin{array}{llllllllll}
S_1 = & ③ & 3 & 9 & 7 & 2 & 8 & 1 & 6 & 8 & \cdots \\
S_2 = & 9 & ⑦ & 2 & 2 & 4 & 6 & 2 & 5 & 9 & \cdots \\
S_3 = & 2 & 3 & ⑧ & 3 & 7 & 9 & 1 & 3 & 8 & \cdots \\
S_4 = & 2 & 6 & 3 & ⑦ & 9 & 5 & 7 & 2 & 3 & \cdots \\
S_5 = & 7 & 6 & 4 & 6 & ⑥ & 5 & 3 & 6 & 7 & \cdots \\
S_6 = & 6 & 8 & 7 & 5 & 3 & ⑦ & 6 & 6 & 4 & \cdots \\
S_7 = & 8 & 9 & 7 & 2 & 1 & 7 & ⑤ & 9 & 7 & \cdots \\
S_8 = & 9 & 2 & 8 & 1 & 9 & 8 & 4 & ② & 5 & \cdots \\
S_9 = & 5 & 4 & 5 & 1 & 4 & 3 & 8 & 2 & ③ & \cdots \\
& \vdots & \vdots & \vdots & \vdots & \vdots & \vdots & \vdots & \vdots & \vdots \\
S_k = & S_{k1} & S_{k2} & S_{k3} & S_{k4} & S_{k5} & S_{k6} & S_{k7} & S_{k8} & \cdots
\end{array}
$$

Figure 2.4 Diagonal construction.

To show that the real numbers are non-denumerable, we need to associate them with the sequences of natural numbers. We can do this in two obvious, and lots of less obvious, ways. First, we can simply appeal to the fact that real numbers all have decimal expansions, and that any such decimal expansion just is a sequence of natural numbers. Second, we can recall from our definition above that every real number has associated with it a convergent sequence of rational numbers of which it is the least upper bound. We can then use our enumeration of rationals given above to construct the related sequence of natural numbers for each real number.

Unfortunately, neither of these automatically associates each sequence with a unique real number. This is easiest to see with the use of decimal expansions as the equivalence of 1.000... and 0.999..., for example, is usually addressed in elementary math classes. The tricky part of the proof, which we're not going to attempt here, is to show that the duplications are at most a countable subset of the sequences. Once we can show that, it is relatively easy to show that the *complement*, the subset of the original set that remains when a specified subset is removed, of a countable subset of a non-denumerable set must be non-denumerable. Simply consider what would happen if we attempted to enumerate the original set by beginning with an enumeration of the countable subset. It should be obvious that if the remainder were itself countable, then the whole set would have to be countable, contrary to our initial hypothesis. Proving this with full mathematical rigor is beyond what we can do here, but if you're having trouble persuading yourself, note the way that we construct the enumeration of the rationals by pasting together enumerations of the positive and the negative rationals![7]

To prove that every continuous interval of the reals has the same cardinality, construct a bijection between any two intervals, (a,b) and (c,d).

To do this, simply construct a linear function between the intervals. For example, consider the intervals (1,2) and (5,8). For any number x between 1 and 2, consider the following:

$$f(x) = \left\{ \frac{(8-5)}{(2-1)}(x-1) + 5 \right\} = 3(x-1) + 5$$

Intuitively, the first term "locates" x proportionally in the second interval and the second term shifts it. Thus, for 1.5, halfway between 1 and 2, this gives 6.5, the halfway point of the target interval. More generally, we can say:

$$f(x) = \left\{ \frac{(d-c)}{b-a} * (x-a) \right\} + c \tag{2.1}$$

This obviously gives a one-to-one correspondence between the numbers in any two intervals. Since such a bijection exists, all open intervals of the reals, those not containing their endpoints, have the same cardinality. We have therefore argued for, although not explicitly proved to full mathematical rigor, three facts about the real numbers:

1 That the continuity of the real numbers results from completing the "gaps" in the rational numbers.
2 That neither the real numbers nor any interval of them can be enumerated by the natural numbers or the integers.
3 That the size of an interval of the real numbers, determined by the difference between its endpoints, is independent of the number of real numbers in that interval.

How does any of this help to resolve Zeno's paradoxes? It does so once we recall that to claim that time is continuous is precisely to claim that it can be put into the appropriate correspondence with the real numbers. Recall, from the beginning of this section, that continuous time is isomorphic to the real numbers. Therefore there are as many moments in every interval of time as there are in the corresponding interval of the real numbers. Just as every interval of real numbers has the same infinite cardinality, every interval of time must contain a continuously infinite collection of moments. However, the length of each such interval, whether of numbers or of time, depends on the difference between the endpoints. Thus, the infinity associated with each interval of time is not paradoxical or inconsistent as long as the corresponding mathematical properties are coherent.

Infinite series and limits

Advocates for the metaphysical significance of the Achilles and the dichotomy sometimes make a slightly different claim than that addressed in the previous section. Rather than relying on the infinite cardinality of the racecourse directly, they argue that the infinite divisibility of the course implies that completing a single finite course is equivalent to completing an infinite sequence of ever-shrinking, but also finite, courses. It has seemed to various philosophers that it should be impossible to complete such an infinite sequence of courses. Just above (cf. p. 23) we saw that the length of a continuous interval does not depend on the number of points in the interval. In addition, any such sequence of ever-shrinking courses is *dense*; for any two courses, of any length, there is another course whose length is between them. Crucially this means that there is no *particular* intermediate course or sequence of courses that I complete in completing the entire course. There is no *next* course that I complete after completing the halfway course for example. We cannot think of the sequence as constructed by sequentially adding on or moving to the next point of the sequence; there is no such next point. Instead, we will illustrate the sense in which given an interval of a finite length, the length of an appropriate subdivision into an infinite number of subintervals of the original interval can be equivalent to the original interval.

To see this, notice that the sequence of sub-races in the Achilles have their duration given by a simple relationship to their position in the sequence, if we take it that the whole race takes 1 "race unit" of time to complete; the nth segment has duration $1/2^n$. Thus, at any stage of the race the runner has been running for:

$$1/2 + 1/4 + \cdots + 1/k^2 = \sum_{n=1}^{k} \frac{1}{2^n}$$

Thus, the time it takes her to complete the entire race is given by the infinite series:

$$\tau = \sum_{n=1}^{\infty} \frac{1}{2^n}$$

which generates an infinite sequence of partial sums:

$$T = \langle 1/2, 3/4, 7/8, 15/16, \cdots, \frac{2^n - 1}{2^n} \rangle$$

Notice two facts about this sequence. Each partial sum is closer to 1 than the previous term in the sequence; every term is less than 1. We call this a convergent sequence, and the series that generates it is a convergent series. The point of this is that such convergent series do not pose any particular conceptual or metaphysical difficulties. The existence of such formally infinite representations of finite quantities is simply a product of the interplay between length and cardinality illustrated above in pp. 39–47. The appearance of infinity is related to the cardinality as above, not to the length of the interval relevant to the completion of the race.

The basic claim here is that the infinite series is merely another representation of the original length; thus, our estimate of the length as represented by the infinite series should not be different. That $1 = 1/4 + 3/4$ doesn't give us any reason to think that it is "larger" than 1 in any interesting sense. What matters is the sum of the terms not how many there are. What is the total of an infinite number of terms? The standard response relies on the concept of the limit of a series.

Just above, we saw that the relevant series approaches arbitrarily close to 1 without ever going over; we say that it converges to the limit of 1 as the number of terms goes to infinity, symbolically:

Definition 2.1. A sequence T converges to a limit L if for any value $\varepsilon > 0$, there is an element of the sequence T_δ such that for all elements of the sequence T_n such that $n \geq \delta$, $|L - T_n| < \varepsilon$.

This captures in a rigorous sense the concept of "arbitrarily close to." Thus, suppose that I want to find the first element of T no more than 0.0001 less than 1, with $\varepsilon \leq 0.0001$. That's the 14th.

In modern mathematics it's generally just taken as the definition of the sum of an infinite series that it is the limit of sequence of partial sums. However, here are two plausible reasons to equate the sum of the infinite series, the limit of the infinite sequence of partial sums and the original finite interval. First, just notice that the interval is the smallest that will contain all the subintervals. Second, extend this by remembering our definition of the real numbers above. The sequence T just is a sequence of rational numbers whose least upper bound is 1! Given the definition of the real numbers, the most plausible interpretation of these equivalences is to think of both the infinite sum and the infinite sequence as merely alternative representations of the same mathematical object.

Derivatives and instantaneous velocity

Before we consider the philosophical consequences of these mathematical results, we need one more result. Resolving the Achilles and the dichotomy requires a consistent account of finite continuous magnitudes. The arrow depends not on the activity of a system *over time* but *at a time*. What is it about the moving arrow at a particular time which distinguishes it from an identical arrow at rest? The standard answer from classical Newtonian physics is that the path of the moving arrow places it at a different location at every moment of time. We call the rate of change of the position of the object relative to time it's speed or velocity.[8] When the arrow doesn't change its position at all in any finite duration, this speed is obviously going to be zero; the arrow is at rest.

But, given what we've already seen about infinite divisibility, every finite interval has finite parts. Couldn't the arrow be moving during some of them and at rest at others? And wouldn't that create precisely the problem we are trying to avoid, with the arrow moving without being in motion at any particular time? The answer to the first question is obviously yes, but we can resolve the problem by invoking the concept of limit again to define the *instantaneous velocity* of the arrow; its speed at every moment of its trajectory.

What follows here is just basic kinematics from an introductory physics course. A quick review, paying particular attention to the definition of a derivative, will be useful to resolve the tensions here. So, the path of the arrow through space, over time, is simply given by a function from time into space, $x(t)$. Given what we said above about functions, it should be clear that some such functions map a continuous temporal interval into a continuous spatial one, allowing us to determine where the object is at any time in that interval. We can define the average speed of the arrow between any two times, t_1 and t_2, as the distance covered between the two times divided by the time difference,

$$\frac{x(t_2) - x(t_1)}{t_1 - t_2} = \frac{\Delta x}{\Delta t} \qquad (2.2)$$

But what is the speed of the object at any one time?

Well, the object certainly doesn't change its position at a time, but we can think of this instantaneous velocity at t as the rate of change as the time allowed for that change shrinks to zero. This limit or instantaneous rate of change is called the derivative of $x(t)$ with respect to t, written $dx(t)/dt = \dot{x}(t)$. Here's the bit that's crucial to contemporary debates over the arrow paradox, but generally skipped over in physics classes. The derivative at t_2 is the limit of the difference quotient given in Equation 2.2 as $\Delta t = t_2 - t_1$ approaches zero. That is,

$$\dot{x}(t_2) = \lim_{\Delta t \to 0} \frac{x(t_2 + \Delta t) - x(t_2)}{\Delta t}$$

Finally, the limit is defined as follows:

Definition 2.2. $\dot{x}(t_2) = L$ if and only if for all $\varepsilon > 0$ there is some $\Delta > 0$ such that for all[9] $\delta \leq \Delta$

$$\left| L - \frac{x(t_2 + \delta) - x(t_2)}{\delta} \right| < \varepsilon$$

The crucial fact about this definition is that while the instantaneous velocity is defined *at* each time, it is only defined for a path through that place at that time. Notice that the arrow is at rest at t, has 0 instantaneous velocity, just in case there is some finite continuous interval containing that time when it is at the same location. This provides a mathematically rigorous formulation of Aristotle's intuition that to be in motion is to be at some place at each time, while being at different places at all other times.

It seems to have been this that led Bertrand Russell to claim, in §327 of *The Principles of Mathematics* that this definition "has at last shown that we live in an unchanging world, and that the arrow, at every moment of its flight, is truly at rest." What Russell means here is that there is no additional physical or metaphysical fact above or beyond the trajectory of the arrow that accounts for its motion. It moves not because of some mysterious force of becoming, but simply by being at each of the places when it is at those places. For reasons to be discussed below, we should be careful about jumping to conclusions; however, if nothing else, modern analysis culminating in this definition of the derivative seems to demonstrate that classical Newtonian kinematics is at least free from obvious contradictions, including Zeno's.

One final note for less-mathematically sophisticated readers. Remember the basic moral of this entire section is that one can represent the path of an object through space at various times as functions of real numbers; once you do so you can help yourself to all of the mathematical effort that went into clarifying the structure of the real numbers and the calculus; and then when one does so one can resolve the apparent contradictions involved in the various conceptions of infinity in Zeno's paradoxes. However, we now need to turn to the philosophical consequences of these mathematical results.

Modern responses to the paradox

Beginning in the late nineteenth century, we can trace three basic reactions to Zeno's paradoxes. The standard response can be seen as similar in spirit to that of Aristotle. As suggested above, in *The Principles of Mathematics* Bertrand Russell claimed that all of the Zeno's paradoxes could be easily resolved through the proper application of calculus. Adolf Grünbaum developed this approach in great detail in a series of articles culminating in his *Modern Science and Zeno's Paradoxes.*

Summarizing the above: according to the modern theory of real numbers, Aristotle was precisely correct to recognize a distinction between the number of moments contained within an interval and its length. Only once we either impose or discover a length measure for temporal intervals can we compare their lengths; all continuous intervals contain exactly the same number of points. The theory of limits demonstrates that the infinite series involved in the paradoxes of division are merely alternative representations of finite intervals. Given the continuity of the relevant quantities, the two descriptions are merely notational variants just as 1 and 3/4 + 1/4 are variant names for the same number. Finally, the theory of the derivative proves that instantaneous velocity is a well-defined concept; the arrow moves simply by occupying different places at different times. What could be the problem?

As we've already seen from the examples of Parmenides and Zeno, there is a deep suspicion of change and becoming in philosophy. Those who shared that suspicion long suspected that the Aristotelian solution was itself a trick. The general suggestion is that the only way in which the completed race could be potentially infinitely divisible is if the actual race is a completed infinity of sub-races. And there are reasons to be suspicious of the claim that the mathematical results discussed above provide a philosophically adequate resolution. At least some philosophers and mathematicians suspect that rather than resolving the paradoxes, this "solution" merely moves it around.

Notice that all infinite sets, whether of the cardinality of natural numbers or real numbers, have an extremely odd property. They have proper subsets, sets containing some but not all of their elements, of the same cardinality as the original set. Think for a moment about how odd this is; these are sets from which it is possible to remove elements, even an infinite number of elements, and yet have precisely the same number of elements remaining. By providing rigorous definitions of the various concepts, especially those that separate cardinality from containment, the underlying theory seems to be free of obvious contradictions.[10] However, philosophers and metaphysicians of a finitist bent have remained suspicious regarding the philosophical foundations of transfinite set theory. They also suspect that one is able to construct a model for time and change using that theory only because it reproduces the underlying metaphysical paradoxes revealed originally by Zeno.

These suspicions have motivated both radically Eleatic and radically Heraclitean alternatives to the usual resolution. For example, worries such as those that motivated Zeno seem to have played a central role in various forms of nineteenth-century idealism. As the philosopher Wesley Salmon reports:

> The absolute idealism of the late nineteenth and early twentieth centuries does bear strong resemblance to the Parmenidean view, both in its conclusions and in its arguments. F. H. Bradley, while making no explicit mention of Zeno, uses thoroughly Eleatic arguments to support the conclusions that space and time, motion and change, are unreal. "Time, like space, as most evidently proved not to be real, but a contradictory appearance." (Salmon, 16)

The Eleatic strand in philosophy thus remains alive and well.

Other philosophers have drawn a fundamentally opposite conclusion from Zeno's paradoxes. Henri Bergson claimed that the Achilles demonstrated not the unreality of change but its reality. For Bergson, change and its accompanying duration is so fundamentally basic that any attempt to analyze it so as to understand it traps us into contradiction. Not because change itself is contradictory, but because its nature can only be felt not understood. As Bergson says, no attempt to understand change from an analytic or rational perspective can possibly do so instead we must

> install [ourselves] within change, and [we] will grasp at once both change itself and the successive states in which it might at any instant be immobilized. But with the successive states, perceived from without as real and no longer

as potential immobilities, you will never reconstitute movement.... But the interval between two consecutive states be infinitely small: before the intervening movement you will always experience the disappointment of the child who tries by clapping his hands together to crush the smoke. The movement slips through the interval, because every attempt to reconstitute change out of states implies the absurd proposition, that movement is made of immobilities. (from Bergson's *Creative Evolution* reproduced in Sellars)

For Bergson, as for William James and Alfred North Whitehead, we fall afoul of the paradoxes of division not because of our tendency to believe in motion, but because we don't believe that motion is fundamental. Each such change occurs as an indivisible whole which we mistakenly attempt to represent as the sum of its parts. Part of the complaint of these philosophers is an overly literal interpretation of the mathematical machinery introduced in this chapter. From this perspective, the definition of a limit used above, for example, must be understood as an inadequate attempt to explicate a fundamentally dynamic process using static properties of sets. According to these process-oriented philosophers, the mathematical results, even if they are accepted as mathematically legitimate, are merely the logical articulation of another inadequate human language, not the mathematical or temporal reality itself.

Although neither Bergson's version of Heraclitean metaphysics nor Bradley's version of Eleaticism have broad adherence today, they remain the best alternatives if we are not able to defang the paradoxes following the model of Russell and Grünbaum. Unfortunately for those hoping that Zeno's paradoxes reveal deep metaphysical problems, it seems clear that without the full arsenal of contemporary mathematical analysis we've no idea how to formulate most of modern physics. While it might be possible to describe the physical world without mathematical formulae that depend on problematic infinite sets, no one has yet done so and prospects seem dim.

Conclusions and open questions

There are two basic conclusions to be drawn from this discussion of Zeno's paradoxes. The substantive conclusion to be drawn is that since modern mathematical analysis does provide a prima facie consistent account of continuous motion, there is no logical bar to recognizing the continuity of time as the structure of change given the existence of continuous change.

Historical Note 8: Process Philosophers: Bergson, James, and Whitehead

While physics prepared to enter a period of upheaval, the last decades of the nineteenth century witnessed a profound philosophical reaction to the Eleatic rationalism of absolute idealism. Friedrich Nietzsche (1844–1900) is today the most famous of these revolutionaries. However, despite his doctrine of the eternal return (cf. Chapter 8, p. 233), his principal interests don't overlap much with the subject of this book. William James (1842–1910) and Henri Bergson (1859–1941) are more important for our purposes.

The American William James, brother of the novelist Henry James, was trained as a physician and is often credited as the founder of psychology as an independent discipline. Philosophically, he was an early defender of pragmatism; he defended a version of radical empiricism according to which the way things seem to be is the way they are for us. Therefore, James's description of our experience as a sequence of discrete happenings, anchored in his promotion of the specious present (cf. Chapter 5), makes him with Henri Bergson among the radical Heraclitean opposition to absolute idealism.

Henri Bergson was the most influential French philosopher of the early twentieth century. Deeply influenced by the advent of evolutionary theories in biology, Bergson came to believe that the world is a source of radical creativity and dynamism. Any attempt to limit that dynamism within rational bounds can only falsify it. Unfortunately, Bergson became involved in an embarrassing technical dispute regarding time dilation in special relativity (cf. Chapter 6, p. 170) with Albert Einstein that badly damaged his legacy outside of France.

The *process philosophy* of Alfred North Whitehead (1861–1947) is the most fully developed Heraclitean reaction in the twentieth century. Whitehead did important early work on symbolic logic as coauthor of *Principia Mathematica* with Bertrand Russell, and his later process philosophy remains influential in philosophy as well as theology. Unfortunately, his most complete statement of his mature positions in *Process and Reality* is extremely difficult to comprehend as the result of his attempt to describe processes and events without referring to any underlying objects.

That leads us to the second, methodological conclusion of this chapter. As should become increasingly clear moving forward, our philosophical account of time turns out to depend on the results from many other apparently distinct disciplines. Here we looked at mathematics, but elsewhere there will be equally important connections to physics (especially in Chapters 6 through 9) and psychology (especially in Chapter 5).

We will end this chapter, as we will most of the chapters of the book, with some open philosophical problems. The first problem is phenomenological; our temporal experience of the world seems to be chunky rather than smooth. As William James says,

> Such seems to be the nature of concrete experience, which changes always by sensible amounts, or stays unchanged. The infinite character we find it and is woven into it by our later conception indefinitely repeating the act of subdividing any given amount supposed. (Quoted in Grünbaum, p. 46)

Even assuming something like the Jamesian doctrine of the "specious present" is correct, a problem that we will look at in Chapter 5, James seems to draw his metaphysical conclusions from the psychological data too hastily. Why should we not comprehend our "chunky" temporal experiences as inadequate experiences of really continuous physical time? What is really at stake here are deep questions about the role of experience in our knowledge of the world. Does the world reveal itself to us in our experience so that our experiences form the shape and boundary of the real? If time reveals itself to us discretely, according to James and Whitehead, or indivisibly, according to Bergson, then any further mathematical structure must be entirely the product of our own creation.

However, there is another kind of empiricism—that practiced in natural science. Here, experiences are taken not as revelatory but merely as data. Around that data, we construct the best theory of the world that we can. As mentioned above, it's clear that our best theories of the natural world treat time as a continuous quantity. In the absence of an equally good physics that treats time as a discrete sequence of moments, the profound predictive success of physics based on continuous time seems to make it reasonable to gamble that time actually is continuous. We'll revisit this relationship between temporal consciousness and temporal metaphysics in Chapter 5.

Finally, there are various interesting philosophical issues raised by the standard solutions themselves. Here are two of them. First, the equicardinality of all intervals seems to make the length of time contained in any interval arbitrary. This is called the problem of the conventionality of the temporal metric. There are literally an infinite number of different mappings from the real numbers onto time, and many of them assign different lengths to every interval in time. Is there any way to restrict these functions and assign a determinate length to temporal intervals? Imagine that every such function is represented by a clock; the equi-cardinality of all such intervals seems to imply that there is no intrinsic notion of size that distinguishes various intervals. At best we might hope that more general physical or theoretical considerations might narrow down the range of legitimate choices. Our discussion, in Chapter 6, of clocks and proper time in the context of Einstein's theory of special relativity will investigate this in more detail.

Second, there is also an ongoing debate in the philosophy of physics regarding instantaneous velocity. Granted, the calculus allows us to determine the value of the instantaneous velocity of a moving system at every time, as long as the motion is smooth and continuous, what is it exactly that we are determining the value of? There are two problems here. The first is a philosophical worry. The motion of the arrow, as represented by the derivative is only defined over neighborhoods around a particular time; how can the state of the arrow at that time be logically dependent on other times? This seems to violate the very philosophical intuitions that motivate the move in the first place. Wasn't the goal to explain the appearance of becoming in terms of the pure states of being of the arrow at each of the separate moments of its existence? Now its existence in that state at those times seems to depend, in some sense, on its whole existence.

In addition, there are hypothetical systems which seem to be moving, but which do not have an instantaneous velocity as defined in this chapter. For example, consider an arrow that simply "popped" out of existence when its tip hit the midway point between the bow and the target. The limit defined above does not exist at that moment, because there are finite temporal intervals around that moment when the arrow is nowhere to be found. This means that the numerator of the velocity function is not defined at those times. This is both a striking illustration of the worries in the previous paragraph, and a puzzle in its own right. It seems odd to claim that the arrow was not moving as it disappeared.

As with the phenomenological concerns with which we opened this section, there are proposed resolutions to these puzzles, but none that have achieved anything approaching universal acceptance. Some of those proposals are listed in the suggested reading below. We turn, now, to an aspect of temporal structure perhaps even more puzzling than its continuity—McTaggart's paradox—and the changing status of times as past, present, and future.

Study exercise #1: Supertasks

In 1954, the British philosopher James Thomson introduced an example which he took to be a variant on Zeno's dichotomy paradox. While it's connection to Zeno's paradoxes has been questioned, the kind of problem situation Thomson described is interesting in its own right.

Thomson described a lamp connected to a toggle switch that could turn the lamp on and off. In the idealized case considered here, assume that it takes no time to turn the switch from on to off, or vice versa. At time $t = 0$, the lamp is off. At time $t = 1/2$ second, turn the lamp on. At 3/4 of a second, turn it back off. In general, for any time, t, less than 1 second, press the switch at $t' = 1-t/2$.

Thomson then asked: what is the state of the lamp at $t = 1$ second? It cannot be on, because at any time less than 1 second when it was on, there's a time when it gets turned off. But, it can't be off, because it always gets turned back on.

Thomson called any such infinite sequence actions a "supertask." A supertask is defined to be any task whose completion requires an infinite sequence of ordinary tasks. Thomson took the indeterminate state of the lamp at the conclusion of the supertask above as proof that such supertasks are logically impossible. He also understood Zeno's dichotomy to have demonstrated that any ordinary trip through space was also a supertask, and thus impossible.

Although it seems plausible that such discreet supertasks are impossible, it is far from clear that Zeno's racecourse involves such a supertask. On Zeno's racecourse, both the course and the time of the race are continuous. As such, there is no actual sequence of discreet actions, only various ways of dividing a single continuous action. However, other philosophers take Thomson's challenge more seriously. Much of the discussion is reproduced in the book edited by Wesley Salmon listed below.

For now I leave you with two questions. Is Thomson's lamp a logically possible situation? And, if so does its possibility or impossibility tell us anything about the nature of time?

Further reading

Pretty much all of the math you need to follow the debates about Zeno's paradoxes can be found in:

Steinhart, E. (2009), *More Precisely: The Math you Need to do Philosophy*, Peterborough, ON; Buffalo, NY: Broadview Press.

Some of the standard works on Zeno's paradoxes include:

Faris, J. A. (1996), *The Paradoxes of Zeno*, Aldershot, Hants, England: Avebury.

A useful discussion of the scholarly issues regarding the interpretation of Zeno in historical context.

Salmon, W. C. (1970), *Zeno's Paradoxes*, Indianapolis: Bobbs-Merrill (The Library of Liberal Arts, LLA148).

An essential collection of classic papers and excerpts on Zeno's paradoxes, including excerpts from both Bergson and Bertrand Russell.

Grünbaum, A. (1968), *Modern Science and Zeno's Paradoxes*, London: Allen & Unwin.

The now standard account of the resolution of the paradoxes using modern mathematical techniques.

Huggett, N. (1999), *Space from Zeno to Einstein: Classic Readings with a Contemporary Commentary*, Cambridge, MA: MIT Press.

Although it focuses on problems of space, the first chapter has an excellent introduction to Zeno's Achilles paradox.

The last 15 years have seen a revival of interest in Zeno's arrow paradox. Among the most important recent papers are:

Arntzenius, F. (2000), "Are there really instantaneous velocities?," *Monist: An International Quarterly Journal of General Philosophical Inquiry*, 83 (2): 187–208.

Arntzenius, F. (2003), "An arbitrarily short reply to Sheldon Smith on instantaneous velocities," *Studies in History and Philosophy of Modern Physics*, 34B (2): 281–2.

Carroll, J. W. (2002), "Instantaneous motion," *Philosophical Studies: An International Journal for Philosophy in the Analytic Tradition*, 110 (1): 49–67.

Lange, M. (2005), "How can instantaneous velocity fulfill its causal role?," *Philosophical Review*, 114 (4): 433–68.

Smith, S. R. (2003), "Are instantaneous velocities real and really instantaneous?: An argument for the affirmative," *Studies in History and Philosophy of Modern Physics*, 34B (2): 261–80.

Discussion questions

1   Rather than begin with a definition of time, you have been offered a list of characteristics but not definitive temporal phenomena.
    a   Do you agree with this way of proceeding? Why or why not?
    b   Can you construct your own definition of time or becoming? How well does it account for the list on p. 24?
    c   Can you think of any plausible additions to that list?

2   Explain why change is such a serious metaphysical problem in its own right. Can you explain why time cannot be identical to any particular processes in the world? Can you explain the difference between time understood as change itself and time understood as the dimension or measure of change?

3   Can you construct your own examples to illustrate Zeno's paradoxes? Why does the combination of Zeno's paradoxes seem to leave Eleatic monism as the only alternative?

4   Mathematical results
    a   Can you explain what it means to claim that time is continuous in the sense intended in modern mathematical analysis?
    b   Explain, in words, the concept of the cardinality of a set? How does cardinality differ from the magnitude of an interval? How does this resolve Zeno's paradoxes of divisibility?
    c   Some actual math problems
        i   Complete the proof that all intervals of the real numbers are of equal cardinality.
        ii   Show why the disappearing arrow does not have an instantaneous velocity.

5   Henri Bergson, William James, and Alfred North Whitehead all refuse to accept standard mathematical resolution of the paradoxes. Can you explain what the basis for their rejection has in common? Can you explain at least one difference between Bergson's position and James's?
6   *Food for Thought:* Do you ultimately think that Zeno's paradoxes are examples of simple logical mistakes, sources of metaphysical profundity, or both?

Notes

1. This is the most metaphysical interpretation of Heraclitus. It is also possible to interpret Heraclitus such that there are not even real patterns in the flux, merely words, the literal meaning of the Greek *logos*, that human beings invent and impose on the flux.
2. This is of course a profoundly idealized version of modern chemistry. Even ignoring nuclear, as opposed to merely chemical, interactions, the modern theory of the chemical bond recognizes that the complex interactions create a real unity within a new compound as profound as that within the original elements.
3. We set aside the problem of tense—the ordering of time by past, present, and future—until Chapter 3.
4. We will discover in Chapter 6 that one of the ways in which special relativity requires a radical reevaluation of our understanding of time is that it violates this principle.
5. The Greek letter Σ, "sigma," stands for summation and tells us to add together everything that follows it.
6. Although there were, of course, debates about the status of π until the eighteenth century.
7. For mathematically sophisticated readers, the construction of the enumeration of the rationals technically only depends on the denumerability of the union of countable sets, but the two facts are closely related. Note that if a countable subset of a non-denumerable set had a countable complement, then one could go the other way and have a union of two countable sets that is non-denumerable. Whether these are precisely equivalent depends on subtle issues in set theory, such as which version of the axiom of choice one has available in a given context.

8. Nothing here hinges on the difference between *vector* or directed velocity and mere speed as an absolute rate.

9. This is technically the derivative of $x(t)$ from above. There are various ways to "take the limit" here; under the appropriate mathematical conditions, the various ways of taking the limit can give different answers. This illustrates the philosophical significance of the appropriate mathematical results; anyone interested in actually doing the mathematics should consult a basic calculus or analysis textbook, or see the relevant chapters in Roger Penrose, *The Road to Reality*.

10. This is not ultimately the case until the naive set theory we have been using here is replaced by some version of axiomatic set theory. But, it can be done.

3

McTaggart's Paradox and the Unreality of Time

After a schematic presentation of McTaggart's argument, we consider the difference between A-series, B-series, and C-series orderings of time and the application of the distinction between realism and idealism to the distinctive problem of time. This is followed by a somewhat detailed explication of McTaggart's original presentations of the argument. The rest of the chapter treats issues arising from McTaggart's argument including: possible defenses of a dynamic theory of change, the role of language and representation in debates about the reality of time, and the attempt to construct B-theoretic accounts of time based on theories of indexicals, like "I" and "here."

More than 2,000 years after the Eleatic assault on becoming, the Cambridge philosopher John Ellis McTaggart mounted his own arguments for "The Unreality of Time." Like Zeno, McTaggart claims that our ordinary conception of the world as evolving in time is self-contradictory. Unlike Zeno, McTaggart does not attempt to derive a contradiction from ordinary material change and motion. Instead, McTaggart's target is time understood of itself and independently from any material foundations.

McTaggart claims that there is a distinctive kind of change characteristic of time. This is the kind of change, later called "pure becoming," undergone as future times cease to be future and become present on their way to becoming past. McTaggart claims that such becoming is both essential to time and impossible (see box). McTaggart offered two apparently canonical presentations of the argument, in a classic article in the journal *Mind* in 1908 and in volume II of *The Nature of Existence* published in 1927.

Unfortunately, the appearance of clarity created by such a schematic presentation largely serves to highlight two fundamental sources of obscurity regarding McTaggart's arguments. The first, and most obvious, is McTaggart's own notoriously convoluted prose. This makes it difficult

---

McTaggart 1 Change is necessary for time.

McTaggart 2 Pure becoming–change in the A-series position of events as past, present, or future—is necessary for objective change.

McTaggart 3 Pure becoming is self-contradictory.

McTaggart 4 Therefore, time is unreal.

---

to understand why McTaggart thinks that "pure becoming" is the only kind of change that counts and, equally problematically, why he thinks it is self-contradictory. In addition, the two canonical presentations are not perfectly consistent, especially in their treatment of the necessity of pure becoming. We will do our best to unpack McTaggart's arguments for these two claims on pp. 71–75.

The second source of difficulty is the intrinsic philosophical difficulty associated with some of McTaggart's concepts. This inherent philosophical difficulty rests in two areas in particular—McTaggart's conception of the force of his argument and his characterization of becoming in terms of the A-series/B-series distinction. Until we have some kind of handle on this philosophical background, McTaggart's argument appears even more opaque than it actually is. On pp. 66–69, we will examine the basic distinction between the A-series and the B-series as introduced by McTaggart. We explicate the basic conception of objectivity and reality which McTaggart presupposes in presenting his argument beginning on p. 68.

There is a further problem that confronts those coming to McTaggart's argument and the literature surrounding it for the first time. Because of the difficulties associated with McTaggart's original presentations, there are many different presentations of something called "McTaggart's argument" or "McTaggart's paradox" in the philosophical literature that are much more clearly understood as what McTaggart could have or should have said than as representing what he did say. For example, in his classic essay, "McTaggart's Argument for the Unreality of Time," the important philosopher Michael Dummett offers an interpretation of McTaggart as arguing that fundamental reality cannot have an indexical component. Unfortunately, while the concept of indexicality turns out to be important for the philosophical debates inspired by McTaggart (cf. pp. 87–91), McTaggart himself does not appeal to it in either of the canonical statements of his argument. Similar problems afflict contemporary presentations of the A-series in presentist or growing block terms (cf. pp. 83–87 and Chapter 4) as changes in what exists. While these ontological moves might resolve some of McTaggart's worries about change, they are not the way that McTaggart resolves them.

Historical Note 9: J. M. E. McTaggart and Absolute Idealism

Following Immanuel Kant, the dominant philosophical trends of the nineteenth century are various versions of idealism. G. F. W. Hegel (1770–1831) is probably the most famous representative of idealism, but F. H. Bradley (1846–1924) is a more accessible figure and more directly influential on the twentieth-century figures important to this book. Bradley's basic metaphysical position is generally called "absolute idealism" and like many of the idealists, he serves to mark a kind of Eleatic vanishing point in the philosophy of time. Unfortunately, philosophers whose system is built around the illusory nature of temporal experience are unlikely to spend much time analyzing the structure of temporality.

Although J. M. E. McTaggart's (1866–1924) most important contributions to the philosophy of time do not appear until the twentieth century, his idealism gives his philosophy the feel of an older era. As a Fellow of Trinity College, Cambridge, McTaggart was also a deeply influential teacher of Bertrand Russell, G. E. Moore, and C. D. Broad among others. Of course his famous paradox is our subject here and is an important influence on all subsequent philosophy of time.

We therefore have two major tasks in this chapter. We must unpack McTaggart's original argument, and we must discover some kind of guide to the post-McTaggart debates about becoming and the A-series. The next three sections focus on the first of those tasks, with pp. 71–75, particularly attempting to explicate McTaggart's own reasoning. I will argue that McTaggart's own argument cannot be salvaged in anything like its original forms. Neither of the crucial second or third premises above can be given a plausible interpretation that also leads to a valid argument.

Fortunately, at least for the sake of full employment for philosophers, that's not the end of the story. Whatever one thinks of its philosophical coherence, the historical significance of McTaggart's argument is immense; almost all Anglo-American philosophy of time takes its terminology and its conceptual shape from McTaggart. I would suggest that this results from three philosophically significant sources. First, the legitimate philosophical insight embodied in McTaggart's distinction between the A-series and the B-series has led many philosophers to look for an important argument "in the vicinity" of McTaggart's paradox. Second, McTaggart's own obscurity makes him a perfect philosophical mirror; other philosophers can construct whatever philosophical interlocutor they need from his text. Finally these lead to serious disagreements about the nature of McTaggart's failure. So-called A-theorists such as Quentin Smith, Michael Tooley, and others agree with McTaggart that becoming is essential to time, but argue for its internal coherence. B-theorists agree with McTaggart that the A-series is contradictory, but defend the conception of time ordered only by the B-series. These debates are some of the most active in contemporary philosophy, and the second half of this chapter is dedicated to providing the basic conceptual toolkit and a map to prepare the reader to jump into and follow these ongoing debates.

A-series, B-series, and the structure of time

Before we can unpack McTaggart's argument against time, we need to clarify the philosophical background assumptions with which he is operating. To do that we really need answers to three questions. First, what is time; what is the model that McTaggart takes to be essential to time? Second, what kind of thing is time; to what metaphysical category does it belong? Finally, what conception of reality does McTaggart employ; what would have to be the case in order to satisfy him that time was real?

The first question is the most straightforward and is the topic of this section. Let's begin with what we already know. In Chapter 2, we characterized time as the dense, continuous linear order characteristic of motion and change. For now, let's set aside our previous concern with continuity and shift our attention merely to the concept of an order of events. Locating each event within this structure allows us to represent quite a lot of information about it. However, nothing about that structure is yet distinctively temporal. To see what's missing, consider the curve that follows the train tracks from Chicago to New York City. This is also a dense continuous linear order, only in this case of locations in space rather than time. My ability to recognize that one of these orders is temporal and the other is spatial depends entirely on our pre-theoretical understanding of the distinction between places and times rather than on any facts about the model itself. They are both merely examples of what McTaggart calls a C-series.

So are there any facts about temporal orders that distinguish them as a special category of linear order? The most obvious feature is that legitimately temporal orders possess an intrinsic direction from earlier to later, what McTaggart calls the B-series. To see this, consider our train tracks from Chicago to New York again. Those are also the tracks from New York to Chicago. However, for any "trip" through time, say riding the train along those tracks from Chicago to New York, the reverse path seems to be impossible. If I leave Chicago at 9:30 p.m. and arrive in New York the next day at 6:30 p.m., I can't leave New York at 6:30 p.m. and arrive back in Chicago at 9:30 p.m. the previous day. For any two elements of a time series, T_1 and T_2, one of them is before the other and there is a path only from the earlier to the later.[1]

Intuitively, there is a second distinctive feature of temporal orders, McTaggart's A-series. Within the A-series, there is always a distinguished element of any time series, the "now" or "present." The present has two important roles. First, it partitions time into the past and the future. Second, one and only one time is present, but it is present only instantaneously and then immediately becomes past; never to be present again. This is McTaggart's famous A-series, always determinate but always changing.

These two features of time, while connected, are logically independent of each other. They are connected in that presentness always flows from earlier to later times, and the past is always earlier than and the future later than the present. However, no knowledge of these relations is ever sufficient to determine an A-series. No knowledge of the order of events making up a train ride to New York tells one whether or not the trip is happening, will happen, or has happened.

Thus, time is the total linear order of events in the universe directed from earlier to later with a single element of the order, an instant or moment of time, distinguished as present. The order is total in that every instantaneous event is associated with, occurs at, one and only one element, and every event or process that takes a nonzero time is associated with a unique subinterval of the structure. What do we mean when we say that such a structure is either real or unreal?

The metaphysical status of time

Once again we begin with the case with which we're already familiar—Zeno's paradoxes. Obviously, if it really were the case that nothing can ever happen in the world, then nothing has this structure. There are much more subtle kinds of reality and unreality though. Let's call our ordinary, everyday picture of a world containing plants and animals, people, built objects like cars and houses, and all the regular stuff of life, the world of ordinary middle-sized dry goods (OMDGs). I don't have to agree with Parmenides or Zeno that I'm wrong about everything regarding these OMDGs in order to recognize that I'm wrong about some of my beliefs about some of them.

In addition, the world of OMDGs does not merely contain objects; those objects have a structure. They have properties that make them similar to other objects, and they have relationships to those objects. Consider a simple case like a coffee cup. Among other things, my coffee cup is a cup; it has a particular shape; a particular color, blue in this case; etc. On the one hand, these properties of or facts about the cup connect it to other OMDGs. There are, or at least could be, completely distinct things, such as a shirt, that are exactly the same color as the cup. On the other hand, there are also cups that have almost nothing else in common with this cup. These *universals,* as philosophers call things likes colors and shapes, seem to exist in a way different from the OMDGs themselves.

On the one hand, universals don't seem to be limited in the same way as *particulars.* My cup can only exist once—when, where, and as itself; the same color can occur in a multitude of different things. On the other hand, each of those occurrences depends on the existence of a particular thing; a color is always the color of something. Philosophers say that each occurrence of a universal is *ontologically dependent* on a particular.

So each instance of a universal is ontologically dependent on the particular that exemplifies it. Is the universal itself ontologically dependent on its instances, and thus on the particular things? Perhaps, or perhaps not. Plato famously claimed that each particular instance of a universal is merely the dim reflection of an ideal form that is ontologically independent of the world of OMDGs. On the other hand, it seems possible to imagine a universe empty of material objects. It has seemed bizarre to many people to claim that such a world, without any color, still contains all of the ideal COLORS.

We're not going to solve the problem of universals here. It is one of the most vexed in all of metaphysics and only tangentially related to the problem of time. The point of this detour is to introduce the way in which questions of ontological independence or dependence lead us to a more complex conception of reality. Thus, someone who believes that the color blue is entirely exhausted by a list of its particular instances might well claim, in certain contexts, that blue is unreal. They needn't, thereby, deny that there are any blue cups in the world.

What does this have to do with time and McTaggart? Consider the structure of time described above. There are two questions suggested by this discussion of ontological independence. First, is the structure ontologically independent of the events associated with it? Would the world have this kind of a directed structure with passage even if nothing else occurred? The most general form of this question is the debate over absolute versus relational theories of time which we will discuss in Chapter 6. However, we will need to say a bit about this to clarify McTaggart's answer to the second question.

That second question is whether time is ontologically independent of our thought and experience of time. Would the world have this structure even if there were no sentient beings to experience it having the structure? In philosophy, those who believe that the world or some aspect of it exists independently of minds are called *realists*. At the opposite end of the spectrum are *idealists* who believe that the world, or some aspect of it again, is entirely the product of human minds in roughly the sense of ontological dependence sketched above. Consider an OMDG such as the coffee cup again and recognize that I never really have direct contact with the cup. Instead, on the common-sense understanding of things, the cup causes me to have certain ideas, to be in certain mental states. An idealist would point out that even if I think there's *something* out there ontologically independent of me, I don't have any reason to think that it's much like my idea of the cup. Therefore, according to the idealist, I'm really better off thinking of the cup as an idea that I have about the world instead of as a thing independent of me.

Unfortunately, our ability to apply this criterion of reality to time is complicated by the fact that time is not a thing within experience. It is neither an OMDG nor a qualitative feature of particular OMDGs. My experience of the blueness of my coffee cup is a part of my particular experience of the particular coffee cup. However, my experience of time does not seem to be a part of the foreground content of experience, but a part of the background structure of experience. This is emphasized by a particular oddity of time. Not only do my experiences of the world represent it as being in time, they are themselves in time. When my experience of a race tells me that it's ten seconds long, that's not a separate part of the content of the experience. I simply have a ten-second–long experience corresponding to the ten-second–long race.

The question then becomes, what and how much of the "temporal" content of our experiences reflect facts about the objects of those experiences and how much is entirely the product of our own mental activity. Consider those distinct mental states most closely associated with the A-series: memory (of the past), perception (of the present), and anticipation (of the future). We ordinarily accept that we remember some event *because it is past*; we treat memory almost as a "perception" of pastness. Memory is our mental capacity to represent past events to ourselves as past. However, according to McTaggart, we have improperly inverted the natural order of things here. We should simply take it as a brute psychological fact that we have this variety of qualitatively distinct mental states. We then, mistakenly, project or invent an underlying structure of qualities of events to account for the structure of our ideas. As McTaggart puts it in his original article in *Mind*,

> The direct perception itself is a mental state qualitatively different from the memory or the anticipation of perceptions. On this is based the belief that the perception itself has a certain characteristic when I have it, which is replaced by other characteristics when I have the memory or the anticipation of it—which characteristics are called presentness, pastness, and futurity. Having got the idea of these characteristics we apply them to other events.

We now turn to the argument that led McTaggart to his extreme claim that all temporal experience is illusory.

McTaggart's argument for the unreality of time

One of the fundamental goals of this section is to explicate McTaggart's own argument as he presents it in his *Mind* article and in *The Nature of Existence* while avoiding, as much as possible, interpretations that depend on what McTaggart could have or should have said. The remainder of the chapter is dedicated to work inspired by or in conversation with McTaggart. Before we begin, we need to introduce some additional terminology. We've already been introduced to the A-series and the B-series. Let's say that the A-determinations are whatever there is about events which distinguish them as past, present, or future. Then, A-change will be change in the A-determination of an event or moment. One more bit of terminology, *an* A-series is what one has when the set of moments is ordered around a single one as the now. *The* A-series generally refers to the complete system of distinct A-series with the becoming present of each distinct moment either constitutive or associated with the passage of time.

We are now in a position to unpack the schematic presentation of the argument given on p. 64 which will allow us to recognize how implausible McTaggart's argument actually is. **McTaggart 1** is, as we saw in the last chapter, relatively uncontroversial on its own. However, the version of this claim that McTaggart requires in order to justify the rest of his argument is controversial. McTaggart clearly requires that change *in* or *of* the underlying events that make up the time series is required for time. In the original article McTaggart offers essentially no defense of this claim; he simply seems to see it as a restatement of the fact that time requires change. Unfortunately, for McTaggart, this is simply a fallacy of equivocation. Those who claim that change is essential to time mean that the events which make up time are themselves changes in objects or substances. Before McTaggart, I know of no hint that the passage of time requires change in changes.

In *The Nature of Existence*, McTaggart does say a bit more regarding this claim. In response to an objection from Bertrand Russell, he suggests that only change in events can ground ordinary change in ordinary entities. McTaggart suggests that we consider an ordinary object, such as a fireplace poker. Suppose that it is heated on October 14 and that is the only time at which it is hot. It certainly seems as though the poker has changed, and this description makes no reference to the A-series. McTaggart claims that this is not a legitimate change in the absence of additional A-series specification of when the poker became or becomes hot. As McTaggart puts it,

> This makes no change in the qualities of the poker. It is always a quality of that poker that it is one which is hot on that particular Monday. And it is always a quality of that poker that it is one which is not hot at any other time. Both these qualities are true of it at any time—the time when it is hot and the time when it is cold. And therefore it seems to be erroneous to say that there is any change in the poker.

Let us grant McTaggart that there are such qualities as "hot on October 14," and that any object with that quality neither gains nor loses that quality. There seems to be a quite simple fallacy in this passage as well. Neither Russell, nor anyone else who believes that the poker changes by being hot on October 14 and at no other time needs to claim that every quality of the poker changes. You simply can't get from something does not change to nothing changes, as a matter of logic.[2] Many philosophers of the Heraclitean bent have sensed an important argument in the vicinity of McTaggart's suggestion. Perhaps, some requirement that real change in individual entities depends on or requires some kind of change in, what we might call, the total constitution of the world. We will examine some of these suggestions on pp. 75–78.

In addition to his problematic assumptions regarding the nature of change, McTaggart makes a further presupposition regarding the A-determinations. He takes for granted that they must be characteristics or qualities of the elements of the time series, whether those are events or moments. As McTaggart does, let us focus on events. In that case, McTaggart requires the A-determinations to be either properties of events or relations between an event and some nontemporal entity.

McTaggart offers basically no argument for this claim. However, our discussion of ontological independence in the previous section allows us to see why one might believe this. Assume that the temporal presentness of a particular event must be ontologically independent of all other events or beings in the world. Properties are simply the only aspect of things that have that characteristic. The problem is that interpreting "pastness" for example as a property of events yields a fairly implausible metaphysical picture. To begin to see how implausible, ask yourself how many such properties there must be to distinguish all of the past events from each other. As we will see, much of the modern debate over "McTaggart's paradox" has focused on identifying the actual logical and metaphysical categories to which the A-determinations belong.

We are now ready to consider McTaggart's overall argument against the reality of time. Begin with the following: from **McTaggart 1** and his conceptions of change and of the A-determinations, we can interpret **McTaggart 2** as follows:

> **McTaggart 2**(a) Time is ontologically independent of human beings if and only if events undergo change in the A-determinations, that is, they instantiate, A-change.

McTaggart doesn't say much to establish A-change, change in the degree of pastness or futurity of events, as the only kind of change in events that can constitute the A-series, but here's a way to make it plausible. Consider some past event, say the first inauguration of Barack Obama as president of the United States. The A-determinations of that event certainly seem to change; it now has the A-determination "pastness." Setting aside, as usual, concerns from relativity theory, nothing can be past without having once been present; having any one A-determination immediately seems to imply that the event has lost at least one of the other A-determinations.

This also seems to be the only kind of change to which events might be subject. As we saw in Chapter 2, any account of change requires a distinction between essential properties that define the identity of the changing entity and the accidental property subject to change. The problem is that all of the features of events other than the A-determinations seem to be essential.

Consider the inauguration again. Any change in the "ordinary" features of the event—the participants, their actions, the setting, and spatial location, even the temporal location relative to other events in the B-series or the C-series—convert it into an event distinct from the one that actually occurred; the only possible variation in the event that leaves it the same event is that it was future, became present, and is past.

So given the other elements of McTaggart's basic metaphysical picture, **McTaggart 2(a)** seems plausible. How does this end up trapping him in the contradiction indicated in **McTaggart 3**? Consider the following:

> **McTaggart 3(a)** Every event has exactly one A-determination.

This seems straightforwardly required by the definition of the A-series; every event is located at one and only location in time. However, McTaggart also claims to offer an argument in favor of the following claim:

> **McTaggart 3(b)** Every event has at least two A-determinations.

Why might McTaggart make such an apparently odd claim? Consider the inauguration again.

Example 3.1 Barack Obama was inaugurated as president of the United States.

Note that example 3.1 predicates two distinct characteristics of a single event: "presentness" and "pastness"; it says both that the inauguration is past in the present and present in the past. In doing so, it seems to commit us to **McTaggart 3(b)**. McTaggart also notes that the explicit predication of the A-determinations is not the only temporal reference in our example. The example at least appears consistent because it predicates the incompatible properties of the event only at distinct times. In general, the possession of incompatible properties generates a contradiction only when one claims that an object possesses them simultaneously, not successively.

Consider color. "Being wholly red" and "being wholly green" are also incompatible properties, but the tomato on my counter was green and is red without any problem. Why is the same resolution not available for the A-determinations?

McTaggart responds that any attempt to unpack along the lines of colors or other sets of incompatible qualities generates either a vicious circle or a vicious infinite regress. Unfortunately, at this crucial moment the obscurity of McTaggart's expression becomes debilitating. He provides three accounts of the "difficulty" or "fallacy" involved in such attempts, none of them particularly clear. He does however seem to take them as manifestations of the same underlying problem.

Rather than unpack the various accounts in McTaggart's article, here's an attempt to diagnose the problem around which he is circling. McTaggart seems to be interpreting his first two premises as implying that nontemporal variation in A-determinations grounds or generates time. If the replacement of the property of presentness by the property of pastness defines change of location in time, McTaggart presumes that there must be an explanation of that variation without any implicit or explicit reference to the A-series position.

Here's another way to see the problem. In order to undergo A-change, given that the A-determinations are properties of events, the inauguration must have been present in the past. That is, it must have the property of presentness at some past time. On this interpretation though, being at some past time just is a matter of having the property of pastness. Therefore, "to have been past" is to have the property of presentness while also having the property of pastness. This does seem to be an example of **McTaggart 3(b)** and to commit one to contradictory treatments of the A-series.

This interpretation at least has the virtue of making McTaggart's argument valid. If we insist that temporal passage must be generated by nontemporal A-change construed as change in underlying objectively real A-properties, then McTaggart is correct. There can be no nontemporal characterization of A-change, and thus there can be no nontemporal grounding of the passage of time. Unfortunately, it does so only at the expense of making McTaggart's view profoundly implausible. I know of no one before McTaggart who attempted to provide such a nontemporal grounding of the past-future distinction and McTaggart's argument that it is necessary depends on two profoundly implausible premises—change in events and his treatment of the A-determinations as qualities of events.

Heraclitean arguments for A-change

There are three basic arguments to be found in the philosophical literature that attempt to "cash out" McTaggart's intuition that a wholly objective A-series is necessary for the objectivity of the passage of time. These include: worries about coherence of certain attitudes and actions on a purely B-theoretic conception of time, attempts to defend McTaggart's claim that change must be something more or other than mere B-series variation in the properties of persistent entities, and semantic worries about our ability to interpret tensed sentences and A-series ascriptions in purely B-series terms. In this section, we consider the two direct arguments for the reality of A-change. We consider the semantics and metaphysics of the A-series later in this chapter pp. 83–87, following another technical interlude to introduce some crucial concepts from philosophy of language on pp. 78–83.

Before we proceed one additional note is in order. The actual division between A-theorists and B-theorists probably has a lot more to do with the personalities of individual philosophers than most participants in the debate are willing to admit. Thus, much of the debate proceeds in reverse order. That is, one either believes that that pure becoming is an absolute feature of reality or not. Only then do arguments begin to get any traction. In any case, here are two standard examples.

A. N. Prior's headache

The most important arguments for A-theoretic accounts of time are a family of arguments designed to prove that only A-change can make sense of our changing attitudes toward various events and another family of arguments designed to prove that only change in events can account for real change in objects.

The most well-known example in the first family of arguments was presented by Arthur Prior in an article called "Thank Goodness That's Over!"

> One says, e.g. "Thank goodness that's over!," and not only is this, when said, quite clear without any date appended, but it says something which it is impossible that any use of a tenseless copula with a date should convey. It certainly doesn't mean the same as, e.g. "Thank goodness the date of the conclusion of that thing is Friday, June 15, 1954," even if it be said then. (Nor, for that matter, does it mean "Thank goodness the conclusion of that thing is contemporaneous with this utterance." Why should anyone thank goodness for that?) Prior (1959)

Consider a headache.[3] Suppose I learn that I will suffer severe migraine tomorrow. As soon as I get such news, I will quite reasonably begin to dread getting out of bed tomorrow morning. However, as soon as it passes, I will feel relief precisely for the fact of its passing. Therefore, as Prior suggests in the passage above, it seems as though there must be some fact about the headache which explains the reasonableness of my differing attitudes. Attitudes which are, of course, mirrored in my actions. Thus, I don't merely dread the future migraine; I prepare for it, while obviously, not preparing for yesterday's migraine today.

I can then run precisely the kind of argument by exhaustion that McTaggart makes in his original article. There must be some difference between the future headache and the past headache which explains my differing attitudes and actions. However, any change in the ordinary characteristics of the headache, for example, it's intensity, turns it into a different headache. In addition, the headache will always be later than today and earlier than the day after tomorrow. If I know when the headache is, I know that too. Those don't change so they can't explain why I change. The only available candidates are the A-determinations.

Change in events as essential to change in objects

The second argument for A-theory is more about dissatisfaction with the alternatives than a particular positive theory. Consider an object that exists across time, say McTaggart's example of a fireplace poker. At some point in time, the poker is taken off the rack and put in the fire—at which time, it becomes hot. A *static theory of change* provides an account of the lifetime of the poker as a sequence of events that the poker participates in, or equivalently of changes that happen to the poker.[4] The poker becomes hot, undergoes a particular change, just in case at some time in the life of the poker it's hot later than having been cold.

Many A-theorists seem profoundly dissatisfied with this account of change. Unfortunately, much of the dissatisfaction manifests itself as philosophically sophisticated table banging rather than argument. By that I mean, A-theorists simply wish to emphasize that being hot later than being cold is not a change, apparently because it involves states of being rather than becoming. There are two general suggestions in the literature as to why not.

First, there is a suggestion originating with McTaggart himself that such accounts of change are unable to distinguish temporal change from mere spatial variation in properties. Why, asks McTaggart, does having different temperatures at different times constitute a change, but being different temperatures at different ends does not constitute a change? The general worry seems to be that such an account of change fails to adequately distinguish time from space.[5]

Second, there seems to be a general sense that real change must involve fundamental change in the contents of the universe as a whole. This is what Michael Tooley has called a *dynamic* rather than a static conception of the nature of the world. The worry seems to be that just as no matter where I am in space, the rest of the occupants of space are, metaphorically, waiting for me to run across them, so the already later states of the poker are equally waiting for me to get to that temporal location. For a philosopher who believes in a dynamic world, it makes no sense to say that my cold poker becomes hot by being hot later because right now that later poker doesn't exist to have any properties at all.[6] Therefore, it seems as though one who wishes to create change in a dynamic way must appeal to something more than merely the B-series to do so.

There's one final way to think about the problem here. Imagine that I had a list of the temperature of my poker at every time at which the poker exists. For example, imagine a poker that doesn't yet exist and won't be made until 2050. Suppose I had a list of the temperatures of the poker at all of the times when the poker exists. In fact, suppose that I know that the poker will become extremely hot after being placed in a fire sometime in 2051. The poker changes when it's placed in the fire, but until that time actually becomes present, it seems plausible to wonder whether anything has yet changed about the poker. Only as the event of the poker becoming hot achieves the appropriate position within the A-series does the world change in such a way as to contain a hot poker. For someone with strong Heraclitean intuitions, it is not the various ways that things are in the world that constitutes change, it is only in coming to be each of those ways that change is real.

Technical interlude #2: Representation, semantics, and metaphysics

Perhaps the most pervasive family of arguments regarding the A-series, both for and against, hinge on the interpretation of tensed sentences. By *tensed sentences* we mean sentences that change their truth-value at different times in ways that are independent of anything except the changing time. Thus, example 3.2 is true only at two times and false at all others. We call these tensed sentences because in Indo-European languages the dominant, but far from only, manifestation of the phenomenon of variable truth-value rests in the tensed inflection of verbs.

Consider the difference between examples 3.1 and 3.2.

Example 3.2 Barack Obama is being inaugurated as president of the United States.

They must make different claims about the world because they are true at different times despite the fact that they seem to be statements about precisely the same event(s). In this section, we will introduce some of the technical machinery developed by philosophers, and others, to address such puzzles about the relationship between our representational structures, such as language, and the world as represented. In the remainder of this chapter, we will use it to examine various proposals about the A-series.

Human beings represent the world to ourselves and to each other. We have beliefs and opinions about the way things are; we draw pictures and construct sculptures; and most importantly for our purposes, we formulate theories and describe the world in language. When we accept such a description as true or accurate, we also accept that the world is the way that it is represented as being. *Semantics* is the study of such representation and has two aspects. First, we would like to know how it is possible that language represents the world. We're going to worry about this problem only tangentially—only to the extent that some answers to the second question seem to make it impossible to answer this one. Our second question concerns the structure of such representation. We would like to identify the rules that would allow us to "read off" the content of such representations.

This might seem a profoundly trivial question. We all speak a language, and we don't generally have much trouble figuring out what other people are telling us about the world. That would be true if all we were interested in was understanding individual statements. However, semantics is about the system of representation and the rules for interpretation. Competent speakers of English do not have any trouble interpreting my statement, "My cup is blue." That does not mean that they understand what they are doing.

To see why not, consider the following two questions. What makes the content of "My cup is blue." and "Meine Tasse ist blau." the same? Do they both directly represent the same facts about an external real world? Do they both trigger the same or similar actions among speakers of the respective languages, English and German? Do they express the same idea or proposition? Second, what accounts for the similarity in the content of "My cup is blue." and "My house is blue."? Is there a single thing, the universal property of "blueness," that manifests itself in the two separate objects? Or am I really making a claim about appearances? Am I claiming that there is not really something that is the same, but merely that the two objects seem similar to me in a particular way?

The problems become even more subtle in the case of time because, as we've already seen, outside of philosophy time shows up largely as part of the way we talk about things rather than as one of the things that we talk about. The A-series largely manifests itself in the different temporal behavior of present-tense, past-tense, and future-tense sentences. What kind of structure must we postulate in the world to account for that behavior?

We need to characterize that temporal behavior. To do that, a technical notion from philosophy of language will be useful. In 1891, the German philosopher Gottlob Frege introduced a distinction between two different aspects of the semantic meaning of a sentence, sense and reference. He did this by considering a puzzle. Since "The Morning Star" and "The Evening Star" both refer to the planet Venus, they both mean the same thing and learning that "The Morning Star is The Evening Star" seems as though it should be a purely linguistic matter. A matter of learning a new name for the same thing, like learning that Chicago is also called "The Windy City." That doesn't seem quite right. The first person who figured out that these really are the same thing discovered a real scientific fact about the world.

Frege suggested that we can divide the meaning of words and sentences into two aspects. Words or sentences pick out things or facts in the world, their reference; they also do so in a particular way or mode, their sense. This allows Frege to account for his puzzle, roughly, as follows. "The Morning Star" means, has the sense of, "the bright green star that I see come up over the horizon just before the sun a lot of the time." Similarly for "the Evening Star." It is therefore a real discovery that these two ways of picking out an object in the world, arrived at independently, happen to pick out the very same object, to have the same reference.

We don't have to endorse Frege's own theory about sense and reference, or even his account of the puzzle of identity, in order to recognize the usefulness of his distinction between two kinds of meaning.(See the relevant references in suggested reading for more discussion of this issue.) For our purposes, it allows us to capture the most difficult aspect of accounting for the A-series—the variable truth-value but the constant meaning of tensed sentences.

Although example 3.2 is false today, there were two times when it would have been true. Therefore, something has to be different today than it was on January 20, 2013. Yet it also means the same thing today as it did then; it has the same sense. We need one more bit of terminology. If names refer to objects, we will say that statements are *satisfied* by facts or *states of affairs*. We will therefore say that a statement is true just in case a state of affairs that satisfies that statement *obtains*. Roughly speaking, *tensed theories* or A-theoretic accounts of tensed sentences explain the variation in truth-value in terms of a change in the underlying facts. According to tensed theorists, example 3.2 is no longer true because the state of affairs that would satisfy it no longer obtains. *Tenseless theories* claim that although the same state of affairs obtains today as it did on January 20, 2013, example 3.2 can only be satisfied when the inauguration occurs at the time of evaluation of the sentence.

That is, tenseless accounts of tensed sentences account for the difference in terms of a difference in the sentence or in terms of a difference between various uses of the sentence. Although we won't make use of them until pp. 87–91, this is a good place to introduce two additional technical concepts central to most B-theoretic or Eleatic accounts of tensed languages.

The first technical device that we require is that of *tenseless predication* or the *tenseless copula*. It is a grammatical fact about English and related languages that we ordinarily specify the properties of objects using verb predicates. It's also a grammatical oddity of such languages, as Quine notes in *Word and Object* and as quoted on p. 87, that every verb requires a grammatical tense. So every ordinary sentence of our language involves us in problems of tense and temporal becoming. Even outside of metaphysical problems about time this can be problematic. For example, my claim that the number two is even or, to use an example from Chapter 2, that a given mathematical series converges should not, even under normal circumstances, be understood as something that happens at a particular time.

We can therefore introduce the tenseless copula to construct grammatically correct sentences while removing the implicit temporal references. Thus, in order to assert the abstract mathematical relationship above, we might say:

Example 3.3 The number two *is-tenselessly* even.

For concrete objects that have spatial location and occupy particular periods of time, things are a bit trickier. Objects such as my car always possess their properties at particular times. However, whether my car has the property of "whiteness" on January 1, 2013, seems to be entirely a matter of the state of the car on that day, and not whether it happens to have that color in the past, the present, or the future. We can thus say:

Example 3.4 My car *is-tenselessly* white *on* January 1, 2013.

This emphasizes that the color of the car on that date doesn't seem to depend on what is happening now, but only on what is happening at certain specifiable times in the lifetime of the car.

Our ability to generate such tenseless systems of representation, of which the predicate calculus of modern symbolic logic is the most developed, is the first clue that B-theorists might be on the right track. The variable truth-value of tensed sentences might be a contingent feature of systems of representation and not a manifestation of underlying structure in the world. Finally, the system of tenseless predication allows us to replace the implicit appeal to temporal structure of verb inflection with explicit temporal indexicals. Thus, example 3.2 becomes:

> **Example 3.5** Barack Obama *is-tenselessly inaugurated* as President of the United States *now*.

Similarly, example 3.1 becomes:

> **Example 3.6** Barack Obama *is-tenselessly inaugurated* at some time earlier than now.

The basic goal of the B-theorist is to provide an account of the A-series in entirely tenseless terms, largely appealing to the B-series. This might seem hopeless given what we said about the train journey earlier in this chapter, but that presumes that the A-series position of the train journey is given only in terms of the B-series features of the *train journey*. The basic B-theoretic strategy is to recognize that there are two sets of B-determinations relevant to specifying the A-determinations of the train journey: those of the train journey and those of the person describing the train journey.

This points toward the basic strategy that tenseless theorists will adopt: the recognition that time and tense are not the only situations in which such puzzles of variable truth-value but constant sense arise. Such linguistic devices as "here" and "there" for space, "I" and "you" for persons, and "that" for objects all manifest the same apparently puzzling features. Such devices are variously called *indexicals*, *demonstratives*, or *token-reflexives*. What all of these have in common is change in reference, without change in the underlying "meaning" or sense, depending on the context of use. Thus, the location indicated by "here" depends on where it is used; the person indicated by "I" depends on who uses it; etc. It is also the case that "here," "I," and the like *mean* the same thing each time. In these cases only the context plus the meaning determines the reference, not the meaning by itself. It is as if such locutions have an incomplete sense, one only completed by some further facts.

The usual way to describe this difference involves introducing one more technical distinction, the type-token distinction. The distinction is deployed in an attempt to clarify an ambiguity in the identity conditions for elements of language, such as a sentence, phrase, or even an entire book. Imagine there are two people in a room, each of whom has a copy of this book, and assume that there are no other books in that room. How many books are there in the room? Depending on the exact context in which we ask the question, both one and two seem be legitimate answers to the question. What philosophers would say is that there are two (book) *tokens* of a single book *type* in the room.

Notice that meaning is fundamentally a property of types; I understand an expression only when I recognize what type it instantiates. Truth or falsehood is fundamentally a property of tokens, especially but not exclusively for any type that involves indexicals; I can't make a true or a false a statement without producing a particular token. Finally, since part of the purpose of specifying the meaning of the types is to give us the rules for determining whether individual tokens are true, the meaning of indexical types must include a reference to facts about the tokens. The various tenseless accounts of the A-series adopt different strategies to account for this.

Both the tensed and tenseless options face their own hurdles. Tensed theories that postulate real A-change must overcome McTaggart's paradox. Tenseless theories must explain how sentences can have consistent meaning but change their reference over time. Let's begin with tensed theories.

Tensed theories of the A-series

There are two categories of tensed theories in general circulation—property theories and existence theories.[7]

Most tensed theories are really hybrid theories. They invoke both a change in the A-determinations of events and a change in the contents of the universe, an ontological difference. Here we're going to examine reasonably pure theories of each type. In *Language and Time*, Quentin Smith defends a theory of A-change that is a direct descendant of the account of the A-series in McTaggart. Smith attempts to account for the flow of time entirely in terms of the changing collection of things that have the property of "presentness." We will then examine the relatively "pure" existence theory defended by Michael Tooley in *Time, Tense and Causation*.

Smith's account of the A-series forms a part of a complex and unorthodox metaphysical system. For example, Smith also claims that existence is a property that comes in degrees, a claim contrary to the mainstream philosophical tradition going back at least to Immanuel Kant. Fortunately, we can largely set aside these general metaphysical concerns. Our interest in Smith's system is as an example of a general strategy for avoiding McTaggart's paradox.

Although it's not clear how many A-properties Smith believes in, there are clearly at least three of them: pastness, presentness, and futurity. Of these the most important is presentness which Smith believes is an implicit logical subject of absolutely every sentence. By this he seems to mean that every statement, whatever it seems to be about, is really a statement about the present and only secondarily about the explicit subject. Luckily, this extreme claim is also independent of Smith's attempt to avoid McTaggart's paradox.

Consider example 3.2 again. According to Smith, this sentence attributes the property of presentness to Barack Obama's inauguration. More precisely, it states that:

Example 3.7 Presentness inheres in the event of Barack Obama's inauguration.

Similarly, for past and future-tense sentences. Consider:

Example 3.8 Barack Obama was inaugurated.

Example 3.8 attributes pastness to the same event as 3.7 attributes presentness. How then does Smith avoid the paradox? Doesn't this immediately commit Smith to **McTaggart 3(b)** (p. 105)? That is, the event described in 3.8 has the property of pastness in the present, which requires it to have the property of presentness. That requires that it either have the *same* property of presentness as it has in 3.7 triggering the paradox, or a different such property triggering an infinite regress.

At this point Smith introduces a twist. If the A-properties are properties of events, some of the events of which they could be properties are the inherence of the A-properties in ordinary events. Thus, in example 3.8 what is present is not the inauguration but the "inherence-of-pastness-in-the-inauguration" and what is past is the "inherence-of-presentness-in-the-inauguration." While there are potential problems with this scheme,[8] the work of Smith and others has made it at least plausible that a sufficient willingness to add metaphysical complexity could yield a version of it immune to McTaggart's paradox. This is because, at the very least, it provides a scheme for nesting tenses which avoids attributing incompatible properties to the same events and does not obviously require an infinite regress of distinct A-series.

Unfortunately, Smith's system is complex in ways often used to give metaphysics a bad name, and does commit us to some rather implausible positions. Among others, it seems that example 3.1 is only indirectly about the actual inauguration, but directly about the property of presentness. Despite this, it illustrates one basic strategy for defending A-change. If one believes that intrinsic change in events is essential to temporal becoming, then some distinctively temporal properties, or perhaps relations, of those events must be changing. In which case, one requires an account of the present truth of statements about the past that never attributes any two of those properties to the same event. Smith demonstrates how to do this more directly and more clearly than any of his A-theoretic competitors with whom I am familiar.

Unfortunately, Smith's theory also illustrates the classical problems facing any A-theoretic attempt to avoid McTaggart's paradox. First, the complicated, metaphysical twists and turns of such theories make it difficult to see how such a complicated, alleged reality produced such a relatively straightforward engagement with time in ordinary language. Whatever else might be going on, ordinary five-year-olds don't have any trouble learning to properly deploy English tenses. Does that mean that they also have an implicit grasp of the underlying metaphysics postulated by A-theorists? That seems implausible.

Second, these A-properties often seem to be almost too pure. They seem to be causally neutral at least relative to any effects on ordinary sense modalities. If I'm using linguistic tenses to track A-determinations, wouldn't I also expect to have an appropriate sense modality that allows me to track them? I don't seem to have any such thing. Finally, all such A-theories are incompatible with Einstein's theory of relativity. Although we will reserve our detailed discussion of this problem for Chapter 6, we can point out now that all such theories require sets of simultaneous events to be absolutely present to each other in a way that contradicts the relativity of simultaneity at the heart of modern physics. This problem afflicts not only property versions of tensed theories but existence-based versions as well, to which we now turn.

Suppose that one finds the property conception of the A-series problematic, even if it's possible to formulate a version that avoids McTaggart's paradox. It might still be possible to identify some feature of the present such that it remains really distinct from all other times. Given our tendency to believe that what is happening now is real in a way that neither past nor future events are, existence seems to be an obvious candidate for such a feature.

We'll reserve a general discussion of the metaphysical status of the future compared to the present and the past for Chapter 4. Here we are only interested in the connection between theories of a nonexistent future and the problem of the A-series. Such theories have an advantage over other tensed accounts in that they do not postulate intrinsic change in events. As the philosopher C. D. Broad, himself a student of McTaggart, said:

> Nothing has happened to the present by becoming past except that fresh slices of existence have been added to the total history of the world. The past is thus as real as the present. On the other hand, the essence of a present event is, not that it precedes future events, but that there is quite literally nothing to which it has the relation of precedence. The sum total of existence is always increasing, and it is this which gives the time series a sense as well as an order. (*Scientific Thought*, Chapter II)

Broad's position is the classical statement of the growing block: at any time the universe consists of everything that has happened up to that time and nothing later than it. Broad accepts that the B-relations are the primitive temporal order, while recognizing the need for an additional fact to ground the A-series. For Broad, that fact is that the present is that time such that at no later time does anything exist.

Michael Tooley's theory, defended in *Time, Tense and Causation*, is probably the purest contemporary descendant of Broad's. Tooley denies that he is an "A-theorist" or a "tensed theorist" because he claims that the only distinctively temporal structure in the universe is the B-series, and that the A-series can be interpreted in B-theoretic terms. However, he also believes that the present is distinguished as the time such that no later states of affairs obtain.

Therefore, unlike the property A-theorists he does not believe that examples 3.7 and 3.8 are satisfied by different states of affairs. Instead, they are satisfied only when the statements are used under the right conditions relative to the relevant state of affairs. This is particularly true for future-tense claims, such as:

> **Example 3.9** Barack Obama will be inaugurated as president of the United States.

In 2007 this was indeterminate, according to Tooley, not because the inauguration lacked some particular temporal status of presentness, but because the inauguration simply didn't exist yet. There was nothing to satisfy the relevant statement at that time.

Presentists, such as Dean Zimmerman, make a similar but more extreme claim. Zimmerman has claimed that "being present" and "being real" are simply synonyms. The present consists of all and only existing things. Once again, we will examine these positions in some detail in the next chapter, but here we should simply note that the presentist response to McTaggart is basically the same as the growing block. In both cases, it is not the case that anything ever has incompatible properties, since the future, and for presentists the past, doesn't exist to have any properties at all.

Growing block or presentist theories offer the most plausible Heraclitean accounts of the A-series. They have an intuitive appeal because they build on our common-sense hesitation in treating the future and the past as real. The fact that the universe as a whole is different, consists of a different collection of facts and/or of things at every moment satisfies the basic Heraclitean intuition that becoming is more fundamental than being. Finally, the changing collection of facts provides natural accounts of the arguments for dynamic change canvassed on pp. 75–78.

They also suffer from serious objections. As we will see in the next chapter, we have good philosophical reasons to be suspicious of the presentist suggestions built into our ordinary language. Worse, as mentioned above, there is no reasonable version of them compatible with special relativity. All such theories require alterations to the most fundamental theory in contemporary physics—Einstein's special relativity.

Tensed language in a tenseless world: The B-theory of time

In his most important book, *Word and Object*, the American philosopher Willard Van Orman Quine complained regarding tenses:

> Our ordinary language shows a tiresome bias in its treatment of time. Relations of date are exalted grammatically as relations of position, weight, and color are not. This bias is of itself in an inelegance, or breach of theoretical simplicity. Moreover, the form that it takes—that of requiring that every verb form show a tense—is peculiarly productive of needless complications, since it demands lipservice to time even when time is farthest from our thoughts. Hence in fashioning canonical notations it is usual to drop tense distinctions.

> *Word and Object* § 36

Quine captures the general attitude characteristic of B-theorists. According to such de-tensers, as they have come to be called, the prominence of temporal becoming is not a marker of metaphysical significance, but is an oddity of

Historical Note 10: Bertrand Russell, C. D. Broad, and Early Analytic Philosophy

Bertrand Russell (1872–1970) was probably the most influential English-language philosopher of the twentieth century and one of the most influential political activists. His early work on symbolic logic and its application to philosophical problems is fundamental to the analytic style of philosophy that remains dominant in the English-speaking world today. That work, combined with his influential writing on social issues, earned him the Nobel Prize for Literature in 1950. Russell's discussion of Zeno's paradoxes in *The Principles of Mathematics,* cf. Chapter 2, is the basis for much later work and remains a model of philosophical clarity. Russell also provides one of the earliest attempts to provide a B-theoretic elimination of tense (cf. Chapter 3).

C. D. Broad is another early twentieth-century English philosopher of enormous influence on the analytic tradition. Although Broad shares Russell's commitment to philosophical clarity and logical rigor, his interests are somewhat different and in some ways more traditional. Broad is particularly interested in understanding the "fit" between our conscious experience of the world and our scientific theories of its structure. In *Scientific Thought* he provides a careful analysis of the relationship between our experience of spatiotemporal phenomena and the physical theories of such phenomena. In Chapter II of *Scientific Thought* he articulates the "growing block" ontology discussed in Chapters 3 and 4. In Chapter X of the same work, he also offers the intriguing account of temporal experience discussed in Chapter 5.

our linguistic representations or perhaps of our linguistic representations combined with our psychological structure. These philosophers claim that, at most, the B-relations are real relations among either events or times, but that the prominence of "the now" is an illusion created by the restricted temporal perspective available to human beings; an illusion no different in principle from the apparent importance of what is nearby over what is far away.

Unfortunately for the B-theorists, stating one's intention to construct a tenseless canonical notation is the easy part of the project. Actually specifying such a canonical notation turns out to be tricky because of the need to mimic the transitory nature of tensed utterances in the permanent idiom of the B-series. How is it possible that "Barack Obama is president of the United States" is true at some times, but not at others without appealing to the presentness or lack thereof of his presidency? According to all versions of the B-theory what changes is not the presidency of Barack Obama, but my location in time relative to that presidency. In this sense, "now" is taken as entirely analogous to such indexicals or demonstrative terms as "here" or "I." The only difference is that while our language requires that we explicitly invoke such spatial or personal references, the grammar of verb conjugation invokes them implicitly in every English sentence.

Consider the two arguments for dynamic change above. What they have in common is that they identify either beliefs or statements which are true only at particular locations in the A-series. This feature, which Heather Dyke has called the "variable truth value" characteristic of tensed statements, is alleged to be the semantic manifestation of the underlying metaphysical specialness of the A-series. Can we account for this variability of attitude, belief, and truth without postulating objective A-determinations?

The obvious proposal is that made by Quine in the quotation above and can be ultimately traced to Bertrand Russell. If there are no objectively real A-determinations, then it seems that it should be possible to simply replace all of our tensed statements with tenseless ones. Why could I not simply replace example 3.1 with a sentence that tells me what time the inauguration takes place? I cannot, because no one such sentence properly duplicates the meaning of my initial example. Suppose that at noon, January 20, 2013, someone tells me "Barack Obama is being inaugurated as president." I therefore understand them to be telling me that

Example 3.10 Barack Obama is-tenselessly inaugurated as president at noon January 20, 2013.

This would be the tenseless statement that seems to be satisfied by the same fact as the initial tensed statement. The problem is that example 3.10 is equally as true today as it was then. Put slightly differently, the tensed sentence communicates different information than any tenseless sentence. Even if I have no idea what time it is or what day it is, the first sentence tells me that I could turn the TV on and watch the inauguration. These and similar problems have led most B-theorists to abandon the plan to replace tensed language with an equivalently descriptive tenseless language.

Instead, most contemporary B-theorists attempt to deploy a more general semantics for indexical terms and statements to prove that the truth conditions of tensed statements do not require us to postulate an objectively real A-series but to identify facts about the context of the particular tokens that determine their truth or falsehood in those contexts. There are two standard proposals for such contextual facts.

The more traditional account of indexicals is as token-reflexive sentences. As the name indicates the meaning of token-reflexive sentence types involves self-reflexive reference to the particular tokens. The meaning of some statement types can only be given by referring to particular tokens. So, the meaning of any statement involving "I" is given, in part, as "the person uttering this token"; "here" is "the place of utterance of this token."

We can use this to produce a completely analogous treatment of the A-determinations. Interpret all present tense statements as involving an implicit indexical "now" as suggested in our treatment of example 3.5. When I produce a token of the sentence, part of the truth-conditions for that token is that whatever state of affairs would otherwise satisfy the sentence holds at the time I produce the token. For past-tense sentences, it must have held at a time earlier than the time of production and mutatis mutandis for the future tense.

The alternative semantics for indexicals is that based on David Kaplan's subtle and complex theory of demonstratives; in the philosophy of time, these are often called "date theories." As has been the case so often in this chapter, we'll barely get to taste the power of this theory. Kaplan's basic strategy is to divide the meaning of indexicals, and the sentences in which they occur, into two parts that he calls the character and the content. Very roughly speaking, the character of an indexical is a map from context to a meaning, the content. The content then directly determines the reference of the indexical and the truth-value of the sentence. We saw above that part of the problem with the simple proposal for handling tense is that different *uses* of the same tensed sentences correspond to different tenseless sentences and have different truth-conditions. Philosophers would tend to say that each use of a tensed sentence expresses a different *proposition*. The character is simply the rule that allows us to determine, based on the context, what proposition is being expressed.

Thus to return to our usual example. Any token of "Barack Obama is president of the United States" is true in a particular context just in case the time of that context is contained within the presidency of Barack

Obama. The context would be determined using whatever complex procedure human beings use to interpret our language. We have no good reason to believe that there is any fundamental difference in that procedure for temporal indexicals than for spatial or personal ones. However one determines which aspects of the spatial properties of a token are relevant to determining the meaning of "here," we use the same procedure to isolate the relevant temporal context. Ultimately, the point is that whatever technique we used to represent the meaning of spatial indexicals, we have no good reason to think that it won't be equally effective in representing the meaning of temporal indexicals. If we have no reason to attribute a special metaphysical status to here, then we have no reason to attribute a special metaphysical status to now.

Conclusion: The metaphysics of B-time

Such indexical accounts of the A-series might seem to confirm McTaggart's idealism. If the boundary between the past and the future is simply defined as the temporal location of various human beings, doesn't that mean that time is unreal? Some defenders of the B-theory of time take this tack and accept that time is part of the way we represent and experience the world rather than part of the world itself. Most recognize that this is not so obvious.

Remember that McTaggart's paradox depends on two premises: the contradictory nature of the A-series and the claim that an objective A-series is required for the existence of time. Unlike defenders of the A-series, many B-theorists accept the first claim but deny the second. Thus in his books *Real Time* and *Real Time II*, D. H. Mellor presents detailed arguments to demonstrate that B-time can account for all of the distinctively temporal aspects of the world except for those directly concerned with the A-series. These include purely B-theoretic accounts of change, causation, and even arguments against time travel.

As an alternative to a strict dichotomy between A-theoretic realism and B-theoretic idealism, consider the possibility that this distinction might be a matter of degree. Toward the beginning of this chapter we explicated the distinction between realism and idealism in terms of ontological independence from human minds. Once we accept that characterization, isn't the right question about in what way and to what extent does a particular apparent feature of the world depend on the existence of human beings? The classic example of such a middle ground problem is the debate over *secondary qualities*.

Secondary qualities are those features that we experience as properties of objects in the world, but whose nature and structure clearly also depend on human sensory and mental structures. Color is the classic example. I experience objects as having particular colors, and those experiences seem to communicate real information about the objects. The difference in my color experience of red apples compared to my experience of green apples tracks a real difference between red apples and green apples. However, much about that experience doesn't seem to have anything to do with the objects, but rather seems to be the product of the structure of my visual system. For example, the fact that red and green don't mix is the product of the way the nerve channels from my retina to my visual cortex are structured.

Given these facts, it seems obtuse to insist that color is either entirely ideal or entirely real. Instead my color experiences are the product of a complex causal interaction between my visual system and objects in the world that I can use to more or less accurately guide my actions. This points us toward a roughly *naturalistic* account of aspects of the world like color and time. On this account, human beings are a part of the natural world and interact with it in all the ways such objects do. Some of our experiences track straightforward properties of other objects or relations between them; some of them are entirely the product of our sensory and cognitive architecture.

Most of them probably track complex causal interactions relevant to our flourishing within this world in ways that don't naturally fall into either category. We are thus better off when it comes to time asking not whether time is real or ideal, but simply trying to describe the ways in which various aspects of our temporal experience and representations do or do not have a ground in the external world. Rather than going for the "big kill" metaphysical argument in the style of the Eleatics, whether classical or modern, simply ask whether we have good reasons to think that the future is ontologically distinct from the past (Chapter 4)? Whether our experience of flow tracks some real phenomena in the world and how (Chapter 5)? Whether the B-relations of earlier and later have a basis in physics or metaphysics (Chapter 7)? And so, on for the other aspects of time, to which we now turn.

Cards on the table

Why I am not an A-theorist

There are two primary reasons why I am not an A-theorist. First, I have an aesthetic objection to the available A-theories. I do not have sufficient tolerance for logical and metaphysical complexity to find anything attractive in the available consistent versions of A-theory. No matter what version of A-theory one endorses, one is immediately in a thicket of universals, varieties of existence, degrees of actuality, variable quantification, and other logical or metaphysical undergrowth. Your mileage may vary, but I would hate to think that the ordinary world of spatiotemporal experience rests on top of such a thicket of abstract metaphysical structure.

Second, there's simply no way to make any version of A-theory compatible with Einstein's theory of relativity. Adopting any such metaphysical theory requires complete revision at the foundations of contemporary physics. However one defines the present, an A-theoretic present must consist of a unique slice of the universe of arbitrarily large spatial extent, a simultaneity slice of the universe. The fundamental consequence of Einstein's theory of special relativity is that there is no unique partition of simultaneity slices. According to special relativity, what time a spatially distant event occurs is no more objective than how fast an object is moving. Detailed discussion of the relativity of simultaneity and its philosophical consequences are in Chapter 6.

Why I don't call myself a B-theorist

Despite its influence, the A-theory versus B-theory debate has had a pernicious influence in the philosophy of time. In dividing philosophers up into teams, it has made it harder to simply describe what one believes and blinded philosophers to a collection of important problems that are independent of McTaggart's paradox. Most importantly, the problem of constructing the basic model of time required in order to even formulate McTaggart's paradox has received almost no attention. This is not to denigrate the real value in some B-theorist's attempts to construct models of B-time; part of the problem with such success is that the A-theory versus B-theory dichotomy begins to look exhaustive even though it is merely one dimension in complex philosophical disputes about time. Rather than making every debate fuel for the fire of McTaggart's paradox, let's examine these various problems on their own terms.

Further reading

Two introductions to the basic issues in metaphysics and the philosophy of language raised in this chapter are:

Dummett, M. (2006), *Thought and Reality*, Oxford: Clarendon Press.

The first chapter of this little book has a nice introductory discussion of facts, statements, and propositions. The rest of it requires a substantial background in philosophical logic.

Loux, M. J. (2008), *Metaphysics: Contemporary Readings*, 2nd edn, New York: Routledge.

This is an excellent introduction to metaphysics as the search for the appropriate categories of existence. Chapters One and Two are a detailed but reasonably accessible account of the variety of standard positions on the nature of universals mentioned in passing in this chapter.

In the conclusion, it is suggested that we think of time as "secondary quality." The distinction goes back to the ancient Greek atomists, but the classic discussion, and the name, is from Book II of John Locke's *An Essay Concerning Understanding*.

For additional reading on the basic structure of McTaggart's paradox, see the relevant chapters in the books by Dainton and Le Poidevin listed in the Further Reading list for Chapter 1. Also see:

Garrett, B. (2011), *What is this Thing called Metaphysics?*, 2nd edn, Abingdon, Oxon: Routledge.

Chapter 5, "Time: The Fundamental Issue" contains a discussion of McTaggart's paradox slightly more simple than this one.

McTaggart, J. E. (1908), "The unreality of time," *Mind*, 17: 457–74.

McTaggart's original paper, which has also been widely reprinted, including in the anthology edited by Westphal and Levenson listed after Chapter 1. The version of the argument from his book The Nature of Existence *can be found in Le Poidevin and MacBeath.*

C. D. Broad's careful discussion of McTaggart's argument in the chapter on "Ostensible Temporality" in his Examination of McTaggart's Philosophy is probably the canonical explication of the argument. Another classical explication is:

Dummett, M. (1960), "A defense of McTaggart's proof of the unreality of time," *The Philosophical Review*, 69 (4): 497–504.

Dummett's paper, which is somewhat less heavy going than most of his work, is largely responsible for inaugurating the modern debate over the paradox. Unfortunately, it's also one of the classic examples of attributing to McTaggart what he should have said instead of what he did say. Reprinted in Westphal and Levenson.

Oaklander, L. N. and Q. Smith, eds (1994), *The New Theory of Time*, New Haven: Yale University Press.

A useful collection of papers on the contemporary A-theory/B-theory debate jointly assembled by a prominent A-theorist, Quentin Smith, and a leading B-theorist, L. Nathan Oaklander. The introduction remains a valuable map to the basic landscape of the debate.

A-theorists

There are many defenses of A-theory. Unfortunately, they generally require substantial prior familiarity with philosophical logic. The introduction in this chapter should be enough to get you started with these.

Smith, Q. (1993), *Language and Time*, Oxford: Oxford University Press.

The most extended contemporary attempt to defend the existence of A-properties.

Craig, W. L. (2000a), *The Tensed Theory of Time: A Critical Examination* (Vol. 293), Dordrecht: Kluwer Academic.

Craig, W. L. (2000b), *The Tenseless Theory of Time: A Critical Examination* (Vol. 294), Dordrecht: Kluwer Academic.

Craig, W. L. (2001), *Time and the Metaphysics of Relativity* (Vol. 84), Dordrecht: Kluwer Academic.

Together, these three books are Craig's magisterial defense of presentism.

Tooley, M. (1997), *Time, Tense and Causation*, Oxford: Clarendon Press.

A contemporary version of the growing block, although Tooley claims that states of affairs, rather than objects or events, come into existence.

B-theories

Quine, W. V. O. (1960), *Word and Object*, Cambridge: Technology Press of the Massachusetts Institute of Technology (studies in communication).

Word and Object *is Quine's most complete articulation of his naturalistic philosophy.*

Williams, D. C. (1951), "The myth of passage," *Journal of Philosophy*, 48: 457–71.

This is the classic argument for the elimination of temporal becoming from our fundamental metaphysics. Only Quine's treatment in Word and Object *is of similar significance.*

Mellor, D. H. (1981), *Real Time*, Cambridge, UK: Cambridge University Press.

Mellor, D. H. (1998), *Real Time II*, London: Routledge.

The two classic defenses of tenseless time. In Real Time II, *Mellor abandons the token-reflexive semantics in favor of a date theory.*

Oaklander, L. N. (2004), *The Ontology of Time*, Amherst, NY: Prometheus Books.

Because this also contains Oaklander's detailed criticisms of a wide range of A-theories, it is a useful reference on the range of options as well as on Oaklander's own views.

There are various skeptical or deflationary treatments of McTaggart's Paradox and the A-theory versus B-theory debates along the lines suggested in the appendix. Here are a few of them:

Harrington, J. (2009), "What 'becomes' in temporal becoming?," *American Philosophical Quarterly*, 46 (3): 249–65.

This develops the skeptical line taken in the appendix in more detail, but also presupposes more background knowledge.

Savitt, S. F. (2002), "On absolute becoming and the myth of passage," *Royal Institute of Philosophy Supplement*, 50: 153–67.

This essay appeared in the important collection of original papers better known by its title, Time, Reality and Experience, *and edited by Craig Callender. Savitt reaches similar conclusions to those suggested in the appendix by a different route.*

Callender, C. (2000), "Shedding light on time," *Philosophy of Science*, 67 (3 Supplement): S587–99.

In this article he urges philosophers to give up hope for "the big kill" in philosophy of time. According to Callender, a large part of the problem in contemporary philosophy of time arises from the hope that it can be reduced to a single philosophical problem and then resolved by a single argument.

Discussion questions

1 How is the experience of time similar to the sensory experience of ordinary middle-sized dry goods? How is it different?
2 Explain the difference between primary and secondary qualities. Do you think that time is more like a primary quality or a secondary quality?
3 Can you explain the difference among the A-series, B-series, and C-series orderings in the standard model of time?
4 Consider the following sentence, "Barack Obama was president of the United States in 2010." Does that sentence primarily express A-series or B-series structure for time? What about, "The presidency of Ronald Reagan is earlier than the presidency of Barack Obama"?
5 Change in events
   a Assume that change in events is essential to time. Why does that require A-change?
   b Can you describe three arguments for change in events?
   c Do you think that real passage of time requires change in events? Why or why not?

6 Why does McTaggart believe that example 3.1 is a contradiction? Can you explain how a property attribution A-theorist like Quentin

Smith might avoid the contradiction? What about a growing block theorist like C. D. Broad?

7 Can you explain the difference between tensed and tenseless interpretations of "the apple is red"? Based on this example, can you explain the general distinction between logically tensed and merely grammatically tensed statements? Can you explain what it means to say that a particular state of affairs is the truth-maker for a particular statement?

8 Is it irrational for a B-theorist to treat the past and the future differently? If so, why? If not, why not?

9 Do you believe that it should be possible to express all of the facts in the world in non-indexical language?

Notes

1. Unless it turns out time travel actually is possible, see Chapter 9.
2. McTaggart makes an additional suggestion in the very next paragraph involving Greenwich Meridian. Unfortunately, that suggestion is even more obscure than the previous one; it's not even entirely grammatical.
3. The actual example of a headache is given by D. H. Mellor.
4. Michael Tooley seems to have introduced the terminology of "static theories of change" as well as of "dynamic theories of change" discussed below.
5. Here I'm going to anticipate the appendix. I have no good sense of what the worry is supposed to be here. We saw on pp. 68–71 that the fundamental difference between a spatial order and a temporal order is that temporal orders are directed. So is change; change is always from one state to another state. Worrying about why we would line up the direction of change with the direction of time rather than with an arbitrary "direction" in space seems bizarre. Two directed things, one direction.
6. On Michael Tooley's ontology, the poker exists at times later than the present; it just doesn't stand in any states of affairs at those times.
7. There are also modal theories that construct the A-series out of the modal concepts of possibility, necessity, and actuality. Even explicating these theories requires a substantial grasp of issues in formal modal logic. Fortunately, the basic strategy for avoiding McTaggart's paradox is very similar to that of the existence theories.
8. Interested readers should consult the relevant chapters of Nathan Oaklander's *The Ontology of Time* for some of them.

4

The Ontology of the Future

Do future or past events or objects exist? Supported by common sense, the philosophical theory of presentism claims that they do not. Eternalism claims that they do; defenders of the growing block claim that the past, but not the future, exists. We also consider what existence means, and consider criteria of ontological commitment. Next we consider arguments for fatalism, the claim that the future must occur in a particular way. The chapter concludes with a survey of alternative logical and metaphysical accounts of the future including three-valued logics and branching time models.

The previous two chapters focused on the relationship between time and change. We saw that while Zeno's paradoxes do not undermine the possibility of change in objects, McTaggart's paradox creates serious problems for any conception of time that involves change in events. Only a conception of the passage of time resulting from changes in what exists seems to avoid McTaggart's paradox. In this chapter we will continue to examine the ontological status of the future, albeit from a somewhat different direction.

The apparent distinction between the past, the present, and the future also matters in profound ways to ordinary language and ordinary life. Our conception of ourselves as agents capable of altering the world seems to be crucially entangled with these temporal concepts. It seems as though I can only act in and on the present; neither the past nor the future are available to me, within the metaphorical reach of my hands. It also seems as though I can only act *for* the future; the actions which I take in the present can only have consequences in the future, not the past.

These considerations, as well as others to be marshaled below, point toward some combination of two metaphysical doctrines. Presentism is the doctrine that only the temporal present exists. Indeterminacy is the doctrine that in contrast to an unchanging and determinate past the future remains indeterminate and subject to our choices.

Although we saw in the previous chapter that these questions about the ontological status of the present and the future are relevant to the problem of becoming, it's worth examining these ontological questions independently of worries about becoming. Our principal concern in this chapter is not with whether or how different moments become present. Instead we are principally concerned with each moment understood as present. In the language of the last chapter, our principle focus is on the status of each distinct A-series, not with the way in which A-series succeed each other to constitute the flow of time.

The next two sections discuss the arguments for presentism and then for the alternative doctrine of eternalism according to which past, present, and future entities are all equally real. After that, we turn to the classical problem of future contingents, also known as the problem of logical fatalism. According to this doctrine, introduced beginning on p. 113, our ability to make some true statements about the future implies that all future facts are as real and unchanging as the past and the present. The chapter ends with a sketch of some alternatives to logical fatalism, and a brief survey of the rather inconclusive conclusions we can draw.

Presentism and the meaning of existence

Our ordinary language and our common-sense worldview distinguish two senses of existence, one of them tensed and the other tenseless to use the language of Chapter 3. In the tenseless sense of existence, we consistently distinguish real from imaginary or fictional entities. In the tenseless sense, Socrates and the Roman Empire are just as real as Barack Obama and the United States, all of which possess a distinct ontological character from the imaginary wizard Gandalf or the Kingdom of Gondor. However, there is clearly another sense in which neither Socrates nor the Roman Empire currently exists. Unfortunately, English does not have a good general term for the class of things which are real but that do not currently exist—a term parallel to the ordinary usage of imaginary above.

So we are going to have to introduce a *term of art* here. We do sometimes say that things which exist now are extant as opposed to those which used to be and which are defunct. The contrast is not perfectly parallel; in ordinary usage to claim that something is not extant implies that it once was. Here we need a term that distinguishes those things which are extant from those which are defunct as well as those which are merely forthcoming.

We thus have a fourfold classification; something could be imaginary, real and extant, real but defunct, or real but forthcoming.

This doesn't quite close out the ordinary range of ontological categories. Some things, for example numbers like π, seem to be real without actually existing at any particular time. Such abstract objects seem to occupy a category of their own (Table 4.1).

We can then see that the basic problem in temporal ontology is precisely to unpack the relationships between these various categories. *Presentists* take the category of extant objects as basic; the only things which are really real are those that are real now. For such a presentist, Socrates is no more real in his own right then Gandalf. Neither of them are part of the current furniture of the universe. Socrates however once was. This allegedly grounds a legitimate, if derivative, distinction between him and the wizard. *Eternalists* take the real/imaginary distinction as basic; Socrates exists in precisely the same way that Barack Obama does. Neither of them have any ontological similarity to Gandalf.

The first problem here is to prevent the debate between presentists and eternalists from degenerating into a merely verbal dispute, as all such debates over ontological commitment seem to be in danger of doing. Since both sides accept a linguistic distinction between two ways of failing to exist—as non-present and as imaginary—the debate seems to be about which kind of "reality" deserves to be *called* reality. The obvious way to make the debate a matter of substance is to introduce a more fundamental conception of existence, one independent of the presentism-eternalism debate.

Table 4.1 Some occupants of the various ontological categories.

Imaginary	Real, abstract	Real, extant
Gandalf	π	Barack Obama
Gondor	God(?)	The United States
Real, defunct		**Real, forth coming**
Socrates		My grand children
The Roman Empire		

What we really need is a rule for ontological commitment. How can I tell what things someone is really committed to? The now standard conception of ontological commitment is normally traced to W. V. O. Quine although Quine himself traces the fundamental insight to Bertrand Russell in his theory of descriptions. The problem can be put as follows. In a debate between a presentist, Z, and an eternalist, H, the eternalist has no problem stating that the presentist fails to recognize some things that the eternalist accepts. However, the presentist should be hesitant to accept that formulation. The problem is that there is no *thing* about which Z and H disagree, according to Z. If Z accepts that they disagree about some *thing* then she seems to have handed the debate to H.

What Quine recognized is that this is a more general version of the problem posed by statements about nonexistent objects, a problem apparently solved by Bertrand Russell's theory of descriptions. Consider the following statement: "The author of Waverley is a poet." What Russell realized is that "the author of Waverley" is, despite first appearances, not an independently referring name. Instead, it is really an incomplete expression, a *predicate* like "being the author of Waverley," which only picks out things in the world in the context of a sentence. In this case we can interpret our example as meaning "there is something that is the author of Waverley and that is a poet and nothing else is the author of Waverley."

Here, the locution "there is something that" functions as the English equivalent of *existential quantification* in modern predicate logic. Quine recognizes that we can explicate the substance of such ontological disputes as that between Z and H in terms of disagreement about the range of such quantification. Consider the English pronoun "something"; what range of objects would we be willing to accept as substitutes for it? The eternalist is perfectly happy to allow it to range over such defunct objects as the long dead Sir Walter Scott, a substitution that presentists have to oppose. As Quine puts it in "On what there is":

> To be assumed as an entity is, purely and simply, to be reckoned as the value of a variable. In terms of the categories of traditional grammar, this amounts roughly to saying that to be is to be in the range of reference of a pronoun. Pronouns are the basic media of reference; nouns might better have been named pro-pronouns. The variables of quantification, "something," "nothing," "everything," range over our whole ontology, whatever it may be; and we are convicted of a particular ontological presupposition if, and only if, the alleged presuppositum has to be reckoned

among the entities over which our variables range in order to render one of our affirmations true.

This brings us to the first problem facing presentists: what to say about past and future objects? There are two basic options available. One might reinterpret all apparent quantification over past and future objects in terms of present objects. A presentist choosing this option might interpret claims such as our example above as not referring to the person "Sir Walter Scott" but to the present objects caused by him. For example, a presentist might try something like this:

Example 4.1 There are copies of a book called *Waverley* and there are records describing the origin of that book that say that the same person who wrote it also wrote poetry.

This is probably too simple to actually get a purely presentist set of ontological commitments, but it should be enough to give you the flavor. Similarly, future statements become descriptions of the present causes of the nonexistent future objects.

This conception of non-present existence seems particularly attractive when combined with a growing block ontology rather than a pure presentist ontology. According to growing block theories, one can quantify over defunct as well as extant objects, but not over forthcoming ones. This resolves a problem posed by past objects. It has seemed odd to many people that statements about "Sir Walter Scott" are not actually about the author, but about his present traces. However, such present-oriented accounts do seem more plausible when applied to future-tense statements. Future statements, that is, predictions, do seem to be projections of current conditions in a way that past ones are not.

Alternatively, one can treat the tenses as context shifting devices. Thus, existential quantification in a past-tense sentence tells me to use the range of quantification that I would have used at the time picked out by the past-tense construction. Thus, "The author of Waverley is a poet." is false, but "The author of Waverley *was* a poet." is true because at some time earlier than the present, one would have accepted "Sir Walter Scott" into one's ontology. This is the basic mechanism of tense logic.

Why be a presentist? The most common and most powerful reason is what we might call the "analytic argument"; to many people it simply seems obvious that being present is simply synonymous with existing.

As St. Augustine of Hippo put it in his *Confessions,* putting into context a quotation we have seen before:

> What is this time? If no one asks me, I know; if I want to explain it to a questioner, I do not know. But at any rate this much I dare affirm I know: that if nothing passed there would be no past time; if nothing were approaching, there would be no future time; if nothing were, there would be no present time. But the two times, past and future, how can they be, since the past is no more and the future is not yet? On the other hand, if the present were always present and never float away into the past, it would not be time at all, but eternity. But if the present is only time, because it flows away into the past, how can we say that it is? For it is, only because it will cease to be. Thus we can affirm that time is only in that it tends towards non-being.

There are two primary additional arguments in favor of presentism. First, eternalism seems incompatible with human agency, our belief that our actions bring about their consequences. The worry is not so much about the classical free will versus determinism debate that we will discuss beginning on p. 109. The worry is, we might say, deeper than that. Even if my writing of the book is determined, even if I didn't really have a choice in the matter, it is still my book because my actions brought it into existence. Since, according

---

Historical Note 11: St. Augustine of Hippo

St. Augustine of Hippo (AD 354–AD 430) is one of the most influential philosophers and theologians of the Christian Latin West. Only Thomas Aquinas is his rival measured in depth of influence and the range of topics covered in his work. As a philosopher, Augustine's principal contribution was his attempt to integrate pagan philosophy, especially Neoplatonism, with Christianity.

Although he was raised in a Christian household in Roman North Africa (modern Tunisia), Augustine was a late convert to Christianity. His *Confessions* utilize a radically new first person literary form to recount his early search for meaning in various forms of paganism and his later conversion to Christianity. The last few books of *Confessions* are a series of philosophical reflections on Augustine's relationship to this God whom he believes himself to have discovered. The reflections on the nature of time remain one of the fundamental starting points for all reflection on the way in which being in time shapes our experience of ourselves as human beings.

to eternalists, the book merely becomes present but has always, tenselessly, existed, presentists wonder how that is possible.

Eternalists, of course, don't understand causation in this way. Since nothing is brought into existence, causation cannot be bringing something into existence. Instead, eternalist causation must consist in relationships of dependence between things that already exist. That is, eternalists would claim that the book is mine because it stands, and always has stood, in certain relationships to me that I don't have, unfortunately, to the books of Stephen King. Presentists object that this is not a solution to the problem, but merely another way of stating it: How can the book be dependent on my actions without being ontologically dependent on those actions?

Finally, presentists worry about eternalist solutions to the problem of temporary intrinsics. This problem is related to some of the problems of change that we have already discussed. Consider the ripe red apple on my counter, once again. Once that apple was green. This seems to create a dilemma for eternalists. Assume that the past apple and the present apple are strictly or numerically identical. The principle of the indiscernibility of identicals seems to be part of the definition of identity; one thing cannot have distinct and incompatible properties. However, if it's not the same thing, then there doesn't seem to be any *change*. Two things having different properties is not a change; it is just variety. According to presentists, the green apple and the red apple are numerically identical, one thing rather than two, but there is never any time where both the red apple and the green apple exist.

As usual, eternalists don't conceive of change in this way. While the apple is the same apple at different times, it is not the same thing at different times. Accordingly, most eternalists are also four-dimensionalists about persistence. According to four-dimensionalists, objects persist through time by having the appropriate relationships to objects at other times. This is analogous to the way objects exist through space by having parts with different locations. See the Study Exercise at the end of this chapter for a brief survey of theories of persistence. Instead we now to turn to arguments in favor of eternalism.

Eternalism and the apparent incoherence of presentism

We have already met St. Augustine of Hippo and his *Confessions*. Here is a more formal introduction. In his *Confessions*, Augustine (AD 354–430) narrates his evolution from pagan aesthete to Christian ascetic. However, the last few sections of this seminal work make what can only strike us as an odd turn from autobiography into philosophical and theological speculation. Book XI, in particular, consists of a series of reflections on the nature of time and eternity. Most significantly for us, in chapter 14 Augustine offers the characteristically elegant, and justly famous, explanation of the tension between the two senses of existence discussed above.

Let's follow Augustine at this stage of his argument in assuming that the distinctive reality of the present is essential to the passage of time. Otherwise, all of Barack Obama, Socrates, and my grandchildren exist together in eternity rather than sequentially in time. What Augustine realized is that presentism seems to be incompatible with various other equally essential features of time.

Augustine focuses on two of these features. First, it is not clear that presentism is compatible with the fact that time involves quantities of more or less. If being past is merely being defunct and being future is merely being forthcoming, how can there be any difference between something 100 years in the past and something 1,000 years in the past? As Augustine puts it, "In what sense can that which does not exist be long or short?" Perhaps, when it did exist it had a particular length. Perhaps it is strictly speaking false to say that the nineteenth century is 100 years long, but correct to say that it was. The analogy here is with the properties of ordinary objects. When speaking casually, we might say that George Washington has false teeth; even though strictly speaking he doesn't have any kind of teeth at the moment.

Unfortunately, this isn't going to solve the problem in the case of time. Of the 100 years of the nineteenth century, none of them were ever present together. Thus in 1850, 1849 was past, 1851 was future and neither of them existed. The same holds true for any subdividable period of time. Only this single indivisible instant can ever be strictly present; an instant that "flees at such lightning speed from being future to being past, that it has no extent of duration at all."

This is not the only puzzle generated by presentism. It also seems to be the case that the past and the future are not *merely* nothing. Past things are moving away from us and future ones toward us. There is a crucial difference between things which are not and have never been real, but will be, and those which are merely unreal in themselves. Augustine brings this out most clearly in his discussion of prophecy, whose reality he takes for granted. However, even in this more skeptical age it seems as though precognitive prophecy is *possible* in a way that direct experience of entirely unreal events or objects, such as Gandalf, are not. I might not believe that anyone could experience the outcome of the next US presidential election before it happens, but I wouldn't automatically take them to be delusional in the way that I would someone who truthfully claimed to have been present at the Battle of Helm's Deep from *The Lord of the Rings*.

Augustine's solution is to link eternalism with a form of idealism about time. All of the past, the present, and future exist together in eternity, for God. According to Augustine, human beings have a more limited form of access to reality. We can experience only a small subset of reality together. As for the rest, we can at best remember it or anticipate it. As Augustine himself puts it:

> But how is the future diminished or consumed when it does not yet exist? Or how does the past, which exists no longer, increase, unless it is that in the mind in which all this happens there are three functions? For the mind expects, it attends, and it remembers; so that what it expects passes into what it remembers by way of what it attends to. Who denies that future things do not exist as yet? But still there is already in the mind the expectation of things still future. And who denies that past things now exist no longer? Still there is in the mind the memory of things past. Who denies that time present has no length, since it passes away in a moment? Yet, our attention has a continuity and it is through this that what is present may proceed to become absent. Therefore, future time, which is nonexistent, is not long; but "a long future" is "a long expectation of the future." Nor is time past, which is now no longer, long; a "long past" is "a long memory of the past."

Our discussions over the previous two chapters point toward an alternative and less idealistic version of eternalism. Defenders of this alternative, usually called four-dimensionalism or the block universe, agree with the Augustinian eternalist that past, present, and future objects all exist, but deny that they exist *together* except in the most metaphorical sense. Instead, they exist by being arranged at various times along the timeline given by the continuous one-dimensional model organized by the B-relations of earlier and later. In this model, existing at different times is closely analogous to existing at different locations in space. Hence the name recognizing time as the fourth dimension of existence.

While time is analogous to a fourth dimension of space in this view, it is not, with all due respect to H. G. Wells's *The Time Machine*, merely a fourth spatial dimension. It is, as we saw in Chapter 2, the dimension of existence particularly associated with change and motion. Earlier states of objects produce the later ones in ways that the merely spatially separated parts of an object do not. In addition, we saw in Chapter 3 that time is distinct from space in possessing an intrinsic direction. As best we can tell every direction in space is the same as every other except for the arrangement of material objects. Time is not like this. If there is a path through time from one event to another event, then there is no inverse path. I can go from earlier to later, but not vice versa. In this, time is unlike space. If I travel from north to south, then I can automatically reverse my path and travel from south to north.

Modern physics places severe pressure on this intuitive understanding of the difference between time and space, as it does on so much of our common-sense worldview. In particular, we will see in Chapter 7 that physics does provide some reasons to believe that the *intrinsic* directionality of time is itself an illusion and that time travel, in some sense, might be possible as we will see in Chapter 9.

The most persuasive direct arguments in favor of four-dimensionalism are its natural compatibility with the representation of time in physics and especially the role of space-time in Einstein's theories of special and general

Historical Note 12: W. V. O. Quine, D. C. Williams, and the Block Universe

In the United States the dominant school of philosophy from the end of the Second World War was what has come to be called "analytic philosophy." American analytic philosophy was deeply influenced by the clarity achieved by Bertrand Russell through logical analysis and the respect in which the logical positivists held natural science. Together these lead naturally to the defense of some version of the block universe. For example, Harvard philosopher W. V. O. Quine (1906–2000), probably the most influential American philosopher of the 1950s and 1960s, developed an unflinching defense of the block universe version of Eleaticism.

Quine and other analytic defenders of the block universe, such as J. J. C. Smart (1920–2012) and Donald C. Williams (1899–1983) recognized the affinities between their metaphysics and relativity theory as a virtue, but their principle defenses of them were philosophical and conceptual.

relativity. While these arguments will have to wait for Chapter 6, the block universe also offers profound philosophical advantages. Most importantly it offers a halfway house between the idealism of Augustine and the Eleatics and the mystery mongerings of presentist Heracliteans. As the philosopher Donald Williams puts it in his celebrated "The Myth of Passage," the theory of the manifold, his name for four-dimensionalism,

> is the one model on which we can describe and explain the foreground of experience, or can intelligibly and credibly construct our account of the rest of the world, and this is so because in fact the universe is spread out in those dimensions.... The homely realm of natural existence, the total of world history, is a spatial-temporal volume, of somewhat uncertain magnitude, chockablock with things and events.

Most importantly, four-dimensionalism provides a model that allows us to describe the world however it might be. Rather than presuppose answers to questions of human agency and other problems of metaphysics in the construction of the basic model of the world, it leaves them to be investigated by examining the world itself. To quote Williams again:

> The theory of the manifold makes a man at home in the world to the extent that it guarantees that intelligence is not affronted at its first step into reality. Beyond that, the cosmos is as it is. If there is a moral responsibility, if the will is free if there is reasonableness in regret and hope in decision, these must be ascertained by more particular observations and hypotheses than the doctrine of the manifold. It makes no difference to our theory whether we are locked in an ice pack of fate, or whirled in a tornado of chance, or are firm footed makers of destiny.

It is to one of those more particular investigations that we now turn— Aristotle's famous argument for fatalism.

Aristotle's sea-battle and logical fatalism

There are a variety of classical philosophical arguments intended to demonstrate the truth of fatalism. Fatalism is, of course, the doctrine that everything that happens is fated to happen in that particular way. The particular philosophical doctrine with which we will be concerned, logical fatalism, must be distinguished from two closely related sets of claims. On the one hand, religious fatalism depends on the belief that the world and everything in it, including human beings, is under the control of some external force—usually a God or gods. On the other hand, causal determinism is the claim that everything in the world is caused to be the way that it actually is by other things in the world, in such a way that it could not be different.

If either or both of these are true, then there is an obvious problem with human moral responsibility. Whether Oedipus was forced to kill his father and sleep with his mother because he was manipulated by the gods or because of his environment and history does not seem to matter. In either case he was forced and could not have done otherwise. Holding him responsible for the outcomes of his "actions" seems as inappropriate as holding him responsible for his inability to fly.

Logical fatalism seems to undercut the significance of questions about divine intervention or causal determination. According to the logical fatalist, everything in the universe is the way that it is just because that is the way that it is. The very question of whether or how something is brought about seems to be undermined by these arguments. There are several arguments that the world must, as a matter of logic, be the way that it is. The most famous of them is Aristotle's sea-battle from his *On Interpretation*.

Aristotle points out that it seems to be a simple logical truth that every sentence of the form "P or not-P" is a tautology, and therefore necessarily true. Consider the question of whether there is a sea-battle somewhere on January 1, 2100. Whether there is or not, that there either is or is not must be true. That is,

> 1. "There is a sea-battle somewhere on January 1, 2100 OR there is not a sea-battle somewhere on January 1, 2100." is a tautology and therefore true *now*.

However, it seems to be part of the meaning of disjunction, "OR," that such sentences can only be true in case at least one of the disjuncts, the sentences joined by "OR," is true. This apparent fact, usually called the law of excluded middle, implies:

> 2. "There is a sea-battle somewhere on January 1, 2100." is true, OR "It is not the case that there is a sea-battle somewhere on January 1, 2100." is true.

Therefore, although I cannot know which is the case, I can know that one and only one of them is the case. If the first disjunct is true, then it has seemed to many philosophers as though it must be true independently of anything that happens between now and the beginning of the next century.

Example 4.2 There is a sea-battle somewhere on January 1, 2100.

That future sea-battle is the truth-maker in the present for example 4.2. In the language of Chapter 3, the occurrence of that future sea-battle is the fact whose obtaining satisfies that sentence in the present.

So, how might it be the case that the tenseless obtaining of that "future" fact in the "present" implies that the sea-battle *must* occur in a way that undermines free will? The first is that it simply seems to elide the distinction between the past and the future. When the sea-battle actually occurs, it seems obviously to be the case that our choices are no longer relevant to its occurrence. As Aristotle puts it, "That which is, is necessary when it is." It seems to satisfy the tenseless claim stated in the first disjunct in a way independent of the time of its use.

Second, we can see this more clearly if we consider the possibility that the sea-battle does depend on events between now and its occurrence, for example on choices that someone makes. Now suppose that someone makes a choice in 2050 incompatible with the occurrence of the sea-battle. That seems to require one of the following three options. Either both facts obtain, or neither fact obtains, or what facts obtain depends on one's perspective. If both facts obtain, then we seem to have a straightforward contradiction. If neither fact obtains, then it's hard to see what makes example 4.2 true in the first place. Finally, perspectival facts hardly seem like facts at all; the point of having a category of facts is to have a class of entities that are not perspectival. There are ways to make variants of these work, some of them discussed in the next section, but as we'll see they require substantial logical and metaphysical complexity.

Before we turn to those responses to logical fatalism, we can take a brief look at two more, formal classical arguments for the necessity of the future. The "master argument" attributed to the stoic philosopher Diodorus Chronos connects the temporal distinction between past and future with the modal distinction between necessity and possibility. The precise structure of the "master argument" is the subject of significant scholarly debate. Because it serves as a primary inspiration for tense logic which attempts to represent temporal features of language using the mechanisms analogous to those used in modern logic to handle modal notions, these debates quickly become very technical. However, the basic premises are well attested in the ancient sources, and from them it is possible to construct a fairly straightforward additional argument for fatalism. These premises are:

Master Argument Everything true of the future is necessarily true.
Master Premise #1 Everything true of the past is necessary.
Master Premise #2 The impossible does not follow from the possible.

From these premises it is possible to prove that anything that happens in the future happens necessarily. Consider that there is now a sea-battle on January 1, 2100. It seems obvious that this would also have been the case

---

Historical Note 13: Diodorus Chronus and a Hellenistic Interlude

The period of Hellenistic cultural dominance, roughly from the conquests of Alexander to the collapse of Roman hegemony in the fourth or fifth century AD, was a period of immense philosophical and religious ferment, culminating in the rise of Christianity. Little of this resulted in much direct influence on the particular debates that concern us in this book. There are two exceptions that need to be mentioned.

Logicians associated with the stoic school are reported to have made sophisticated contributions to the logic of future contingents and related areas throughout this period. Unfortunately, very little of the stoic's technical work in logic and metaphysics survives. Diodorus Chronos (died c. 284 BC) whose "master argument" features in Chapter 4 is the best known of these. Unfortunately, little is known about him; even his association with the stoics and the dates relating to important events in his life are contested.

The other crucial development, for our purposes, is the development of various late Neoplatonic philosophical systems, most famously by Plotinus and Porphyry in the third century AD. These systems replaced the more rationalistic and mechanistic systems of Plato's *Timaeus* with a more mystical account of the relationship between the worlds of being and becoming that was deeply influential on Augustine and his idealistic theory of time. Those interested in more information on the profoundly rich philosophical legacy of Neoplatonism should consult the useful article at *The Internet Encyclopedia of Philosophy.*

yesterday. Then it is now necessarily the case, since the past is necessary. It's therefore impossible today to make it not the case that the sea-battle occurs without violating the second premise above.

Finally, there is a historically important theological argument for fatalism. While the argument is most famously associated with the Christian Boethius in Book VII of *The Consolation of Philosophy*, all of the Abrahamic religions teach that God is omniscient. In particular, God knows what will happen at all times: past, present, and future. This seems to be incompatible with human free will. If God now knows that I will have Chinese food for dinner tonight, then it seems impossible for me to choose to have Mexican. Because if I did, then God would turn out to have been mistaken. This is obviously incompatible with divine omniscience.

As with the other arguments, this seems to undermine our entire conception of a difference between those events which are necessary and those which are merely contingent. The argument seems to show that whether particular events are past, present, or future, and whether those events are caused by other things in the world or not, everything must be exactly the way that it actually is.

Whatever their details, all of the forms of fatalism create two crucial problems. First, they turn the problem of determinism and free will, which should be a substantive metaphysical issue, into a trivial matter of logic. Second, they directly attack our understanding of ourselves as agents bringing about our own fates. All of the various responses attempt to resolve these problems. As Aristotle puts it, all of these positions seem to imply that "there would be no need to deliberate or to take trouble (thinking that if we do this, this will happen, but if we do not, it will not)."

Alternatives to logical fatalism

There are three basic lines of response to the arguments for logical fatalism: these can be classified as deflationary, compatibilist, and logical-metaphysical responses. The deflationary responses argue that logical fatalism generally fails to distinguish between the truth of statements about the future and the necessity of such statements. The simplest version of this response points out that many versions of the sea-battle argument involve a modal fallacy. Consider that what you really seem to require for Aristotle's argument is an argument that gets you to:

Example 4.3 Necessarily, there is a sea-battle on January 1, 2100.

from

> **Example 4.4** Necessarily, there is or there is not a sea-battle on January 1, 2100.

However, that inference seems to generally involve one in various modal fallacies. For example, the immediate inference from 4.4 to 4.3 is a straightforward modal fallacy. Example 4.4 requires that in every possible world *exactly one* of the options holds, but it does not require that the same one hold in every such world. In general, the deflationary accounts depend on the fact that 4.4 does not depend principally on the way that the actual world is, but on the range of possibilities available at the times when it is true. Another way to get at a similar worry is that it is not clear that the law of excluded middle can be applied directly to 4.4 in any meaningful way; logicians would say that the disjunction is not the *main connective* of the sentence. More intuitively, necessity, not disjunction, is the controlling feature of the sentence.

Unfortunately, for the deflationary accounts you don't seem to need 4.4 to get the argument off the ground. If it is necessarily true, then the disjunction is true. And, we saw above that the mere truth of the disjuncts creates problems. So we turn to the alternative responses.

The compatibilist response assumes that the principal problem with fatalism is the apparent threat to free will. Boethius and those who follow him, therefore, attempt to show that there is no such threat from fatalism. God may know what I will do this evening, but he does not bring it about that I will do what I do. According to Boethius and others in the compatibilist tradition, questions of deliberation and free will concern *how* something is brought about, by my action and deliberation or otherwise.

Boethius appeals to a now famous metaphor to explicate the difference. A spectator watching a race may well know the winner, but the way in which he/she knows the winner, through vision, has no effect on the outcome of the race. Since his/her knowledge is not part of the cause of the race, the outcome of the race still depends entirely on the actions of the racers. Boethius claims that the theological argument from omniscience to fatalism depends on an equivocation; defenders of the argument fail to distinguish the way in which human beings know about the future from the way in which God knows about the future. Human beings carry out predictions from current causes, but God knows the future by some divine analog of pure perception. Unlike God, human beings can only know the outcome of the race if they can make an absolutely certain prediction, which requires that the outcome of the race be causally determined.

Historical Note 14: Boethius

The late Roman aristocrat and Christian Boethius is one of the most important intermediaries between Greek philosophy and the Latin Middle Ages. His translations of Aristotle's logical works and accompanying commentaries and textbooks were a crucial part of the curriculum throughout the Middle Ages. At some point he agreed to become "Master of Offices" for the Ostrogoth king of Italy, Theodoric. This led to his imprisonment and execution, probably in 526, for treason and practicing magic. Before his execution he composed *The Consolation of Philosophy*, still one of the greatest works of prison literature. In it he proposed his resolution of the apparent conflict between free will and divine omniscience discussed here.

Any historical account of the philosophy of time must acknowledge the extremely sophisticated medieval debates, involving Jewish, Christian, and Muslim thinkers, over future contingents, the nature of motion, and the eternity of the world. Unfortunately, the scientific background to those debates is so different from ours and the logical and mathematical language so unfamiliar that they have been largely relegated to specialist scholarship. Except for a brief discussion of the debates about creation in Chapter 8, we set them aside in this book.

This can be given a nontheological gloss in terms of our failure to distinguish the thin sense of necessity involved in the arguments for fatalism from the kind of causal necessity implicated in the freewill debate. The thin necessity, according to which everything can only be the thing that it is and not something else, simply doesn't tell us anything about how it became that way. In this conception of free will, questions of responsibility hinge only on whether our actions and deliberations are part of the causes of their outcomes, not on whether those outcomes could have been metaphysically different. This version of free will, sometimes called *compatibilism*, has been ably developed by the philosopher Daniel Dennett, especially in his books *Elbow Room* and *Freedom Evolves*.

The Boethian response is probably a minority position in the long history of the debate over logical fatalism and the problem of future contingents. Many philosophers have found the compatibilist theory of free will to be too weak: Absent a metaphysical account of our ability to change the future, how is it possible to be free? To such philosophers it does not matter that my choices are part of the causes of their outcomes if the choices themselves could not be otherwise. In addition, even those who might be tempted by compatibilist accounts of free will have worried that the fatalist arguments destroy any basis for our general sense that there must be a difference between the past and the future.

So the final response is to block Aristotle's sea-battle argument by proposing an alternative logical or metaphysical picture of the future. The *logical* strategy blocks the argument from Aristotle's premise number one above to the two separated disjuncts, generally by offering an alternative to the law of excluded middle. The *modal* or *branching* strategy blocks the inference from the tautological status of Example 4.4 to the necessity of the disjuncts.

The logical strategy normally proceeds by reinterpreting the logical operations of negation and disjunction, usually by considering how to interpret them in cases where the component sentences are neither true nor false. To see how this works, consider the ordinary case. The logical operation of disjunction, represented by ∨, takes any two sentences and generates a new sentence that is true whenever one of the original sentences is true. In this way it operates just like "either ... or ... " in English. Similarly, negation, normally represented by ¬ or ~, takes any sentence and generates a true sentence when the original sentence is false, and vice versa when it is true. For all possible combinations the alternatives are given in Table 4.2.

From these we can tell both why Aristotle's sea-battle sentence is a tautology and why it seems to require that one of the two components be true. However, what if we wanted to say that future sentences are neither true nor false, but of indeterminate truth-value? Would that allow us to

Table 4.2 Truth-tables for negation and disjunction

P	Q	P∨Q
T	T	T
T	F	T
F	T	T
F	F	F

(a) Disjunction

P	~P
T	F
F	T

(b) Negation

avoid this trap? Quite a few philosophers have followed the great Polish logician Jan Lukasiewicz in believing that it would. Suppose that it is now indeterminate whether there will be a sea-battle on January 1, 2100. What should we do with the disjunction? We might go with our intuition that the disjunction is still true, giving us Table 4.3(a).

By creating a third way to make the disjunction true, the truth of the disjunction no longer guarantees the truth of either of the components. Alternatively, we could choose the second table so that the disjunction remains indeterminate so long as the components do.

While such three-valued logical systems offer an alternative to fatalism, they do so only at what has seemed to many to be an unacceptably high cost. Among other problems, such three-valued logic prohibits many standard argumentative strategies involving disjunction, such as arguments by elimination, and endorses many patterns of inference that intuitively seem incorrect. The detailed debates over many-valued logic are fascinating but also quickly become quite technical. Interested readers with the appropriate background should pursue them in the sources listed at the end of the chapter. Ultimately, there doesn't seem to be any sign of a definitive resolution of these questions. One must decide whether the advantages of such alternative interpretations outweigh their disadvantages. This is an area where evidence and argument matters, but so does the strength of one's commitments to other core doctrines.

Table 4.3 Three-valued truth-tables for negation and disjunction

P	Q	$P \vee_{strong} Q$	$P \vee_{weak} Q$
T	T	T	T
T	I	T	T
T	F	T	T
F	T	T	T
I	T	T	T
I	I	T	I
F	F	F	F

(a) Disjunction

P	$\sim P$
T	F
F	T
I	I

(b) Negation

Rather than introduce an additional truth-value, branching theories suggest that future contingent statements, such as that about the sea-battle, simply don't have a truth-value at the present time. In addition, if they do have a truth-value in the present, they don't have it necessarily; it could change before we get there. There are various versions of such theories; the simplest to describe are the branching time theories. The most well-developed contemporary branching time theory is that of Storrs McCall. According to McCall, at each time we can visualize the universe as consisting of a single trunk leading to the present representing the fixed past with a cluster of branches like a tree coming out of the present representing all of the possible outcomes still available to us.

Given this picture, we should only accept as true those claims that hold in every possible branch. Otherwise we simply don't know, and the present doesn't determine, what the future holds. However, now consider our original sentence from Aristotle (refer to the quoted text numbered "1." 'There is a sea battle somewhere...' on p. 110). If time branches, some of those futures contain sea-battles and some don't. However, they all contain one or the other. That commits us to the truth of the disjunction, which is true in every branch, without committing us to either outcome. The actual metaphysical commitments of branching resolutions to the fatalism problem vary widely. Some of them primarily deal with branching or divergence among the available possibilities at different times in the actual world; branching space-time theories postulate the branches occurring at space-time points in an attempt to integrate such theories with modern space-time physics of the kind discussed later.

For all of their metaphysical messiness such theories have real advantages. Most importantly, they completely avoid fatalism and allow us to articulate a very metaphysically strong conception of free will and having been able to act differently from the way one actually acted. In addition, they also bring a new level of logical rigor to Heraclitean metaphysics, avoiding many of the worries about mystery mongering expressed by Williams above. As usual, I leave it to the reader whether the apparent solution creates more problems than it solves.

Conclusions

The conclusion drawn at the end of the previous section that the decision whether to combine a relatively weak conception of free will with fatalism or to adopt messy revisions to logic or branching time comes down to a matter of judgment rather than proof should not be surprising at this point. The last three chapters have addressed the classical attempts to go for "the big kill" in the philosophy of time. This way of doing philosophy—the phrase "the big kill" is borrowed from contemporary philosopher of physics Craig Callender—has, as we have seen, a long and distinguished history.

The Eleatics, especially Zeno, attempted to cut through the mess that is the world of OMDGs with that one knockdown argument. Yet there is always that crucial bit of contested metaphysics that gets smuggled into the premises and creates wiggle room. For Zeno himself, it's his relatively unsophisticated theory of continuity and infinity. For the neo-Eleatic McTaggart, it's both his characterization of time itself and his conception of what it would mean for it to be real or ideal.

For the Heracliteans of this chapter, it's principally a relatively naive conception of how one derives a metaphysical theory from ordinary common sense. The principal case for presentism requires us to place primary ontological significance on the common-sense distinction between extant and forthcoming or defunct entities. Although this is not entirely implausible, it does face serious problems from other aspects of our common-sense conceptions of both existence and time. Similarly, the arguments for a metaphysically open future considered in the previous section require us to endorse without question our introspective sense of our own agency. The reliability of that introspective sense of our own agency depends on substantive metaphysical and empirical psychological questions.

In all of these cases, instead of the logical clarity originally sought we discover a morass of theoretical advantages and disadvantages. As we've seen, in many cases it's not even clear that Heracliteans and Eleatics can agree on the difference between advantages and disadvantages. In some of these debates, it's not clear whether particular aspects of theories are features to be highlighted or bugs to be eliminated. Worse, there does not even seem to be clear agreement on the data that these theories should be responsive to.

That is where we now turn. The next several chapters sketch the best available accounts of the temporal phenomenon available to us from psychology, and related disciplines such as neuroscience, as well as the role of time in physics. Merely as a first hint as to how much this should change our conception of the problem, consider the result of a recent study in the field of psychology, according to which the human population seems to be relatively evenly divided between those who picture time moving past them and those who picture themselves moving through time. We'll consider this experiment in a bit more detail in the next chapter, but it is certainly intriguing to consider the possibility that the difference between A-theorists and B-theorists might be a matter of brain wiring rather than metaphysics.

Study exercise #2: Persistence

Let's say that entities *persist* just in case they exist through time, or equivalently if their lifetimes take some nonzero time to occur. Persisting entities include such OMDGs as tables and chairs, houses, animals, and people. They also include larger objects such as stars or solar systems, and smaller ones such as cells or molecules. However, they also include processes and events such as pregnancies, elections, and courses. The metaphysical problem of persistence is to identify the mode of existence across time of all of these things. Under what conditions do I have the same table, dog, election, or course at two different times?

The fact that these entities seem to manifest two radically different modes of persistence makes the problem particularly pressing. Objects like tables seem to persist through identity; numerically the same object exists at two different times. Processes or persisting events seem to persist by having parts of themselves at different times. Over the course of the Second World War, there is no particular time at which all of the Second World War exists. Instead, the Second World War is constituted out of a sequence of events happening at different times, for example the Battle of Britain and the invasion of Normandy. The various events that make up such an extended process, its temporal parts, are part of the same whole because the earlier parts are part of the causes of the later ones. In the philosophical literature, this mode of persistence is usually called *perdurance*.

In this way processes seem to exist through time in much the way that objects exist through space. My dining room table occupies an extended region of space by having parts, legs and a top for example, at different places, but properly connected to each other. However, the table itself seems to be entirely present at each time when it exists. Unlike perduring things, yesterday's table is not a separate thing properly connected with today's table, perhaps as part of its cause. Instead, yesterday's table just is the same thing as today's table. This mode of persistence is usually called *endurance*.

The philosophical problem of persistence is the attempt to identify the relationship between these two modes of persistence. Perdurantists, or four-dimensionalists, claim that the apparent difference between objects and processes is an illusion. Tables and chairs persist in precisely the same way that wars do, by having different parts at different times properly connected to each other. Endurantists claim that there must be some objects in the world that endure and form what we might call the structural unity of the world across time. Endurantists are also called three-dimensionalists because they claim that there are some things that are only extended in the three spatial dimensions and not across time.

Do you think that enduring objects must form a basic ontological category distinct from perduring processes and events? If so, do you think that OMDGs such as tables and animals endure or perdure? Why or why not?

In addition, while they are not necessarily connected, positions on persistence generally cluster together with positions in the philosophy of time. Although there are presentist perdurantists, can you see why perdurantists are also generally eternalists and endorse a B-theory of change? Similarly, can you see why endurantists are generally presentists and endorse A-theories of change?

Further reading

The articles on "Future Contingents" by Peter Øhrstrøm and Per Hasle and "Fatalism" by Hugh Rice in *The Stanford Encyclopedia of Philosophy* are the obvious next steps for those wishing to pursue these issues. Section 6, "Presentism, eternalism and the growing universe theory," of the main article on "Time" by Ned Markosian, a prominent presentist, is useful as well.

Classical sources for the debates over temporal ontology and fatalism:

Aristotle (1962), *The Categories and On Interpretation*, Cambridge, MA: Harvard University Press; London: Heinemann.
The sea-battle is discussed in Book IX of On Interpretation.

Augustine (2007), *Confessions*, New York, NY: Barnes & Noble Classics. Augustine; [edited by] George Stade. Barnes & Noble Classics.

Boethius and Slavitt, D. R. (2008), *The Consolation of Philosophy*, Cambridge, MA: Harvard University Press.

All three of these works are available in many editions and translations, with a number of them freely available on the internet. The freely available translations are usually not the most up to date, but are often adequate for students.

Despite the concerns about physics mentioned above and discussed in detail in Chapter 6, presentism remains a widely defended position in contemporary philosophy. Dean Zimmerman, Ned Markosian, and Jonathan Tallant are three of its most prominent defenders. Here is a somewhat representative sample of their work:

Markosian, N. (2004), *A Defense of Presentism*, Oxford: Clarendon Press.

Tallant, J. (2013), "Quantitative parsimony and the metaphysics of time: Motivating presentism," *Philosophy and Phenomenological Research*, 87 (3): 688–705.

Zimmerman, D. W. (2005), "The A-theory of time, the B-theory of time, and taking tense seriously," *Dialectica*, 59 (4): 401–57.

Zimmerman, D. W. (2008), *The Privileged Present: Defending an "A-Theory" of Time*, Malden, MA: Blackwell Publishing.

The growing block theory, sometimes under the guise of "no-futurism," also has defenders in addition to Michael Tooley, including:

Button, T. (2006), "There's no time like the present," *Analysis*, 66:2 (290): 130–5.

Forrest, P. (2006), *General Facts, Physical Necessity, and the Metaphysics of Time*, Oxford: Clarendon Press.

In addition to the B-theorists discussed in the previous chapter and D. C. Williams' "The Myth of Passage," reprinted in Westphal and Levenson, some of the most important defenders of eternalism, aka the block universe, aka four-dimensionalism include:

Balashov, Y. (2010), *Persistence & Spacetime*, Oxford: Oxford University Press.

Le Poidevin, R. (1991), *Change, Cause, and Contradiction: A Defence of the Tenseless Theory of Time*, New York: St. Martin's Press.

Sider, T. (2001), *Four-dimensionalism: An Ontology of Persistence and Time*, Oxford, New York: Clarendon Press; Oxford University Press.

Smart, J. J. C. (ed.) (1987), "The reality of the future," In *Essays Metaphysical and Moral: Selected Philosophical Papers*, 92–99, Oxford: Basil Blackwell.

Contemporary introductions to the issues involved with fatalism:

Taylor, R. (1992), *Metaphysics*, Englewood Cliffs, NJ: Prentice Hall (Foundations of Philosophy Series).

Especially Chapters 4–7

Pike, N. (1965), "Divine omniscience and voluntary action," *Philosophical Review*, 74: 27–46.

A relatively contemporary discussion of Boethius's worry about divine omniscience.

Some more technical introductions to anti-fatalist theories:

Since worries about fatalism and the status of future contingent statements have been primary motivators for the development of philosophical logic for more than 2,000 years, debate in this area quickly becomes extremely technical. Here are some of the least technical contemporary introductions to alternative logical systems that attempt to avoid fatalism and its relatives. Even these require a certain comfort with formal languages and, probably, a first course in predicate logic. So I open with two standard textbooks in formal logic:

Jeffrey, R. C. (1967), *Formal Logic: Its Scope and Limits*. McGraw-Hill, New York.

Vander Nat, A. (2010), *Simple formal logic: with common-sense symbolic techniques*. Routledge, New York.

Haack, S. (1974), *Deviant logic: some philosophical issues*. Cambridge University Press London, New York.

Chapter 3 discusses the costs and benefits of alternative, "deviant" as Haack calls them, logical systems, including three-valued logics and truth gaps. Chapter 4 covers future contingents and fatalism. Haack's discussion is more technical than the one in the current chapter, but still fairly accessible by the standards of this literature to anyone comfortable with taking the time to learn some logical notation.

McCall, S. (1976), "Objective Time Flow," *Philosophy of Science*, 43: 337–62.

McCall, S. (1994), *A Model of the Universe: Space-time, Probability, and Decision*, Oxford, New York: Clarendon Press (Clarendon Library of Logic and Philosophy).

In these two works, McCall attempts to articulate a theory of branching time compatible with Einstein's theory of relativity.

Prior, A. N. (1953), "Three-valued logic and future contingents," *Philosophical Quarterly*, 3: 317–26.

Prior, A. N. (1968), *Papers on Time and Tense*, Oxford: Clarendon Press.

Thomason, R. H. (1970), "Indeterminist time and truth-value gaps," *Theoria: A Swedish Journal of Philosophy*, 36: 264–81.

Belnap, N. (1992), "Branching space-time," *Synthese: An International Journal for Epistemology, Methodology and Philosophy of Science*, 92 (3): 385–434.

Discussion questions

1   Can you explain the distinction between eternalism, presentism, and growing block ontologies in common-sense terms? Can you explain why the dispute is in danger of becoming merely verbal? How does Quine's criterion of ontological commitment help us to avoid that problem?

2   How might a presentist explain the difference between abstract objects, fictional objects, and non-present objects? What about eternalists? Can you think of any examples that create problems for either or both of these alternatives?

3   Can you explain the difference between idealistic and block universe versions of eternalism?

4 How may various positions regarding the ontology of the future have implications for problems of human agency and ethics?
5 Can you describe three arguments for fatalism? What is the difference between fatalism and determinism?
6 What is the "Boethian" response to fatalism? Why might one find such an alternative unsatisfying?
7 Why do three-valued logics allow us to avoid fatalism? What about branching time theories?

5

Flow, Change, and the Phenomenology of Time

Two aspects of the experience of time are discussed—the experience of presentness and the experience of flow—and distinguished from more general concerns regarding the role of time in our experience. We consider how our experiences can feel present when they combine sensory data emitted from sources at different times. Next, several versions of the "specious present" are introduced. Much data from modern neuroscience and cognitive psychology raises issues for the relatively simple accounts of time experience characteristic of philosophical accounts. The chapter concludes with a discussion of "spotlight theories" that attempt to provide eternalist accounts of experience.

This chapter serves a dual purpose. Explicating our experience of time, especially our experience of temporal flow, is the last of what we might call the purely philosophical problems addressed in this book. Beginning with Chapter 6, our focus will shift to those problems for our ordinary conception of time raised by contemporary physical theory. This is the last problem for which it seems possible to derive the data from a relatively straightforward act of introspection. However, part of the lesson of this chapter is that such introspective data need to be handled with extreme care.

Various results from cognitive psychology and neuroscience indicate that our experiences can be misleading about their own nature in, at least, two ways. Aspects of our experience that seem to us to be fundamental and therefore universal have turned out to be neither. In *Time Warped*, Claudia Hammond describes the results mentioned at the end of the last chapter. Someone tells you that your class presentation, previously scheduled for

Wednesday, has been moved forward two days. What is your first instinctive response to the question of what day the presentation is now scheduled?

Some people naturally respond that the presentation has been rescheduled to Monday. Others, just as naturally, expect that the presentation has been moved to Friday. While the particular answer the subject gives depends in complicated ways on culture, language, and context, it's clear that neither answer is "right." For example, if the second answer were extremely rare, we might decide that those who see time differently do so as the result of some kind of neurological or cognitive oddity. However, the natural division seems to be right about 50–50.

How does this connect to philosophy? Well, the people who relocate the meeting to Monday seem to be using a different model of motion through time than do the Friday subjects. The Monday subjects are using what Hammond calls "the time moving metaphor." They see time as flowing, carrying the future toward them; they are natural Heracliteans. The Friday subjects are using the "ego-moving metaphor." They see themselves as *moving* through time toward a fixed future; they seem to be natural Eleatics. Perhaps even more surprising, Hammond notes that it's possible to manipulate the subject's dominant metaphor. For example, subjects riding a train seem to be more likely to invoke an ego-moving metaphor then they would otherwise.

I don't think anyone is claiming that these experiments settle or dissolve the metaphysical disputes between A-theorists and B-theorists. As we've already seen, these disputes involve a lot more than the phenomenology of becoming. However, it does introduce us to a theme that will become ever-more prominent over the next several chapters; one must be extremely careful not to confuse a failure of imagination with a truth about the world or human experience.

In the remainder of this chapter, we are going to examine two aspects of temporal experience often taken as evidence for Heraclitean views—the presence of experience and the experience of flow. These aspects of our experience are ideal candidates for beginning to explore the intersection between philosophy and psychology. They have often been treated as the fundamentally temporal aspects of our experience capable of being explained only on Heraclitean grounds. However, there are many results from psychology and neuroscience that create problems for such views. Therefore, the remainder of this chapter proceeds in three phases. In the next section, we examine classical Heraclitean accounts of phenomenological presence and the experience of flux. After that, we will introduce various results from the psychology of time that create problems for such accounts. We'll conclude by considering the possibility of alternative accounts of the phenomenology that don't involve the metaphysics of flux.

Presence, flux, and the micro-phenomenology of time

The role of time and temporality in our conscious experience of the world can be approached under two different aspects. Time seems to function as the fundamental organizing principle of our mental lives. To think, choose, and act is to do so under the guise of temporality. This role of time as, what Immanuel Kant calls, "the form of inner intuition" or as the subject of what contemporary philosopher Barry Dainton calls the "macro-phenomenology of time," is not our topic in this chapter.

On the one hand, it is the subject of the whole book. Throughout, we are examining various ways in which time shapes our experience and evaluating whether they require us to give it a special metaphysical status. On the other hand, we have philosophers who see the whole project of slicing out bits of the problem of time for independent analysis as deeply misguided. Such philosophers often share many of the concerns of radical Heracliteans such as Bergson, although the phenomenological tradition from Husserl to Heidegger often expresses it in a very different philosophical idiom. Because of that distinct philosophical idiom, and because they generally reject the separation of the problem of time into a collection of relatively well-defined puzzles which provide the structure of this book, we do not pay them as much attention as they deserve. Some examples of such radically different approaches to time can be found in the suggestions at the end of this chapter.

Here we focus on the second guise under which time manifests itself in experience. Two issues in the micro-phenomenology of time will be our particular focus: the presence, or presentness, of experience and the experience of temporal flow. Why is it that our experiences seem to be or even seem as though they must be present? Why is it that I don't seem to ever experience anything as past or as future, but only as present? In addition, certain sequences of experiences seem to possess an interconnected structure that goes beyond mere sequencing. When I hear the melody of a song, I don't merely hear each note in sequence. I hear the earlier notes becoming, turning into, the later ones.

Historical Note 15: Edmund Husserl and the Phenomenological Tradition

Edmund Husserl (1853–1938) is the father of phenomenology. Husserl's phenomenological method went through many transformations in his long career, but it was always focused on the attempt to understand what things in the world are *for us* while "bracketing" questions of what they are in themselves. Certainly, the greatest of these mysteries is to understand what *we* are to ourselves. It should be clear that time or temporality is a crucial aspect of our being for ourselves, and it is a central concern of both Husserl and his successors in the phenomenological tradition, especially Martin Heidegger (1889–1976), whose most famous work is the classic, and classically difficult, *Being and Time*. Other than a brief discussion of Husserl's influential theory of time consciousness in Chapter 5, the phenomenological tradition does not feature in this book. Their conception of the structure of the problems and their philosophical language simply doesn't fit naturally into this format.

The presence of experience

That all of our experiences are present to us might seem too obvious to be surprising. However, a bit of reflection can reveal how surprising this actually is. There are two related aspects of presentness that have often seemed to be of phenomenological and philosophical significance. First, all of my experiences seem to be present to me at their time of occurrence and no other. Second, those experiences represent both themselves and their objects to me as present. The phenomenal presence and the intentional presence of experience are deeply puzzling in their own right and even more so when we attempt to explore the connections between them.

To see why, we should consider the general distinction between thoughts, including experiences, and their contents. When I look at my coffee cup, I have an experience; I undergo a transition into a particular mental state. That mental state has properties of its own; it lasts a particular length of time, it feels a particular way to me, and it is at least correlated with certain activity within my central nervous system. None of those properties, by themselves, seem to be enough to make that mental state into an experience *of my cup.* To see why, consider what we would say if we created the same mental state in ourselves by direct electrical or chemical manipulation of our brain. Despite having, in one sense, precisely the same experience, it would be a mistake to describe it as an experience of the cup. We therefore need a distinction between the phenomenological features of an experience and its intentional features.

Now consider the way in which time is odd. It might seem tautological to point out that I only have experiences in the present. At what other time could I have an experience, other than the time at which the experience happens? However, consider the difference with space. Obviously, there must be some sense in which our experiences happen where we are and not elsewhere. However, the "here-ness" of the experience is not part of the phenomenology of the experience. It's not merely that my experiences are happening now, but that they *feel* like they are happening now. Think about a memory, for example. Part of the difference between memories and experiences seems to be the disconnect between the phenomenological presence of the active memory and the intentional pastness of its object.

In addition, this phenomenological presence seems to bleed through into the intentional content of our experiences. The compellingly present nature of the experiences themselves seems to compel us to treat their objects as present. When I see my cup, I see it now. Even in the case of events that I consciously know are in the past, like a distant lightning strike, my mind represents that event as present along with all of the objects of my other current experiences. My mind constructs a picture of the world present to me at each time out of the collection of phenomenologically present experiences.

Finally, there seems to be a deep connection between this presence of experience and our ability to act in the world. We saw in Chapter 3 that one of the distinctive features of tensed, as opposed to tenseless, representations is that tensed representations have distinctive action-generating features depending on their time of use. Our present experience of a situation requiring action, triggers immediate action unless we have the opportunity to prevent ourselves from acting. Think about our tendency to flinch at the sound of thunder even though we know that the lightning must be past.

This loop from the presence of the events to the presence of our experience to our present actions emphasizes the powerful role that "presentness" plays in our conscious lives and makes it seem obvious to many philosophers that something both objective and fundamental must be responsible for the presence of experience and its role in conscious awareness. We will see in the next section that contemporary psychological research raises serious problems for the idea that the presence of experience straightforwardly represents the presence of its objects. First, though, we take a look at another aspect of temporal micro-phenomenology—the experience of flow.

The experience of flow

If our first phenomenological problem is the presence of experience in general, the problem of flow involves the felt structure of that experience. In particular, how is it possible for the past to remain present? To see what this means, consider three examples. Imagine watching a golf ball fly away from you or the second hand of a clock sweep around your watch. Compare that experience with watching the minute hand on a clock. Unlike the minute hand of the clock, I do not merely experience the ball or the second hand as occupying a succession of positions at different times. Instead, I experience the ball at each moment as moving. The motion of the ball in the present is part of my present experience of the ball.

If that's correct, then we have a puzzle. If anything like an at-at account of motion (cf. Chapter 2) is correct, then the immediately past positions of the ball or of the second hand must be present in my current experience. I'm not experiencing the ball as being in two places though; at each time the ball is clearly in motion at the place it currently occupies, not blurred between many places.

A similar auditory example illustrates this as well. Consider three different experiences of the notes C, E, and G played on a piano. Suppose I first play them in order with a two-second separation between them. You experience each note as a distinct phenomenon. Next, suppose I play them simultaneously—you have a single experience of a C major triad. Finally, I play them in rapid succession, and you hear a C major arpeggio. Crucially, you hear the three notes of the arpeggio quite distinctly from each other, but as part of the arpeggio. My experience of each of the notes is transformed in some way by their position in a sequence. The C that I hear as the first note of the arpeggio is somehow transformed by the fact that it will be followed by E. Obviously, it can't be that the note itself is transformed. Somehow my experience of the notes of the arpeggio involves the presence of the immediately past and perhaps future notes, but I experience those other notes as past and future. The arpeggio is also distinct from the chord.

These examples both involve the role of our experience of flow in shaping our experience of material transitions. Philosopher Barry Dainton suggests that we also need to pay attention to manifestations of flow without qualitative change, what he calls "imminent phenomenal flow." Dainton uses the example of laying on our backs looking up into a cloudless clear blue sky. If it gets quiet enough, and one's inner monologue also gets quiet, one might very well be able to lay there having a sequence of qualitatively identical experiences. However, it remains the case that the present experience is not merely present to us as itself. We are aware of it as the latest in a sequence.

This example is more problematic than the first two. This experience of imminent flow seems to be stronger in some people than others. Some people report a very strong sense of themselves as continuously located in time independently of the qualitative contents of their awareness; others do not. In addition, shutting down one's inner monologue is rare and difficult. It is one of the principal goals of many forms of meditation. One of the principal goals of shutting down that inner monologue is to become wholly present. Many practiced meditators report that in the absence of this inner chatter, time sense is largely absent as well.

However, most people do report in most circumstances something like a sense of imminent flow. And the fact that one must work so hard to shut it down might be taken as evidence of its central role in consciousness.

Before we consider three traditional attempts to account for the structure of temporal consciousness, it's worth pointing out one obvious alternative that cannot be correct. Since flow seems to involve the past carried forward into the present, it is tempting to think that memory must play a crucial role in the phenomena. However, my experience of the later notes of the arpeggio proceeding from the earlier ones is distinct from my memory of those earlier notes. Musicians should be able to recognize the phenomenological distinction between hearing the interconnection of the notes of a melody as one plays it while also remembering and evaluating each of those notes independently as one moves forward.

Whatever accounts for the presence of experience described in the last section, the experience of the motion of the ball or the second hand possesses that presence just as much as the experience of the position of that object. That my mind keeps track of where the ball was as well as where it is must play some role in the construction of the experience of flow, but that primitive tracking facility is phenomenologically and intentionally distinct from ordinary memory. Since my memory of past positions is clearly distinct from my present experience of flux, there must be some distinctive mental faculty or activity that keeps track of such flow. In the next section, we will examine three classic models of temporal micro-phenomenology. All of these involve, in various ways, the idea that my current awareness has a duration of its own, either phenomenologically or intentionally.

The specious present and models of temporal flow

If the analysis above is correct, then our experience of change requires that each of our experiences somehow involves temporally extended contents. The most obvious way to achieve such extension is for each of our experiences to itself be temporally extended. This is the suggestion that our experience of the present is really that of a "specious present." Although first introduced by the psychologist E. R. Clay a few years earlier, the proposal was first clearly described in William James's *The Principles of Psychology* in 1890.

James's basic proposal is that our experience of the world is not a continuous stream, but is a sequence of temporally extended pulses. There's more than a bit of ambiguity in James's treatment of the specious present and in the discussion of it over the next century; for example, James sometimes treats it as something more like the span of short-term memory than as the immediate content of present experience. However, there is good reason to expect that the contents of immediate experience are also temporally extended, perhaps nearly a second long. For example, there are pretty clear lower thresholds for temporal discrimination although the details depend on the exact sensory modalities involved. We will discuss these in more detail in the next section.

Here we are more concerned with whether the specious present can explain our experience of motion. At first glance, it seems as though it should. Since each of my sequential experiences of the ball includes a little bit of the ball's motion, it is actually moving within each present experience. Similarly when the arpeggio is played in sequence, the tail end of the previous note occupies the same specious present as the beginning of the next. In each of these cases, the specious present seems to allow for the interconnection required by the experience of flow.

Unfortunately, such a simple model can't possibly be right. Consider the following two problems. Remember that the specious present is supposed to be present to me simultaneously or uniformly. If the end of the tone C and the beginning of E occupy the same specious present, I shouldn't be experiencing them sequentially but simultaneously. We are back to the chord instead of the arpeggio. Similarly for the ball. I shouldn't see it smoothly moving through its path, but blurred between all of the places it occupies within each specious present.

Second, this model seems to imply the existence of a difference which is not phenomenologically present. If the experience of motion is the way in which my mind represents change within a specious present, then shouldn't I be able to detect the jumps at the boundaries between specious presents? There is no evidence of such boundary phenomena between specious presents.

Perhaps the bonding between elements of experience takes place at a higher level of abstraction. Something like this seems to be the suggestion of C. D. Broad. The basic material of experience consists of a continuous stream of sensory information; Broad calls elements of this stream the "sensa." However this stream of data from the senses is processed below the level of consciousness. To use a modern computer metaphor, the brain preprocesses the continuous stream of data from the sense organs into structures that higher mental functions can make use of.

Each act of conscious awareness, each experience, is like looking through a temporally extended window at this stream. If a qualitative change takes place quickly enough that it could appear within a single such window, we experience it as one of these active transitions. Thus, our actual conscious experience is the active representation of the contents of a kind of sliding window onto a field of phenomenal contents. In this model, our minds represent the contents of each window to us as either changing or stable depending on the content of each window. We become aware of slower kinds of change via differences between the windows.

We need to remember that the size of this window is basically that of the specious present and so is significantly less than a second. There are therefore many of these per second. This model certainly solves both the blurring problem and the boundary problem associated with the simple specious present model. Unfortunately, it suffers from a fatal phenomenological flaw. If the processing of the window at each moment *is* the act of conscious awareness, then I should "hear" multiple copies of the notes in the arpeggio corresponding to the multiple acts of awareness of the same note. Each time I rechecked the same phenomenal content, which I must be doing in order to avoid the boundary and blurring problems, I should also be reexperiencing it. But that's obviously not the case.

There is one more classical version of the specious present strategy to account for our experience of change. In this model, rather than each act of experience having a temporally extended structure, each instantaneous experience "contains" in some sense its immediate predecessors, and perhaps successors. There are two versions of this strategy—a phenomenal version usually associated with C. D. Broad and an intentional version due to Edmund Husserl.

In 1938, Broad introduced the idea of "presentedness": at any moment my immediate new experience has maximum presentedness. That same experience manifests its immediate predecessors with a slightly lesser degree of presentedness, and its predecessor with even less, etc. The idea here is that each experience becomes a kind of fading background to its successors—shaping the way in which we apprehend them. Unfortunately, it is not clear what this property of reduced "presentedness" is supposed to be. Is it just the property of being slightly past? That seems to undermine its explanatory power. It was supposed to explain how the past can influence present experience. Saying that it does so by being past seems viciously circular.

Edmund Husserl is the founder of phenomenology which became one of the dominant philosophical schools of the twentieth century. Phenomenology takes as its fundamental project the first person characterization of what it is like to be a human being in the world. Among the major philosophers associated with phenomenology, in at least certain periods of their careers, are Edith Stein, Hannah Arendt, Martin Heidegger, and Jean-Paul Sartre. Obviously given the problems we have examined so far, the problem of temporal consciousness is a central phenomenon and problem for lived experience and therefore significant within the phenomenological tradition. Unfortunately, as mentioned above, the general phenomenological approach to time is very different from that taken here.

Fortunately, there is one aspect of Husserl's account of time consciousness from relatively early in his career that has been deeply influential beyond phenomenology and can give us a taste of his approach. Like Broad's later model, Husserl's model is two-dimensional. That is, our present experience does not merely contain past experience, but it contains, or in Husserl's case represents, immediately past experiences as past in varying degrees.

Husserl's proposal differs from Broad's in that Husserl takes the intentional structure of temporal objects of consciousness more seriously. As Husserl himself puts it,

We can make self evident assertions concerning the imminent Object in itself, e.g., that it now endures, that a certain part of the duration has lapsed, that the duration of the sound apprehended in the now (naturally, with the content of the sound) constantly sinks back into the past and an ever new point of duration enters into the now or is now.

What Husserl seems to be indicating here is that part of experiencing a sound as being in time is that the experience refers to its own immediate past. Consider a spatial analogy. I don't experience my coffee cup as a collection of two-dimensional visual images. I experience my coffee cup as a three-dimensional object—for example, as one that has a back side. However, that three-dimensional model is constructed out of an immense number of two-dimensional images collected by my eyes integrated with kinesthetic information that tracks the moving position of my eyes. While it would be a mistake to say that the immediate object contains all of those images, it refers to them because it is constructed from them.

Retention is Husserl's name for this act of integrating the immediate past into the present experience. Therefore, since the C is within the horizon of retention of the E, the E is represented as following the C. Notice that this solves the repeated contents problem. The experience of C is not contained within the experience of E; it's not that the experience of C is present with a slightly different qualitative feature. Instead, C forms part of the retained content of the experience of E. The difference between experience and retention is not a difference of more or less present; it is more like the difference between belief and doubt. Two very different ways of orienting oneself toward the same potential content.

Protention is the analogous integration of later contents into the present experience. A certain amount of care is needed in interpreting Husserl's conception of protention. At some places, Husserl and his followers write as if protention involves a kind of precognition. When they are being careful, it is clear that nothing particularly mysterious is going on. The formation of the conscious experience lags behind actual stimulation of the sense organs, and each such conscious experience integrates information from stimulations that are objectively later than the subjective time of the experience.

Husserl's model also avoids the circularity worry attached to Broad's model. Remember that Broad's problem is to identify or explain why the particular qualitative difference between experiences that he calls degrees of presentedness should be temporal. Husserl's retentions are by definition the way in which the mind represents the immediate past to itself as past in the present. Husserl is simply not concerned with how this connects up with the temporal ordering of the external world. On the one hand, his phenomenological method deliberately "brackets" all questions about the connection between experience and the world in favor of careful description of the structure of experience. On the other hand, like all those deeply imbued with German Kantianism, Husserl sees time as principally the mode through which the mind represents *itself* to itself; it belongs, in Husserl's terms, principally to the "imminent sphere."

Unfortunately, as we will see in the next section, contemporary empirical work seems to indicate that time consciousness is even more complicated and messy than the early phenomenologists believed.

The empirical psychology of time perception

Psychological research over the past century or so might best be summarized as the ongoing discovery of complexity in the psychology of time. For our purposes, it is useful to divide the relevant material into two categories. There are a collection of psychological phenomena and faculties, such as memory, which are temporally involved. There are also a collection of directly temporal experiences, including our experience of the present and of flow as described in the previous section as well as our experience of the passage of time and our ability to estimate duration.

In this section, we will focus on those more central phenomena. Even in this more restricted realm, we will discover that detailed examination of the phenomena makes it difficult to avoid the conclusion that there is no such thing as the time sense. As psychologist William Friedman puts it,

> At least from a psychological point of view, it seems far more productive to consider the many things that time is in the world and the many ways in which humans experience it. Our environment is rich in temporal structures— in music, in language, in the characteristic duration of familiar events, and in the recurrent cycles of nature and our own activities. To define time as some unitary dimension that cuts across all of these features is to lose sight of the special challenges they pose for perception and cognition. [5]

The philosopher Daniel Dennett warns us to be cautious of the metaphor of a unified locus of consciousness, what he calls "the Cartesian theater."

Even those who grant the complexity of the neurological and psychological processes involved in temporal experience sometimes presume that they must ultimately come together into a single coherent conscious model of the temporal structure of the world. The evidence canvassed below should lead us to take seriously the possibility that there might not be any such thing as a singular temporal experience.

The psychological processes of temporal consciousness, as well as their neurological correlates, remain objects of study. We almost certainly have more questions than answers; it remains possible that we haven't yet figured out the right questions to ask. So it remains eminently possible that we live in a Heraclitean universe whose flux is tracked by a multiplicity of distinct psychological capacities. However, it is also entirely possible that the appearance of a unified psychological model of time is itself an illusion. If nothing else, as we will see in the next section, this evidence opens the door to a block universe account of temporal experience.

Timekeeping, duration, and internal clocks

Under ordinary conditions, human beings are pretty competent at estimating the duration of temporal intervals of anything from a few seconds to many days. Unfortunately, there is no consensus regarding the psychological or physiological basis of this capacity. There are some time cycles, most famously the circadian rhythm, that almost certainly have a biological basis and play some role in our estimates of duration. As one might expect, such biological clocks are fairly robust relative to changes in external stimuli, but are subject to various kinds of physiological or biochemical distortions.

The most notable manifestation of the circadian rhythm is our sleep-wake cycle. Anyone who has suffered jet lag has experienced the independence of this cycle from immediate external cues. Our body tells us to sleep not based on where the sun is, but based on how long it's been since our last sleep, based on our internal cycle. That cycle also responds, however sluggishly, to external cues. Within a few days, our cycle shifts so as to reflect the local day-night cycle.

What happens if we are denied such external cues? While the evidence is equivocal, as it is for many of the phenomena discussed in this section, certain very intriguing temporal illusions seem to arise amounting to a decoupling of our internal cycle from that of the external world. Since the circadian rhythm is actually closer to twenty-five hours than twenty-four hours, the first thing that happens is a shift in wake times relative to the external world. Suppose that before entering such an isolation experiment, one's natural sleep cycle is from 10 p.m. to 6 a.m. Following one's natural circadian rhythm, sleep time will shift forward a bit less than an hour each day until it moves all the way around the clock. For example, within a few days one will go to sleep at about 10 a.m. and wake at about 6 p.m.

Something even odder happens in at least some cases. Subjects sometimes extend the cycles of the natural rhythm as well as shifting their location relative to an external clock. While still believing and reporting that they are sleeping for eight hours and waking for about sixteen, they are actually sleeping for about sixteen and spending thirty-two hours awake. Consider another experiment described by Claudia Hammond in *Time Warped*. After spending two months underground, the geologist Michel Siffre discovered that his internal time sense had become almost entirely disconnected from external clocks or calendars. When his support team informed him that it was time to return to the surface, he believed that he still had twenty-five days left in the experiment.

Intriguingly, this disruption in our large-scale biological rhythms seems to involve disruptions of our time sense even on much shorter scales. For example, Siffre reported an inability to listen to music because he could not interpret the temporal structures of melodies. William Friedman reports that in some temporal isolation experiments when the sleep-wake cycle has decoupled from external time, duration judgments of as short as thirty seconds also become distorted.

There is evidence that some other biological clocks might also play a role in time perception. Although the circadian clock seems to be relatively immune to changes in temperature, in many, but not all, experiments individuals with elevated body temperature underestimate durations while those with decreased body temperature overestimate them. Of course, LSD and other drugs infamously interfere with time sense.

Unfortunately, it seems unlikely that our time sense can be entirely based on unconsciously counting the cycles of some biological clock, even one subject to distortions. This is because the cognitive situation in which we make our time estimate seems as important as the physiological. The watched-pot illusion is probably the most famous of these. When we put ourselves into a condition of waiting for some future event, we systematically overestimate the amount of time it took to occur. In fact, simply having a future orientation seems to distort our time sense. In some experiments, individuals who are told in advance that they will be asked to estimate the length of a certain time interval systematically overestimate its length compared to those who have not been so primed.

Similarly, we are all familiar with the fact that time speeds up when we are engaged with the present task. Thirty minutes watching a comedy feels much shorter than thirty minutes on the elliptical machine at the gym. Other such illusions include the fact that time speeds up as we get older, and that our duration estimates seem to depend on how many identifiable units the period contains. For example, a sporting event divided into four quarters seems longer than one, of the same length, divided into two halves.

For more detailed discussions of these temporal illusions, see the works by Claudia Hammond and William Friedman listed below. For now, the only reasonable conclusion is the lack of consensus on any unified, systematic account of time estimation.

Temporal discrimination and the experience of the present[1]

Here we examine a few of the phenomena that should lead us to consider whether the "presentness" of experience might not be a kind of illusion itself. As we saw above, there is a profound temptation to interpret the immediacy of our experience as resulting from the distinctive presence of its objects. Even a little reflection should show us that that can't be precisely right. Once I accept the finitude of the speed of light, I must also accept that the collection of events which I am experiencing together take place at a variety of different times.

Of course, in terrestrial settings those time differences are well below the level of discrimination. In particular, the time difference between the nearest and the furthest events contained within a single visual stimulus is much less than the 0.5 seconds it takes the brain to process that stimulus. Especially since these stimuli are *synchronous*—all of the light is hitting the retina together—the hypothesis of *visual simultaneity* seems plausible. If our experiences always consisted of a set of synchronous signals, even if they were from asynchronous sources, there might be something left of the idea of an objective present of experience. That is not the case.

Our mind routinely integrates and sometimes even unifies asynchronous signals into a single experience. The most familiar examples of asynchronous inputs unified into a single experience involve sound. Except in very special situations, sound reaches each of our ears at different times, but we consistently hear a single sound. In fact, the temporal difference in arrival is a primary cue for the spatial location of the sound. We can test this experimentally, and many have, by having subjects wear a pair of headphones. If we feed a simultaneous sound in both the left and right ears, the subjects hear a single tone, as we would expect. If the two tones are separated by a very small interval, less than 2 milliseconds (ms) say, subjects still hear a single tone but with the apparent source of the tone closer to the first ear that was stimulated. As the timing of the sounds gets farther apart, subjects will begin to hear two distinct tones. The discrimination threshold is between 2 milliseconds and 5 milliseconds; it increases with age but seems otherwise fixed for each person. In addition, order discrimination, recognizing which tone came first, takes a much larger separation, about 20 milliseconds. There are similar thresholds for the other sensory modalities.

There are many other examples of active temporal integration of experience; many of them discussed in the paper by Craig Callender listed in the Further Reading section. Here is one more for your consideration. Most people are familiar with the ventriloquism affect. When we hear someone speaking, we associate the source of the sound with a moving mouth. For example, it often seems as though sound is coming directly from the screen in a movie theater, despite the fact that the speakers are well off to the side. The general explanation for this is that our brains rely on vision for the most reliable spatial information and correct the apparent source of sound to match the relevant visual stimuli.

Hearing provides the most accurate temporal information, and as we might expect there are similar "illusions" of temporal ventriloquism. In general, a visual stimulus immediately preceded by an audible one will be judged to occur earlier than it did and similarly a visual stimulus succeeded by an audible one will seem to occur later than it actually did. In fact, we can experience this phenomenon when the soundtrack and video track of a movie are just slightly out of sync. As long as they're not too far apart, our minds bind the visual and auditory stimuli, and do so using the auditory as the principal control.

Phi, Tau, and the experience of motion

Just above we saw evidence that present experience is a result of the active integration of multiple asynchronous stimuli. That should make us suspicious of any interpretation of the presence of experience that treats it as a straightforward experience of presence. Not all of those asynchronous stimuli or their causes can be present in any metaphysically significant sense. In this section, we will examine some evidence that our experience of flow is the result of similar active processes.

In particular, we introduce a series of phenomena that illustrate the mind's tendency to process sequences of distinct stimuli into an experience of a continuous process. The *beta phenomenon,* responsible for moving pictures and video, is the most familiar. As a historical aside, one does wonder how strong Heraclitean intuitions could have survived in a culture immersed in video.

Even if we grant that considerations from Zeno's paradoxes (cf. Chapter 2) provide us with good reasons to treat such videos as discrete samples of continuous processes, we still need to resolve whether the felt difference between changing experiences and the experience of change marks a fundamental metaphysical difference. Beta, by itself, seems to provide excellent grounds to treat the experience of change like other secondary qualities; it is principally the product of the way we construct our experience not the product of a quality already present in the object. Here are three additional phenomena that point in the same direction.

Phi phenomena are closely related to beta, but rather than a sequence of static images, we create the illusion of motion via sequences of flashing lights against a stable background. In the simplest case, experimenters simply flash two lights on a screen, causing subjects to see a single spot move from the location of the first light to that of the second. Perhaps the most puzzling version of this is the so-called "color phi" phenomenon. Here, one flashes two lights of different colors. Subjects experience a single light moving from A to B, changing colors about halfway in between. Obviously, this requires input from the final state in order to construct the experience of the transition into that state.

This is not an example of psychic time travel! Instead, the kinds of latency and integration effects that we saw at work above are in play here too. The two stimuli are so close together that the mind-brain constructs a single experience using both stimuli. In essence, it treats them as frames in a film, as discrete samples of a continuous process rather than distinct stimuli.

Here are two related phenomena that seem to indicate that this is a general feature of experience. First, the tau and kappa phenomena indicate a connection between time and space in experience. Suppose I have three lights, X, Y, and Z, arranged in a line with Y closer to X than to Z. When I flash the lights at the same interval, subjects routinely and robustly report less time between X and Y than between Y and Z. This is the kappa effect. Alternatively, one sets up the tau effect with equidistant lights; variation in the timing of the flashes results in changes in the apparent distance. Even if we make the spatial separation or the flash intervals large enough to suppress phi, these effects seem to be the result of the mind treating these lights as three "samples" of a single process moving across the screen at a continuous velocity. This interpretation seems to be confirmed by the fact that kappa is stronger when the sequence of lights is moving downward, which is normally explained by the expectation of acceleration in falling bodies.

The "cutaneous rabbit illusion" is our final example of a continuous experience generated from discrete stimuli. This tactile illusion is generated by tapping the subject rapidly in three locations on their arm. Suppose I were to tap you, rapidly, three times on your wrist, three times on your elbow, and once on your upper arm. What would you feel? You might expect to feel three clusters of taps at the three locations. Instead, you experience a sequence of taps evenly spaced up your arm. Hence, the cutaneous rabbit illusion of a small animal hopping up your arm. All of these illusions indicate that while our experience is not completely independent of external stimulus, it also depends on substantive expectations built into our cognitive architecture.

Of the classical accounts considered above, Husserl's seems closest to being "on the right track." However, even he seems to radically underestimate the complexity and diversity of cognitive processes generating temporal experience.

"Spotlight" theories of temporal consciousness and the block universe

The psychological evidence in the previous section makes it at least plausible that there is no immediate inference from our experience of flux and presence to a Heraclitean metaphysics of flux. At the very least, it introduces the seemingly paradoxical fact that scientific investigation often reveals empirical evidence that things are not the way they seem to be. The evidence that, at least in detail, our temporal experience does not operate the way it seems to when it is subjected to even the most careful phenomenological inspection, is the first example of something we will see again and again in the second half of this book: the manifest image of ordinary experience subjected to systematic analysis in competition with and perhaps replaced by the radically different scientific image.

The context, however, makes the problem somewhat more pressing in this case. Here we are dealing directly with the explanation of particular experiences in terms of a radically different metaphysics. Let's assume that the world is a tenseless, eternal, Parmenidean block. Why does it seem to be a world of radical Heraclitean change?

Notice that the Heracliteans still have an easy rejoinder to these problems, even given the complexities introduced above. According to them, the world seems to be in flux because it is. The details are a matter for perceptual neuropsychology and perhaps some evolutionary biology. The defender of the block universe has no such easy out; for her the devil is in the details.

Even in the absence of such a detailed account, the strategy is clear. The modern eternalist must appeal to something like a "spotlight" theory of temporal awareness. The original metaphor seems to come from the mathematician and physicist Hermann Weyl but it has now become standard. Think of each human being as spread out in time along their life-time (or, as physicists call it, world-line). At each moment along the line, the bit of the person located then is aware of the bit of the universe perceptually available to them at that time via the kinds of mechanisms described above. From our inside perspective, it is as if each of those momentary acts of awareness lights up sequentially. We can imagine a metaphorical spotlight moving along the world-line of each person sequentially illuminating and thereby activating the temporally arranged acts of awareness.

From a God's eye view, all of those temporally arranged bits are indistinguishable from each other. The me-part from two years ago exists and has the same awareness independently of one's temporal perspective. The me of two years ago no more ceases to exist because I am not then, than my office ceases to exist because I am not there. Remember, from Chapter 3, that the point of the tenseless account is to enforce a nearly complete symmetry on temporal and spatial indexicals.

The Heraclitean raises an obvious objection. Don't spotlight theories just move the problem around rather than solve them? If the point of such theories is to eliminate fundamental flux from our metaphysics, then any such theory seems doomed to failure. It might have eliminated radical change from the wider world, but only by relocating it to consciousness itself. My consciousness is not distributed throughout my life, nor does it jump around randomly. Instead it flows, perhaps even grows, along with my life-line. Why? What is the source of this basic change in awareness? I suggest that this is the fundamental problem for neo-Eleatics and one that none of them have successfully met.

Eleatics do have an obvious rejoinder; one which basically amounts to modern physics. As we will see over the course of the next four chapters, modern physics gives us profound reasons to take block universe hypotheses seriously. In fact, as we will see in the next chapter any attempt to take modern physics seriously as an account of reality may very well require some version of the block universe. If that's correct, the relatively patient wait-and-see attitude toward an Eleatic theory of temporal consciousness may well be justified.

Study exercise #3: Libet's experiments and backward referral in time

In the early 1980s the neurologist Benjamin Libet reported an extremely odd phenomenon that raises serious problems for naturalistic accounts of temporal phenomenology. Libet reported on experiments in which the time order of neurological events and the conscious awareness of those events seem to become dissociated. Despite problems replicating his results, Libet's experiments remain puzzling.

Much of our knowledge about the structure of the brain results from the fact that brain surgery is often performed under local anesthetic with the patient wholly conscious. The patient is therefore able to report on the felt consequences of stimulating various parts of the brain. Libet identified a particular brain region such that stimulating it directly caused patients to report a particular sensation in their finger. Libet arranged a situation such that he could trigger that sensation either by direct brain stimulation or by stimulating the relevant finger directly.

Libet decided to take advantage of the fact that it takes about 500 milliseconds for the nerve signal to propagate from the finger to the brain to investigate the relationship between the time order of neurological events and the consciousness of the time order of events. Libet stimulated the patient's finger, and then before that stimulus could trigger a change in the brain also triggered the direct brain stimulation. What do you think happened?

Most people's initial reaction is that the patient should first experience the result of the direct brain stimulation and then the finger prick. Instead, Libet reported the opposite. Somehow the "mind" built in a delay based on the signal lag from the peripheral nervous system. Libet and others interpret this result as providing profound evidence for mind-body dualism. They thought that he had identified a case where the underlying neurological processes do not determine the mental contents of consciousness.

There seems to be a general agreement that this is too simple. In particular, Libet seems to have assumed that the neurological events he has identified must be identical with the experience on any materialist account. That's clearly not right; it is entirely possible that the neurological events Libet identified merely trigger other neurological processes that result in the experiences. However, these results and others like them remain more than a bit puzzling both for attempts to resolve the general mind-body problem and our more particular attempt to understand the relationship between the external time order of physical events and our conscious awareness of them.

In order for our temporal awareness to be considered accurate, must there be some sequence of physical events whose time order is identical to that represented in our conscious awareness? What, if any, philosophical consequences should we draw from situations in which the time order of events of which we are consciously aware routinely differs from that of the objective time order of the events themselves?

Further reading

Starting points for further investigation:

Despite ultimately suggesting very different conclusions, the discussion here is deeply indebted to that in Chapter 7, "Time and Consciousness," of Barry Dainton's *Time and Space*. Dainton is also the author of the article "Temporal Consciousness" at *The Stanford*

Encyclopedia of Philosophy (SEP). For a somewhat different perspective, also consult "The Experience and Perception of Time" by Robin Le Poidevin, also at the SEP.

Sean Enda Power has a useful recent survey of the ambiguities in the "specious present" in:

Power, S. E. (2012), "The metaphysics of the 'specious' present," *Erkenntnis*, 77 (1): 121–32.

Callender, C. (2008), "The Common now," *Philosophical Issues*, 18 (1): 339–61.

This is a useful and empirically informed account of presentness from a B-theoretic perspective.

The Phenomenological Tradition

Edmund Husserl's views on time consciousness evolved continuously throughout his long career. The version discussed here is from *The Phenomenology of Internal Time Consciousness* based on lectures given in 1918. An excerpt is included in Westphal and Levenson.

In *Time*, Philip Turetzky usefully explores the relationship between the more analytic approach to time taken in most of this book and the phenomenological approach inspired by Husserl. The phenomenological tradition takes center stage in chapters XI–XIV of this useful historical survey of philosophies of time. Another approach is to engage some of the more approachable work by Husserl's student Martin Heidegger. Heidegger is both one of the most influential philosophers of the twentieth century because of his unquestioned brilliance and one of the most controversial because of his support of Nazism in the 1930s. Some of his most important and reasonably accessible writings are collected in:

Heidegger, M. and Krell, D. F. (2008), *Basic Writings: From Being and Time (1927) to The Task of Thinking (1964)*, New York: Harper Perennial Modern Thought (rev. and expanded edition).

Psychic time travel?

Libet's experiments as well as other intriguing psychological and neurological data on time perception are discussed from a materialist perspective in chapter 6, "Time and Experience" of:

Dennett, D. C. (1991), *Consciousness Explained*, 1st edn, Boston: Little, Brown and Company.

There are various surveys of the psychology of time. Here are three to get you started:

Poppel, E. (1988), *Mindworks: Time and Conscious Experience*, 1st edn, Boston: Harcourt Brace Jovanovich.

Although somewhat dated now, this remains a classic work on these issues.

Friedman, W. J. (1990), *About Time: Inventing the Fourth Dimension*, Cambridge, MA: MIT Press.

Hammond, C. (2013), *Time Warped: Unlocking the Mysteries of Time Perception*, New York, NY: Harper Perennial.

Discussion questions

1 Can you explain the difference between the general role of time in our mental lives and the particular experiences of time?
2 What is the difference between the phenomenal and the intentional content of an experience?
3 Identify three consequences of the presentness of experience. Do any of these require a phenomenal property of "presence"? Why or why not?
4 Explain the difference between a succession of experiences and an experience of succession. Why does the experience of succession create a particular explanatory problem in philosophy and psychology?
5 What is the specious present and how might it explain the experience of succession? What is the difference between one-dimensional and two-dimensional accounts of flow?
6 Describe each of the following and explain why they are evidence that the experience of time is the result of active cognitive processes rather than a variety of passive receptiveness to temporal phenomena: (a) spatial and temporal ventriloquism, (b) phi and color phi, and (c) the cutaneous rabbit illusion.

7   How might a spotlight theory of temporal consciousness explain the experience of flux? Do you believe that any such theory of temporal consciousness could completely eliminate objective flow?

Note

1. I am deeply indebted to the essay "The Common Now" by Craig Callender in preparing this section.

6

Time as a Physical Quantity

Two philosophical problems of time result from its role in physics–one from Isaac Newton and one from Albert Einstein. In *Principia*, Newton claims that time must pass absolutely, independently of any changes in the material universe; is such absolute time even conceivable? As a result of his theory of relativity, Albert Einstein claims that time must be a relative quantity; the time of events and the duration of processes are dependent on the frame of reference from which they are measured. This leads to the replacement of time, as distinctive element of physical reality, with the combined space-time of modern physics.

So far, and with the partial exception of our discussion of Zeno, we've largely focused on philosophical problems of time that can be understood independently of results in natural science. These problems—the reality of time and the relationship between the A-series and the B-series, the nature and reality of change, and the relationship between experience and reality—are all problems primarily connected to our ordinary experience and our common-sense understanding of a world of OMDGs. They are problems within what philosopher Wilfred Sellars called "the manifest image." The manifest image, while not merely the common-sense picture of the world, is what we get when we bring logical order and standards of philosophical rigor to bear upon the ordinary common-sense picture of the world. As Sellars puts it in his classic essay "Philosophy and the Scientific Image of Man," "The manifest image is a refinement or sophistication of what might be called the 'original' image; a refinement to a degree which makes it relevant to the contemporary intellectual scene." Alternatively, it can be understood as "the framework in terms of which, to use an existentialist turn of phrase, man first encountered himself—which is, of course when he came to be a man."

I hope it's clear to what extent all of our problems so far are problems within the manifest image; the world presents itself to us in a particular way, but does so in a way which makes it difficult to see how the world could be that way. It's also clear that all of these problems can be seen as versions of the classical debates about realism vs. idealism; they all ask us whether the world is, or even could be, the way that it seems to be independently of that seeming? Thus, all of these might be understood as problems that we encounter as we attempt to construct a manifest image of the world.

The seventeenth century introduces an alternative image of the world to compete with the manifest image. The scientific image does not evolve organically out of the original common-sense image of the world as does the manifest image. Instead, its fundamental premise is that the manifest image and its sources in the original image are not confused but mistaken. As Sellars puts it, "From [the scientific] point of view the manifest image on which it rests is an 'inadequate' but pragmatically useful likeness of a reality which first finds its adequate (in principle) likeness in the scientific image."

It's worth reminding ourselves just how self-consciously early defenders of the scientific image set themselves against the manifest image and its accompanying perennial philosophy. That René Descartes grounds his defense of the scientific method in radical skepticism may be too well known to need mention. However, the allegedly more empiricist strands of the Scientific Revolution have no more use for the manifest image than Descartes does. As Francis Bacon, one of the founders of the new science, characterizes his method in his *Novum Organum*:

> The doctrine of those who have denied that certainty could be attained at all has some agreement with my way of proceeding at the first setting out; but they end in being infinitely separated and opposed. For the holders of that doctrine assert simply that nothing can be known. I also assert that not much can be known in nature by the way which is now in use. But then they go on to destroy the authority of the senses and understanding; whereas I proceed to devise and supply helps for the same. (Francis Bacon, *Novum Organum* §xxxvii)

It's not my intention to resolve the conflict between the manifest and scientific images of the world, or of humanity. The metaphysical austerity,

Historical Note 16: The Scientific Revolution and the Scientific Image

The conflict between the manifest image and the scientific image identified by Wilfred Sellars has deep roots in the methodological and philosophical debates that swirled around the Scientific Revolution. In science, the widespread acceptance of the heliocentric Copernican system of the world forced philosophers to engage the possibility that the actual facts of the world are radically different from what they appear to be. Despite the appearance that the world stands still and the stars move around it, we now know that the Earth spins through space at several thousand miles per hour. From this, various philosophers suggested that this disconnect between appearance and reality might be a general feature of the world.

Among those promoting some version of this divide, Sir Francis Bacon and the polymath René Descartes are probably the most well known. In his *Novum Organum,* or "new tools," Bacon introduces his doctrine of the Idols, according to which our ordinary language and concepts of the world are fundamentally deceptive about its actual nature. As an alternative, Bacon proposes a new "scientific method" of experimental practice proceeding without presuppositions. However, in his *Discourse on the Method of Rightly Conducting the Reason and Achieving Truth in the Sciences* and in *Meditations on First Philosophy,* René Descartes famously proposes that only the absolute certainty of abstract metaphysics and geometry can serve to counteract the skepticism associated with ordinary sense experience and reflection. Whatever their varying prescriptions to escape it, the major methodological innovators of the Scientific Revolution all see the manifest image as a trap to be escaped.

some might say poverty, of the entirely measurable world described in physics might be the fundamental philosophical problem of modernity. Instead my goal here is merely to signal a transition. The modern scientific role of time challenges all attempts to understand time merely within the manifest image.

In our most basic physical laws, time functions as the fundamental independent parameter; physics is almost entirely an attempt to predict the state of a physical system at other times based on our current knowledge of that state. However, time also functions as a measured quantity in physics;

using clocks we measure the amount of time that passes in a way that seems directly analogous to the measurement of mass with balance scales or distance with measuring sticks. Of course, these two roles—as parameter and as quantity—are not independent; it is precisely our ability to measure the passage of time, and therefore the rates of change of various other quantities, which makes time an attractive parameter in physics.

However, this physical role of time, as the abstract whatever-it-is measured by clocks and represented by "t," generates a variety of distinctively philosophical problems within the scientific image. So, in this chapter and the next, we are going to focus on a cluster of problems particularly related to the role of time in the scientific image and growing out of the role of time in physics. In the next chapter we will consider the nature of the distinction between the earlier and the later directions in time and examine various attempts to provide a physical basis for the distinction—the problem of the arrow of time. This chapter addresses two problems about the nature of time which take on particular urgency given the role of time in physics—the absolute versus relational debate and the apparent relativity of the length of temporal intervals. We will also begin to come to grips with the elephant in the room—Albert Einstein's theory of special relativity.

Clocks and what they measure

The widespread use of mechanical clocks, especially as scientific instruments, transforms the philosophy of time. Classical philosophy of time, as we've seen, focuses on the need to reconcile the appearance of flux with reasons to believe that reality is radically different. However, clocks belong to the world of material flux and as such they force us to ask a slightly different ontological question about time. The question in front of us is not about whether the appearance of becoming gives us reason to believe in actual becoming, but about the material basis of becoming within the natural world.

While this was not an entirely new question in the seventeenth century—Aristotle seems to have considered a version of it—it first becomes clearly distinguished as a separate question in that period. It gains its first clear statement in Isaac Newton's "Scholium to The Definitions" of his *Mathematical Principles of Natural Philosophy* (*The Principia*). Newton distinguishes the "absolute true and mathematical time" that functions as the ideal parameter of his new physics from the "relative, apparent and common time" measured by clocks and calendars. This absolute time "of itself, and from its own nature, flows equably without relation to anything external." Relative time is merely "some sensible and external (whether accurate or unequable) measure of duration by the means of motion." This immediately imposes the question: since the appearance of motion seems to be the only possible basis of my knowledge of absolute duration, such as it is, what basis do I have for believing in this absolute duration rather than merely in a collection of motions? Newton suggests two basic arguments in favor of absolute time—one of them particularly temporal, the other more general. Newton's direct argument for the existence of absolute time begins from considerations about temporal measurement, especially in astronomy. Consider the fact that we know that the length of the solar day, the time it takes the sun to return to its zenith, varies over the course of a year. In the simplest case we recognize this by comparison with the sidereal day, the length of time it takes for a fixed star to return to the same position above the horizon. In classical, or Ptolemaic, astronomy, the Earth sits at the center of the universe while the stars, literally affixed to a rotating sphere, spin around us. In such a universe it is perfectly reasonable to take the rotational period of the stars as an "absolute" time standard, which is used to judge the accuracy of all other potential standards, whether astronomical or terrestrial. It's this absolute character of astronomical motion that makes the proposal by Plato to identify their motions with time, discussed in Chapter 2, seem initially plausible.

Unfortunately, the advent of modern, Copernican astronomy radically undermines this interpretation of time measurement. The motion of the stars is no longer an independent celestial clock; it is merely the manifestation of another terrestrial motion, in this case the motion of the Earth itself. Newton's worry here is not merely about the loss of a particular standard clock, but with the coherence of judging the accuracy of one clock by reference to a second clock unless we have access to a perfect clock. How could it be reasonable to correct a reading of solar time using a factor derived from sidereal time when the sidereal time itself might very well be simply another irregular motion? Or to correct sidereal time using a pendulum clock, or even a modern atomic clock? Newton quite reasonably concludes that the need for and reasonableness of such corrective equations implies that all such clocks provide more or less accurate approximations to some nonmaterial quantity, "absolute duration."

Most readers also see a second, indirect argument for absolute time in Newton's Scholium—an argument from absolute motion. Newton offers

Historical Note 17: The Newton-Leibniz Dispute

The intellectual feud between Sir Isaac Newton (1643–1727) and Gottfried Leibniz (1646–1716), and no other word but "feud" does the vehemence of their disagreement justice, may be the most significant intellectual dispute in history. Beginning with a priority dispute over the discovery of calculus—Newton alleged that Leibniz stole it when visiting England in 1673—the feud came to represent the tension between two quite different conceptions of modern science and modern philosophy.

The importance of this debate is amplified by the scientific and political importance of the participants. Leibniz was a member of the court and advisor to George Ludwig, elector of Hanover and later king of England. Leibniz's general metaphysical system is a version of idealism according to which everything in the universe is a collection of mind-like monads or simple substances. Isaac Newton, coinventor of the calculus and discover of the principle of universal gravitation, is universally recognized as the most important scientific thinker since ancient Greece. Only Charles Darwin comes close to being considered his equal. In addition, Newton had been a member of Parliament, was master of the Royal Mint, and president of the Royal Society.

In *Philosophiae Naturalis Principia Mathematica* (1687), *The Mathematical Principles of Natural Philosophy* or just *Principia*, Newton articulated an austere version of absolutism about both time and space. According to Newton, the true passage of time is entirely independent of both material change in the physical world and human experience of change. Infamously, Newton himself never provides any clear metaphysical account of how such absolute time works. Instead he claims that its reality is required to make sense of his new physics. This led to a series of letters by Leibniz criticizing the metaphysical coherence of Newtonian physics, which was defended by Newton's friend Samuel Clarke.

In his famous debate with the Newtonian Clarke, Leibniz defended a relationalist account of time rather than an entirely idealist one. In his letters, Leibniz seems willing to grant that temporal relations are real relations between physical objects. However, since Leibniz's more general metaphysical position also denies that such physical objects are real substances his idealism and his relationalism might be compatible.

several examples in which it seems to be possible to distinguish real or absolute from merely apparent or relative motion; Newton's bucket is the most famous of these, cf. Figure 6.1 on p. 164. Consider a bucket hanging from a rope by its handle. When the bucket first starts to spin clockwise, I seem to have two equivalent descriptions of the system.

Either the bucket is spinning in a clockwise direction, or the bucket is at rest and the water and the rest of the universe is spinning in a counterclockwise direction. Once the bucket has been going for a while, the water will pick up some of that motion and start to spin with the bucket. Newton's crucial point is that I can easily tell the difference between the real spinning of the water clockwise with the bucket and the merely apparent counterclockwise spinning of the water early in the experiment. How? Because when the water is really spinning, the surface of the water is no longer flat; as anyone who's ever spun water in a bucket knows, it's climbing the walls of the bucket and dropping in the center.

What's the basis of the difference between the two situations? The obvious conclusion that Newton intends us to draw is that in the first case the water is merely moving relative to some other material body, which is itself in absolute motion. In the second case, the water is in motion relative to absolute space and absolute time, with that motion manifesting itself in motion relative to other bodies. While the bucket example itself is more directly related to Newton's conception of absolute space, it's easy to see how an overreliance on material clocks without an absolute standard can have similar consequences. Thus, a slowing pendulum creates the appearance of accelerated motion in what is actually uniform.

Both the practice of time measurement and the theoretical demands of the new physics seem to require Newton's distinction between absolute and relative time, space and motion. Unfortunately, as Newton's great contemporary and rival Gottfried Leibniz pointed out in correspondence with Newton's friend Samuel Clarke, it's not clear that the distinction is even coherent. Most significantly, Leibniz and his relationalist followers claim that the reality of absolute time implies certain metaphysical absurdities. First, absolute time implies the possibility of time without change. Suppose that everything in the universe froze at 3 p.m., May 15, 2013. Now ask: how much time passed before it unfroze? If absolute time is real, then there must be some determinate fact of the matter about the duration of such freezes. However, that seems absurd. Whatever else it is, time is connected to change, motion and becoming. Absolute time seems to imply that "becoming" could happen without any *thing* actually becoming.

Second, relationalists object that absolute time imposes a real difference between situations which should be merely verbally distinct. To see what Leibniz is concerned about, consider the following example. Since Superman and Clark Kent are the same person, for anything that Superman can do, so can Clark Kent. Lois Lane might believe that something had to happen to Clark Kent in order to make him able to fly. However, that's merely an illusion generated by her ignorance of Clark's real identity. The distinction between Clark Kent's ability to fly and Superman's is a *merely verbal distinction*. Now consider a world in which absolute time flowed exactly half as quickly as it does in the real world. Assuming, plausibly, that this means that every process takes precisely twice as long in that world as it does in this one, that world would be indistinguishable, to its occupants, from this one. Why? The "doubling" in the "duration" of the processes seems to be equivalent to what physicists call a gauge transformation; it's equivalent to simply changing the scale of the measurement used to measure the duration.

Similarly, absolute time seems to require not merely absolute duration, but absolute position in time. There must be some particular moment of absolute time at which everything that happens happens. Again, we ask: could everything in the universe happen one year earlier than it actually does? As with the above case, the absence of any possible consequence of such a shift makes it far more plausible to treat this as a merely verbal disagreement about the choice of temporal origin than as a disagreement about the time of occurrence of events.

At the heart of the Leibnizian objections lies a profound commitment to the principle of sufficient reason (PSR). In the seventeenth century, this was traditionally formulated in theological terms: nothing can happen in the world unless God had a reason to make it that way rather than some other way. The principle seems to be separable from the theological background; it's just a way to formulate the intuition that everything in the world fits together to make up a world. Everything in the world happens that way because that's the only way it could happen given the rest of the world. In this context, it allows one to rule out apparent changes as merely illusory because they don't require any changes in the rest of the world to bring them about. In Chapter 9, pp. 246–251, we will see a different use of the principle to rule out certain real changes that are not properly integrated into the rest of the universe.

That's about where the debate stalls. Newtonian absolutists simply accept that, despite its puzzling metaphysical properties, absolute time is a necessary presupposition of a functioning physics. While there are some attempts to provide a coherent metaphysics of absolute space and absolute time in the

Newtonian tradition, for example Newton's own suggestion that absolute space and absolute time are the physical manifestation of divine omnipresence, such metaphysical questions largely become submerged under the necessary physical work. Leibnizian relationalists and idealists, more troubled by the apparent metaphysical absurdities, sought an adequate account of time immune to those problems. The most significant such attempt at a metaphysically coherent version of absolute time is given by Immanuel Kant in his transcendental idealism.

Earlier, we encountered Immanuel Kant's claim that time is the form of "inner sense." This is a central component of his general philosophical system called "transcendental idealism." Kant's transcendental idealism is one of the most influential and most difficult philosophical creations ever. Very roughly speaking, Kant attempts to locate a middle ground between absolute and relationalist theories of time, as well as a middle ground between realists and idealists in general. He agrees with the Newtonians that the world appears to us to be organized in absolute time. We must therefore, in some sense, believe in absolute time. However, he also agrees with the Leibnizians that such a structure cannot be present in reality separately from anything else. Kant concludes that the physical world is organized in absolute time only insofar as it has been so organized by us. According to transcendental idealism, absolute time is neither an aspect of the physical world nor of the divine presence, but it is an aspect of human cognitive architecture. And that's about all I'll have to say regarding transcendental idealism. Kant's philosophy is so significant that one feels compelled to at least mention it, but so difficult that there are really no natural stopping points in between a mere mention and a multi-chapter exposition. Kant reigns almost unchallenged as the most important, but also the most difficult, philosopher of the last several centuries. Kant's range of influence is almost incalculable, and includes work in ethical theory, politics, aesthetics, and metaphysics which remains important today. Instead, we're going to skip on to the twentieth-century versions of the absolute versus relational debates.

Contemporary versions of the absolute versus relational debate

Contemporary versions of the absolute versus relational debates, taken in the broadest senses, divide into two streams. One of them, more purely philosophical, attempts to directly resolve the metaphysical challenges directed against absolutist, or relationalist, positions; many of these are versions of objections going back to the original Leibniz-Clark correspondence.

First a warning. These debates engage some of the most abstract and technical issues in contemporary metaphysics. It is not possible to give more than the flavor of the debates here, and interested readers are urged to pursue these issues in the list of works given in the Further Reading section.

We saw above that one of Leibniz's central objections to absolute time was the possibility of temporal vacua, periods of time in which nothing happens but which last a determinate duration. In 1969, Sydney Shoemaker published his landmark essay "Time without Change" in which he argued directly that we could have good reason to believe that some substantial period of time, for example one year, could have passed between immediately successive events. Shoemaker considers a possible universe that is divided into three regions, A, B, and C. According to Shoemaker, it certainly seems to be possible that from the perspective of regions B and C, region A undergoes a year-long period of complete stasis every third year. Therefore, to an occupant of region A, a year will have passed despite the fact that nothing has happened in region A.

However, plenty of things have happened in the other two regions to lead us to believe that a year has passed even in region A. Now Shoemaker complicates the example. Why couldn't there be similar freezes in region B every four years and in region C every five years? That however leads to a total freeze of all three regions every sixtieth year. Therefore occupants of our freeze-verse should, or at least could reasonably, believe at the beginning of the sixty-first year that an undetectable year has just passed. Whether the immediate plausibility of the example leads to an actual argument for the possibility of time without change quickly takes us into deep waters; to settle the debate we must establish in precisely what sense the freeze-verse is possible. Instead, we now turn to modern debates about the metaphysics of relationalism.

The principal objections to relationalism have always been that there are temporal facts which seem to be independent of the relations of simultaneity and succession between material events, which are the only temporal facts relationalists recognizes. For example, in his objections to Leibniz, Samuel Clarke argued that time is a quantity not a relation. By this he means that we not only know that time passes and in what order events occur, we know how much time has passed. In one sense, Clark's objection has lost much of its force. It would seem that the modern relationalist could simply make use of the modern logic of relations to invoke a complicated algebra of relations such that events are not merely earlier or later then each other but are some particular duration earlier or later than each other.

However, this seems to miss the real force of Clarke's objection, which is that the time not occupied by the events matters. If event X is ten minutes later than event Y, then there must be ten minutes of time between them, whether or not anything else happens during that time. It's the fact that time behaves like a substance of which there can be more or less which seems to be at the heart of the objection.

Consider a modern relative of Clarke's objection; it too seems to show that the temporal features of the universe depend on more than merely the actual occurrences. The objection rests on the fact that relationalists seem to be committed to the idea that moments of time are merely sets of simultaneous events.

Suppose that John arrives at my office to discuss his paper at 4 p.m. It certainly seems possible that he could have arrived at 4:30 p.m. However, in the real world of the example, 4:30 p.m. consists of a particular set of events that does not include John's arrival. Therefore, John could not arrive at 4:30 p.m. because if he did, then the time that is 4:30 p.m. in the actual world no longer exists. Only a different time, otherwise very similar to 4:30 p.m. in the actual world, exists.

Once again, we see time functioning more like a substance, in this case a container, that can be filled up with various different events rather than as a mere relation between actually occurring events. Thus, both the objections —Clarke's quantity objection and the modern modal objection— seem to identify temporal features that do not properly vary with changes in events as relationalism seems to require.

A modern relationalist, such as Graeme Forbes, might resolve this by appealing to possible as well as actual events. That is, the moment marked as 4:30 p.m. involves not merely the actual events that occur then, but all events that could be simultaneous with the events that are actually simultaneous as well. As with the case of time without change, this quickly takes us beyond the scope of this introduction—in this case, into the metaphysics of modality and possible worlds. However, this does show us one important fact; the advantage of metaphysical simplicity does not automatically attach to relationalism as it sometimes seems to. It sometimes seems as though the relationalist is getting by with nothing but ordinary material objects, while the substantivalist must add time and space to his/her ontology. If the relationalist must include a collection of robust possibilia in his/her ontology, the balance seems far more even.

In the end, this balance between philosophical arguments seems appropriate. Einstein's theories of relativity of 1905 and 1915 are the culmination of a development that began with Newton. The structure and nature of space and time cease to be matters of philosophical speculation and become matters for physical theory.

Special relativity and the structure of time

In this section, we examine those consequences of Einstein's theory of special relativity most directly relevant to issues in the philosophy of time. This is not a general introduction even to the consequences of the special theory of relativity (STR); let alone an introduction to the theory itself. We will not even discuss its most famous consequence, $E = mc^2$!

The principal difficulty involved in any brief, nontechnical presentation of STR is that it is both profoundly simple and profoundly far-reaching in its consequences. Simple, in that it is merely the working out of the logical and mathematical consequences of two fairly straightforward physical principles, the principle of relativity and the constancy of the speed of light. Most of those consequences can be derived with no mathematics more sophisticated than secondary school algebra and geometry. The subtlety arises because the resulting consequences have an impact on everything in physics. Ultimately, STR is either a new theory about the nature and structure of physical theory or equivalently a new and radically different theory of the spatiotemporal context of all natural phenomena.

In the remainder of this section, we answer two questions. First, why did Einstein and others believe that STR marks the ultimate victory of a relational over as a substantival theory of space and time? Second, why, independently of the debate over substantivalism, does STR support some form of a block universe metaphysics? To answer these questions we proceed in stages. I begin by explaining the two basic postulates of relativity. Next, we investigate three crucial consequences of those postulates for philosophical theories of time. We will look particularly at:

Relativity of Simultaneity The time order of spatially separated events depends on the frame of reference in which it is measured.

Time Dilation and the Twin Paradox Moving clocks run slow and the elapsed time between events, even those intuitively occurring at the same place, depends on the path taken between them.

Stein's Theorem There can be no physically significant global boundary between the past and the future; presentness cannot be a relation between spatially separated events.

Einstein's two postulates

Einstein, in his article, "On the Electrodynamics of Moving Bodies," demonstrates the mathematical compatibility of the two "only apparently irreconcilable" postulates that "the same laws of electrodynamics and optics will be valid for all frames of reference for which the equations of mechanics hold good" and "that light is always propagated in empty space with a definite velocity c which is independent of the state of motion of the emitting body." The only such reconciliation which Einstein discovers involves a radical alteration in our conception of space and time. To understand why, let us first look at the two postulates independently and examine the reason for their apparent incompatibility, beginning with the principle of relativity.

The principle of relativity

To understand what Einstein means by a "frame of reference for which the equations of mechanics hold good," let us return to Newton's bucket. This allows us to construct frames of reference in which the laws of mechanics do not apply. Remember that we have a bucket suspended above a point on the surface of the Earth and spinning around an axis through that point. Now imagine yourself standing on the rim of the bucket examining a float on the surface of the water and remove all external references, such as the Earth, the stars etc.

As before, there are two apparently equivalent descriptions of the situation, two frames of reference. In one, BUCKET, you are standing still, as you seem to be, on the rim of the bucket, watching the float spin around the central axis counterclockwise. In FLOAT, the bucket spins around the resting float in the clockwise direction. Is there any way to tell the difference between these situations? Yes, because only in FLOAT do all of the forces obey Newton's laws of motion.

In BUCKET, the float violates Newton's first law of motion. As it spins around the central axis it is constantly accelerating, constantly changing its

Technical Note 4: Newton's Laws of Motion

In reasonably traditional form, Newton's laws of motion are:

1. Any body maintains itself at rest or in motion in a straight line at constant speed, unless a force is impressed upon it.
2. The total force acting on a body is proportional to the acceleration of the body; $F = ma$
3. Any force exerted on a body is accompanied by a force exerted by the body equal in magnitude and opposite in direction.

direction of motion relative to an observer standing on the rim of the bucket. However, there seems to be no material force acting on the float; no matter how carefully we look we will never find anything pushing the float around the center. Similarly, you, the observer, are subject to forces that violate Newton's third law of motion. Anyone who has ever experienced motion in a circle knows the feeling of being pushed out away from the center. However, that force has no source; there is no thing pushing on your shoulders against which you are pushing back.

The appearance of such pseudo-forces is a quite general marker that motion is being described from a perspective, a frame of reference, which is itself accelerating. Consider the surface of the Earth. If I suspend a large pendulum from the dome of a building and set it swinging, the plane of its

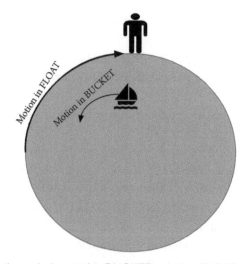

Figure 6.1 Motion relative to the BUCKET and the FLOAT.

motion will appear to "magically" precess over the course of the day. Such a Foucault pendulum provided the first clear terrestrial demonstration of the motion of the Earth. Similarly, water dropping straight down through a drain swirls and wind pushed straight across the surface of the Earth forms cyclonic hurricanes due to those Coriolis pseudo-forces.

Now consider the movements of and apparent forces on the components of the systems as described according to FLOAT, the frame of reference in which the floating boat is at rest. Since the float is at rest by definition in FLOAT, it is not subject to any forces; there are no more pseudo-forces at work on it. What about the observer on the rim of the bucket? She is not being pushed outward by pseudo-forces with no apparent source. She is being pulled in toward the center by the interaction with the bucket. Ultimately, all of the forces measured in FLOAT end up as perfectly mechanically sound interactive forces.

So far this seems, as Newton suggests, to support an absolute theory of space and time as a basis for our description of motion. There seems to be some absolute sense in which the bucket is moving and the float is not. However, Newton's second law complicates things. It says that the forces on an object depend only on its acceleration and its mass. Consider a reference object moving in a straight line at a constant speed relative to the float, and therefore not accelerating. Obviously, the velocities measured relative to this third object will be different from those in FLOAT. However, all such velocities differ by the same constant factor, so the differences between them are unchanged. Therefore, the accelerations are unchanged and so are the forces. Therefore, if I have one such *inertial frame of reference*, then I can easily define an infinity of them. None of which can be distinguished as the rest frame via any mechanical test.

This points back toward a more relational conception of motion. Real motions, in this conception, are not motions relative to absolute space and absolute time. Instead they are motions relative to some special class of objects; a class picked out dynamically, in terms of forces, rather than kinematically, in terms of motion relative to absolute space and time.

To make this more rigorous, physicists define a frame of reference in terms of three components. A frame of reference consists of:

1 A reference object, O, sometimes called an observer, that defines the center point of the frame;
2 A global clock that determines the time of occurrence of every other event in the universe relative to the occurrence of some origin event in the lifetime of the reference object;

3 A system to determine the spatial location of everything else in the
   universe relative to the reference object.

Thus the reference object itself is always located at zero distance from itself,
so we can treat it as the origin of a three-dimensional system of Cartesian
coordinates (X, Y, Z) at every moment when the reference object exists.
Taking this coordinate system together with the global clock, I can assign a
position at every time to each thing in the entire universe. For each thing,
therefore, I can determine its changing position—its motion—as well.

Now suppose that I have another such reference object, O', with its
associated coordinate system, (X', Y', Z') and global clock assigning time, t'.
Also, suppose that O' is moving with a velocity v in the X-direction relative
to O. What are the relationships between the O-system and the O'-systems,
cf. Figure 6.2? Start with time. Once I have a global clock in the O-system,
there's no reason not to treat the O' clock as simply a copy so that the time in
O' equals that in O, $t' = t$. However, any quantities involving position or
velocity will obviously be more complicated. Begin with velocity. Consider a
third object, U, moving away from O in the same direction as O' with
speed u. What is its velocity measured relative to the O'-system? Obviously
it's moving away from O' with a velocity $u' = u - v$.

What about the position of U relative to O'? For simplicity, let's assume
that there was some time, $t = t' = 0$, when O' and U were both located at the
same place as O. At that time then $X_U = X'_U = 0$. At any later time t, U will be
at $X_U = ut$ and

$$X'_U = u't = (u - v)t = X_U - vt$$

in the O'-system.

Any two systems of physical laws which yield the same predictions for all
such frames of reference are said to exhibit Galilean invariance or to satisfy
Galileo's principle of relativity. Since our reliance on such frames of reference
seems to make all specification of spatiotemporal location a matter of the
relation to a reference object and associated system of measurement, it seems
to vindicate the Leibnizian suspicion of absolute space and time. However,

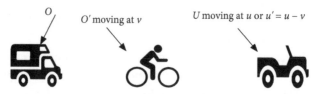

Figure 6.2 Relative motion in multiple frames.

although spatial location and temporal location may be frame-relative notions in classical mechanics, the spatial and the temporal intervals remain absolute. Both the instantaneous spatial separation of objects and events and the time between events are equivalent across all inertial frames, given the transformations above. It is this invariance that makes forces depending only on instantaneous spatial separation such attractive candidates for fundamental forces in Newtonian physics. The paradigm example of such a law is certainly Newton's own law of universal gravitation, according to which the gravitational forces exerted by one body on another at a given time depends only on their masses and their distance at that time.

In special relativity, both spatial separation and temporal duration become frame dependent, much as velocity is in Galilean relativity. Initially that makes Einstein's theory seem like a victory for the relationalist program. That would be a hasty assumption. It is precisely the fact that at least one velocity, that of light, is not a well-behaved classical velocity that leads to this relativization of space and time. Only by "de-relativizing" at least some velocities is Einstein able to relativize spatial separation and duration.

The constancy of the speed of light in a vacuum

It should be obvious from the previous section that no velocity-dependent law can satisfy the principle of Galilean relativity. More precisely, no force which depends on the absolute velocity of a system can satisfy this requirement. Unfortunately, it's quite clear that the laws of electricity and magnetism do involve such absolute-velocity dependence. Perhaps the simplest demonstration of this fact is related to the one with which Einstein opens his original paper. An electric charge in motion is surrounded by a magnetic field proportional to its velocity; an electric charge at rest is not.

However, for our purposes, let's begin by thinking about the role of the constant c in the theory of electromagnetism. On the one hand, c functions as a fundamental constant of the theory determining the strength of the fields, and therefore the forces, in a vacuum. On the other hand, it is also the speed of propagation of light and other electromagnetic waves in a vacuum. Together these two roles immediately imply that electromagnetic theory is not Galilean invariant. In order for the theory to be Galilean invariant, c must be the same in every inertial frame; otherwise the electromagnetic forces will be different in different frames. Then it seems obvious that this can no longer be the speed of propagation of light. How is it possible for two observers, occupying different rest frames, to agree on any velocities at all?

Historical Note 18: James Clerk Maxwell and the Electromagnetic Revolution

In *A Treatise on Electricity and Magnetism* (1873), James Clerk Maxwell (1831–1879) presented a complete set of equations governing the electric and magnetic fields and predicting the existence of electromagnetic waves. As early as 1864 Maxwell had suggested that light might be the oscillations in an underlying medium of transmission, the ether, caused by such forces, analogously to the transmission of sound through air for example. The existence of such waves and their equivalence to light and radio was demonstrated in a series of experiments by Heinrich Hertz (1857–1894) performed from 1886 to 1889.

The hunt was on to detect this underlying electromagnetic ether. As the observed speed of sound varies with the motion of the air, one expects the detected speed of propagation of such electromagnetic radiation to differ as the speed of the detectors and emitters change relative to the ether. It was this "ether drift" effect that Albert Michelson (1852–1931) and Edward Morley (1831–1932) were looking for, and failing to detect, in their famous experiments. Their failures, and those of others, lead first to attempts to define compensatory forces making ether drift undetectable, most famously by the Dutch physicist Hendrik Lorentz (1853–1928). Ultimately, it led Einstein to the theory of relativity.

It seems as though the dual role of c requires that there be a unique electromagnetic rest frame in which the laws of electromagnetism apply. However, by the first decade of the twentieth century, it had become clear that even if such a frame existed it was not empirically detectable. As Einstein put it, these "asymmetries … do not appear to be inherent in the phenomena." Although in some frames, they are due to electrical forces and in others to magnetic forces, in all cases the actual motions and forces are the same. Perhaps even more puzzlingly, all attempts to detect the electromagnetic rest frame directly, via variations in the speed of light, exhibited a null result. The most famous of these "failed" experiments are those of Michelson and Morley.

The actual design of Michelson's interferometer is deceptively simple. It consists of a system of mirrors which first split a single beam of light into two perpendicular beams via the half-silvered mirror in Figure 6.3.

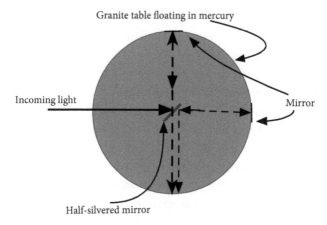

Figure 6.3 Michelson-Morley interferometer.

The other mirrors reflect them back and recombine them into a single beam (see Figure 6.3). The whole apparatus is mounted on a large slab of polished granite to minimize environmental interference. That assembly is made to float in a large pool of liquid mercury so that it can be rotated to test the speed in various directions. If the travel times for the two separated beams are precisely the same, then they simply recombine into a single beam and project a spot onto the screen. However, if the beams are no longer in phase, if the peaks and valleys of the light waves no longer "line up," interference fringes, patterns of light and dark rings, will appear. Obviously, since the Earth itself is moving through the ether, the hypothetical medium of propagation of electromagnetic waves, the speed of the light in the two wings of the interferometer should be different. Since the speeds are different, and assuming that the apparatus is properly calibrated so that the two wings are the same length, the time to complete the two paths will be different. Thus the light beams will come to be out of phase, and the interference fringes will appear. Even if they don't appear immediately, they should appear if one simply waits for the Earth to change its state of motion or even if one rotates the apparatus as a whole. *This will, however, occur only as long as the speed of light depends on the frame of reference in the way that all other velocities do.*

In a series of increasingly sophisticated and precise experiments performed in the last decades of the nineteenth century, Michelson, Morley, and others failed to discover any dependence of the speed of light on the motion of the apparatus. No matter what they did, the interference fringes did not appear. Let's stop for a moment to consider how strange this result is.

Consider the flash of light emitted from a camera held by you. Obviously, the light from the flash moves away from you at the speed of light. At the same moment, Superman runs past you at 10,000 kilometers an hour in the same direction the camera sent the flash of light. He also sees the flash moving away from him at the same invariant speed of light, not at 10,000 kilometers per hour less! This bizarre result demands an explanation.

One option, and the first one explored by physicists, is to refuse to generalize the result in this way. Perhaps, there really is a variation in the speed of light in the two wings of the interferometer. The physicist Hendrik Lorentz suggested that the variation in speed is exactly compensated for by changes in the length of the two wings due to some force that also depends on the motion relative to the ether. Perhaps the wing of the experiment in which the light travels more slowly is also shrunken just enough so that the travel time is the same as the faster moving light. Such suggestions are largely a footnote in the history of physics—part of the groping toward Einstein's more radical solution.

Einstein—young, brilliant, and a relative outsider—was able to take seriously the idea that the speed of light really is a constant and, therefore, was able to embrace a world in which neither the time between events nor the spatial separation between objects are absolute, frame-independent quantities. It was Einstein who was able to accept that if the speed of light is a constant, then the time order of events is not. As Hermann Minkowski— one of Einstein's teachers—was to say three years later, in the universe bequeathed to us by Einstein "space by itself, and time by itself, are doomed to fade away into mere shadows, and only a kind of union of the two will preserve an independent reality." To see how and why Einstein leads us into this new universe, let's begin where Einstein did with the concept of simultaneity and of a global clock.

Consequences of Einstein's postulates

Clock synchronization and the relativity of simultaneity

In our discussion of the principle of relativity, we made an apparently innocuous but crucial assumption as part of our description of a frame of reference. We assumed (see p. 245) that we had access to the actual time of occurrence of every event, no matter where they occurred. Unfortunately, we don't actually have access to such a global clock. At best, we have access to a local clock, one located where we are and carried with us in our frame of reference, plus signals from clocks located elsewhere. In the ideal case we have such signals for every event.

What Einstein realized is that those clock signals are useful to determine the time of an event only if I've already synchronized the distant clocks with my local clock. Determining that fact is much more difficult than it seems at first glance. For how do I know that even if two clocks were synchronized, they remain so after they've been "shipped off" to wherever they're going to be reporting from? Ultimately, all such judgments of synchronization are judgments of distant simultaneity. To know that a distant clock B is synchronized with the local clock A is just to know for any reading t_B of the distant clock what reading t_A is simultaneous with it.

How can I ascertain whether a pair of separated clocks is synchronized? Einstein suggested the following method, using his second postulate. Suppose that a light signal is sent from clock B to clock A, departing at T_B as measured on B and arriving at T_A as measured on A. If A and B are synchronized, then the difference between the two readings should be the same as that for a signal sent from A to B because of the constancy of the speed of light.

However, what about moving clocks? Suppose that I have two systems of clocks, each of them at rest in a particular frame, but in relative motion. Would they generate the same relations of simultaneity and synchronization? Surprisingly to those unfamiliar with special relativity, the answer is a resounding no. And, given the principle of relativity no such system of simultaneity can be preferred to any other. This is the result illustrated by the famous "train and the embankment."

A set of three clocks synchronized as above are mounted on the station platform, A_0 in the middle and A_1 and A_2 at opposite ends. Just as a train passes the station, lightning hits the opposite ends of the platform. An observer located at A_0 sees in the flash of light that the two clocks have the same reading, and since they are properly synchronized concludes that the two lightning flashes occurred simultaneously. Observer A also notices that the flash from the right-hand strike reaches observer B before that from the left. There's nothing particularly puzzling about this so far. Because B is moving from left to right with velocity v, the right-hand flash does not travel as far before reaching her.

Now consider the description of the situation in the B frame of reference. She also agrees with A that the two lightning strikes occurred equidistant from her in her own frame of reference; she also agrees that the two clocks read the same time. However, she is not moving toward the lightning strike; she is standing still. The light from the right-hand strike reaches her first, travels the same distance as that from the left, at the same frame-independent speed of light c. The only possible explanation is that the right-hand lightning strike happened first and that the clocks are not properly synchronized.

When we apply the principle of relativity, we need to fight against our tendency to think of the surface of the Earth as providing a privileged frame of reference. There is *no difference between frame$_A$ and frame$_B$*. A correctly judges that the events are simultaneous and B equally correctly judges that they are not. The time order, the apparently fundamental B-relations of distant events, are no more absolute than the velocities of Galilean relativity.

Time dilation and the twin paradox

The relativity of simultaneity leads almost immediately to the Einsteinian principal of time dilation—that moving clocks run more slowly. To see this, consider adding another clock, B_0, to Figure 6.4. Let's make two assumptions about this clock. It's a properly synchronized clock for frame$_B$, and as it passed A_1 it was synchronized with that clock as well. The only way that it can properly report the lightning flash as earlier than the time on A_2 is if it runs more slowly from A_1 to A_2!

To see just how much more slowly, let's consider a classic simple thought experiment. We can define a clock using a light pulse bouncing back and forth between a pair of mirrors; each round-trip is a tick of the clock. In essence this is what we are doing with the wings of the Michelson

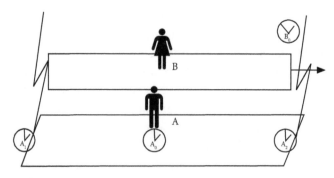

Figure 6.4 Einstein's train and the embankment.

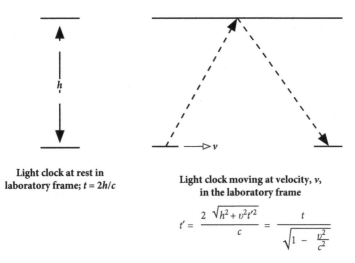

$$t' = \frac{2\sqrt{h^2 + v^2 t'^2}}{c} = \frac{t}{\sqrt{1 - \frac{v^2}{c^2}}}$$

Figure 6.5 Moving clocks run more slowly.

interferometer; timing the trip of one light ray with another. An even simpler version can be seen in Figure 6.5.

Most importantly, this result does not depend, either theoretically or experimentally, on the particular composition of our toy system. Theoretically, for any physical system which exhibits regular time dependence, the requirement of the principle of relativity applied to electromagnetism implies that moving copies of otherwise identical systems evolve more slowly relative to the rest frame. Although tiny, time dilation is both experimentally measurable and practically relevant in high precision applications. For the International Space Station, which has an average velocity relative to the surface of the Earth of about 7,700 m/s (27,000 km/h), v^2/c^2 is about 0.00000000065. However, it is large enough to, for example, interfere with GPS navigation if not corrected for. Similarly, it is responsible for our ability to detect cosmic rays at sea level. Muons have a mean lifetime in their own rest frame of about 2.2 micro seconds; even traveling at 99 percent of the speed of light, they shouldn't travel more than about 600 meters from their creation in the upper atmosphere. The actual flux at sea level is about 10,000 per square meter per minute.

Finally, it is this effect which is responsible for perhaps the most infamous consequence of special relativity, the so-called "twin paradox." Unlike some of our other paradoxes, this one really doesn't deserve its name. It is simply a well-confirmed empirical consequence of one of the best confirmed theories ever formulated. The setup is the following. Consider two identical clocks A and B synchronized and located at the same position in a frame of reference, frame$_B$. Clock A is now moved around a smooth path at a constant speed, relative to frame$_B$, and reunited with clock B. Clock A will have marked off $\frac{1}{2}tv^2/c^2$ less than clock B, where t is the elapsed time according to B.

In addition to the universal empirical confirmation of the time dilation effect in general, the twin effect was directly tested by flying atomic clocks around the world and measuring the difference in elapsed time. When properly corrected for other effects, the time difference is precisely that predicted by relativity.[1]

It is sometimes suggested that the paradoxical nature of the twin paradox rests in the asymmetry between the two systems. If the "traveling" twin is younger than the "home" twin, shouldn't the principle of relativity imply that the "home" twin is also younger than the traveler. Of course, for inertial frames the time dilation effect is completely symmetric; clocks at rest in given inertial frame are slowed relative to all other inertial frames relative to which they have a nonzero velocity. However, the twin situations require that at least one of the clocks is not at rest in an inertial frame throughout the test; inertial frames are by definition moving at a constant speed in a constant direction relative to each other.

The only way we could compare them directly *again* is if at least one of them turns around and returns, undergoing a substantial acceleration in the process. In the classic "twin paradox," the ultimate comparison is only possible because the traveling twin expends substantial energy to *turn around*; during the turn-around boost phase there is no inertial rest frame for the spaceship.[2]

After 100 years of experimental testing, it's not really accurate to think of time dilation and the twin paradox as *consequences* of Einstein's theory. Rather it is a basic empirical fact that, for any ensemble of otherwise identical physical systems all initially at rest relative to each other, any of them that are ever in motion relative to that initial frame will have experienced less elapsed time when the ensemble is reassembled. Elapsed time depends on one's spatial path through the universe.

The Putnam-Rietdijk argument against presentism and an indeterminate future

As if things aren't bad enough for the traditionalists in a world where every object defines its own frame-dependent temporal perspective on the universe, we now know that even restricting the passage of time to each frame-dependent time might not be enough to salvage the passage of time. One might be tempted to claim that the "present" represented by the simultaneity relation in each frame of reference represents the passage of time for the world from the perspective of that frame. Unfortunately, for the traditionalist, a family of arguments, pioneered by Hilary Putnam and C. W. Rietdijk and formalized by Howard Stein, seems to undermine any attempt to attach real significance to any frame-dependent simultaneity relation.

Suppose that one defines a frame of reference as above such that some event is in the future according to the time defined for that frame. One can prove, as I'll explain below, that there are other frames of reference in which that same event is present and others in which it is in the past. This seems to undermine any attempt to articulate a metaphysically significant distinction between the past, the present, and the future. Suppose, for example, that one believes that the crucial distinction is between a determined past and an undetermined future. Since every event is past relative to some present event and some reference frame, then one seems to have, as Rietdijk claimed, a new proof of determinism. Similarly, Putnam claims that he has found a new proof of eternalism. Even if only the present is real, the fact that everything is present in some frame of reference combined with the principle of relativity seems to require that everything is real.

The basic structure of the argument depends only on the relativity of simultaneity and on carefully enforcing the principle of relativity. A somewhat more rigorous version, dependent on the space-time formulation of relativity and attributable to Howard Stein, is introduced below beginning on p. 177. In its original form it begins by considering two events, e_1 and e_2, that are not simultaneous in any inertial reference frame. Such pairs of events are often said to be *time-like separated* from each other, and they can be characterized physically as pairs of events that can be connected by the paths of material objects or causal influence traveling at less than the speed of light. If one is a presentist, then the later of such pairs of events are good candidates for being unreal when the earlier ones become present.

Now suppose that one is a relativized presentist and that there is a natural inertial frame associated with e_1; perhaps e_1 is an event in the lifetime of an object at rest in some inertial frame, call that frame **O**. The natural claim is that when e_1 becomes real, so does everything simultaneous with it in **O**. Even if we invoke the principle of relativity and allow that everything that could be simultaneous with e_1 in *any* inertial frame becomes real, this doesn't seem too disastrous for presentism. e_2 for example would not be real on this account.

What Putnam and Rietdijk realized is that this conclusion fails to apply the principle of relativity with sufficient care and generality. The events simultaneous with e_1 can be arbitrarily far from it as measured in the "space" of O. That implies that there can always be another event e_3 and frame O' such that:

1 e_1 is simultaneous with e_3 in O as represented by the horizontal dashed line in Figure 6.6.
2 e_2 is simultaneous with e_3 in O' as represented by the angled dashed line.
3 O and O' have a relative velocity less than that of light.

Now the relativized presentist faces a serious hurdle. From e_3, e_1 is real relative to O but e_2 is real relative to O' despite the fact that e_2 is later than e_1 in every frame of reference. And that seems a good reason for an "observer" at e_1 to take e_2 as also real. The only alternatives to such radical eternalism seem equally or more implausible. One might jettison the transitivity of reality. Suppose that e_1 is real; e_3 is real relative to e_1; but e_2 is only real relative to e_3 and *not to e_1*; this is despite the fact that, in the relevant sense, e_1 and e_3 occur at the "same time." Whatever one means by real in that sentence seems to have very little to do with the robust notions of existence that motivated the presentists of Chapter 4. Alternatively, one might restrict the relevant notion of the present to the immediately present; when linked with presentism this claim that only each event is real relative to itself seems to involve an absurd solipsism.

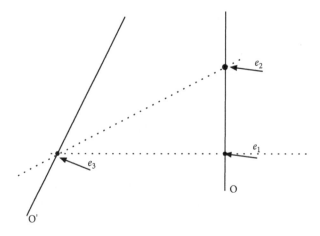

Figure 6.6 Event e_3 simultaneous with two time-like separated events in two reference frames, O' and O.

Finally, one might choose to jettison the principle of relativity and claim that only certain frame(s) of reference give us access to the actual state of existence; this is the move made by various contemporary presentists and growing block theorists concerned to salvage some connection to physics. (See the Further Reading section.) Unfortunately, history is on the side of physics here; when philosophers have allowed metaphysical concerns to trump physics, it has not ever turned out well for them. We might call this the Simplicius problem, after the ill-fated defender of Aristotelian physics in Galileo's *Dialogues on Two New Sciences*. Simplicius might be a fictional character but philosophers marshaling purely philosophical arguments against physical theories never turn out much better than he does.

Special relativity is one of the most rigorously tested and precisely predictive theories in science and stands at the foundations of all twenty-first-century physics; it will take something more than metaphysical quibbling to dislodge it. To see a bit more about why that is the case and to develop a slightly more formal treatment of these results, we need to introduce the concept of Minkowski space-time.

Technical interlude #3: Minkowski space-time and the block universe

In 1908 Hermann Minkowski proposed an alternative formulation of Einstein's theory of relativity. He suggested that rather than formulate it as a claim about the relationships between the formulation of physical theories in various frames of reference, we can reformulate it directly as a claim about the structure of space and time. What he calls his "world hypothesis" is today better known as the claim that the spatiotemporal structure of the universe can be represented by *Einstein-Minkowski space-time*. Minkowski's "world hypothesis" has two components. The first is the suggestion that we consider the universe as the four-dimensional collection of events, rather than as the three-dimensional collection of objects in space existing at various times. Second, he demonstrates that there is a particular geometrical structure on that collection of events compatible with the postulates of special relativity.

Slightly more technically, Minkowski shows how to formulate physics in terms of a *four-dimensional real manifold* of events. To understand what a real manifold is, remember the way that we used the structure of the real numbers to represent the structure of time in the "Technical Interlude" of Chapter 2. Anyone who has had analytic geometry has seen how to do the same for a two-dimensional Euclidean plane or three-dimensional Euclidean space using ordered pairs or triples of real numbers as coordinate systems. These are examples of one-, two- and three-dimensional manifolds, respectively. In general, an *n*-dimensional real differentiable manifold is any set that has such a coordinate representation using ordered *n*-tuples of real numbers, called a chart.[3]

Now notice that any frame of reference, whether inertial or not, can be seen to provide just such a chart on the collection of all events in the universe. Every frame provides three spatial coordinates and a temporal coordinate to every event in the universe. By itself, this recognition isn't worth much; that I can identify the spatiotemporal location of events using four coordinates is as true in Newtonian physics as in Einsteinian physics. The difference really shows up when we examine the difference in the *geometrical structure* associated with different physical theories.

One of the advantages of the fact that the world of events can be represented as a real manifold is that we also know that at least some of its subsets also correspond to substructures of R^4, the set of ordered quadruples of real numbers, in an interesting way. The most important of these are *curves* which are *isomorphic* (cf. Chapter 2) to the real numbers themselves.

When modern physicists and mathematicians ask about the geometry of a given manifold, it is usually the structure of and relationships between such curves that they are interested in. Just as in elementary geometry, there are various questions of interest. For example, we might want to know whether there is a distinction between straight lines and other curves on the manifold. Which curves, if any, are parallel to each other? When they intersect, what is the angle between them? Do they have length, and if so are there shortest curves connecting two points on the manifold?

The most straightforward way to construct this geometry is *via* a distance function on the manifold of interest. Consider ordinary three-dimensional Euclidean space. Analogously to the metrics on time that we considered in Chapter 2, a metric, *g*, on a higher dimensional space obeys four conditions (Figure 6.7).

For any three points in the space, x, y, and z

1 $g(x,y) \geq 0$
2 $g(x,y) = 0$ if and only if $x = y$ (Non-singular)
3 $g(x,y) = g(y,x)$ (Symmetry)
4 $g(x,z) \geq g(x,y) + g(y, z)$ (Triangle inequality)

Figure 6.7 Conditions for a distance relation on a manifold.

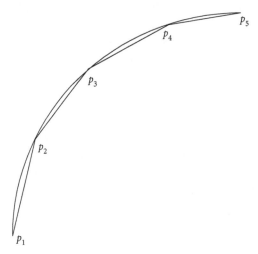

Figure 6.8 The rectification of a curve γ: $\gamma \approx \mathbf{g}(p_1,p_2) + \mathbf{g}(p_2,p_3) + \mathbf{g}(p_3,p_4) + \mathbf{g}(p_4,p_5)$.

Once I have such a function, I can approximate the length of the various curves using *rectification* to approximate the length (cf. Figure 6.8). The more closely together the points of the curve are located, and the more segments I consider, the more accurate the approximation. Certainly, since the curve is continuous, no *finite* approximation is exactly the length of the curve. However, I can use integral calculus to "sum up" all of the infinitesimal distances along the curve. I can then define straight lines in the ordinary way as the shortest curves connecting two points. Obviously the ordinary distance function on Euclidean space given by the Pythagorean theorem obeys these conditions and gives one the ordinary geometry. That is, I just assume that the distance between points along the coordinate axes of a system of Cartesian coordinates correspond to the absolute value of the differences between the coordinates. I can then give the distance between any two points as:

$$\mathbf{E}(p,q) = \sqrt{(q_x - p_x)^2 + (q_y - p_y)^2 + (q_z - p_z)^2} \qquad (6.1)$$

Once I have that, I have all of the ordinary geometric facts about lines, planes, circles, and other shapes in ordinary Euclidean space.

There is one final piece of this puzzle. I can give the geometry of Euclidean space directly via a distance function as I did above. But, I can also give it indirectly by specifying the family of coordinate systems that correctly represent the geometry. In Euclidean space, assume that I have a single Cartesian coordinate system. Any other such system which is merely a shift of the origin, a *translation*, or a rotation around any axis would leave the distances defined in 6.1 the same. We could then define the Euclidean geometry of the space as those structures that are *invariant* under the appropriate transformations of coordinate systems.

This should be starting to sound familiar. It is basically what we did when we identified the equivalence of inertial frames above. In the classical case of Galilean relativity we identified two distinct invariants, a temporal duration and a spatial distance. We can therefore define classical physics on a four-dimensional space-time whose geometry is given by the invariant spatial distance and temporal duration. Classical space-time may be formally four-dimensional but it's fairly easy to see how this four-dimensionality is merely a bookkeeping device for keeping track of two distinct structures: three-dimensional space and one-dimensional time.

Technical Note 5: Classical Space-times

We can define a classical space-time in one of, at least, two ways. In *neo-Newtonian* space-time there is a well-defined spatial distance between *all* events, including those that happen at different times. This means that the spatial "distance" function doesn't quite obey the conditions on distance functions given above; different events happening at different times in the same place have zero spatial distance between them. This is equivalent to postulating a true Newtonian absolute rest, but it gives a natural sense to the principle of inertia according to which free bodies follow straight paths. Alternatively, *Galilean space-time* only has spatial distances defined between events at the same time. This requires an additional structure to specify straight paths for inertial motion. For more details, see John Earman's *World Enough and Space-time* in the Further Reading section.

This is no longer true once we move to special relativity and Minkowski space-time. This is because the corresponding invariant is no longer a distance but a velocity, the velocity of light. As we saw above, Einstein demonstrated that jointly satisfying the principle of relativity and the constancy of light requires that space and time transform differently than they would if Galilean relativity held. Just as the Galilean transformations represent the fundamental physical facts of classical physics—spatial separation, temporal interval, and acceleration—as equivalent in each reference frame, so the Lorentz transformations do the same for Einsteinian physics. In their simplest form, for systems of coordinates $X = \{x, y, z, t\}$ and $X' = \{\xi, \eta, \zeta, \tau\}$ where the origin of the X' system is moving with velocity v relative to the X-system along the x-axis of that system, they are given in Figure 6.9. Now let's consider the speed of a light pulse emitted from the joint origins of two such coordinate systems at time zero in both frames. Einstein's postulate states that the speed of light in each frame must be the same, as represented in Equation 6.7:

$$\xi = \beta(x - vt) \tag{6.2}$$

$$\tau = \beta(t - vx/c^2) \tag{6.3}$$

$$\eta = y \tag{6.4}$$

$$\zeta = z; \tag{6.5}$$

$$\beta = 1/\sqrt{1 - (v/c)^2} \tag{6.6}$$

Figure 6.9 Lorentz transformations for a system moving with the velocity, v.

$$\frac{\sqrt{x^2 + y^2 + z^2}}{t} = \frac{\sqrt{\xi^2 + \eta^2 + \zeta^2}}{\tau} = c \tag{6.7}$$

A little bit of algebra can get us:

$$x^2 + y^2 + z^2 - c^2 t^2 = \xi^2 + \eta^2 + \zeta^2 - c^2 \tau^2 \tag{6.8}$$

A little more work, which we're not going to do here, allows us to demonstrate that the Lorentz transformations plus translation (of the origin) and rotation in the spatial dimensions are, given a few other fairly weak assumptions, the only transformations that leave this quantity invariant.

This quantity should seem familiar; it's just a distance function on four dimensions, except for the minus sign in the time coordinate term. Therefore, it doesn't satisfy the first or second conditions above, and it can take any value, positive or negative. Relative to each point in the manifold, it partitions the remainder of the manifold into three regions—those with zero, positive, or negative separation from that point. The set of all events with zero space-time separation from a given event is the path of a light pulse emitted at the place and time of that event or from which a light signal would have been detected. This set of null or light-like separated events forms the outer surface of the two lobes of a four-dimensional cone marked by the expanding sphere of the wavefront of the light, just as a circle of constantly increasing or decreasing radius marks the surface of a three-dimensional cone (Figure 6.10 shows this for two dimensions, one space-like and one time-like).

The interior of the cone consists of events with a negative separation from the baseline event; for all such *time-like separated events* there is some inertial frame in which they are at the same spatial location but not at the same time. The forward lobe of the cone consists of events that can be reached by causal signals propagated at less than the speed of light. The backward lobe contains those events from which causal signals could have reached the origin event. Finally, the space-like separated regions consist of those events with a positive space-time separation from O and are causally isolated from it; these are called space-like separated events because there is some inertial frame in which they are simultaneous with but spatially separated from each other.

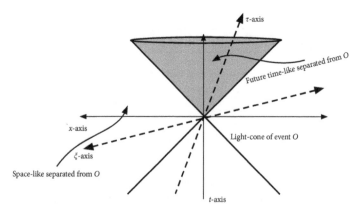

Figure 6.10 The space-time diagram for an event O in two dimensions.

The principle of inertia then states that bodies not subject to any force follow *time-like geodesies. Geodesics* are a generalization of the concept of a straight line, defined as the shortest distance between two points. However, in the context of a Lorentz metric, this becomes somewhat complicated since the existence of negative "lengths" means there's no lower limit to the possible distances between points. Instead, we say that geodesics are *extremal* paths between points; relative to other paths between points they can be either the longest or shortest. In the case of Minkowski space-time, the time-like geodesics are *most negative length* paths connecting time-like separated events.

This gives us, basically, the whole structure of Einstein-Minkowski space-time and should make it reasonably clear in what sense Minkowski's "world hypothesis" just is equivalent to Einstein's original theory. It also demonstrates why that theory has long seemed to be, on its face, incompatible with Heraclitean becoming. Unlike the case of classical space-times, there simply is no intrinsic division into space and time. To see this even more clearly, let's revisit the twin paradox and the Putnam results from the previous section.

We first need two additional bits of terminology. First, we say that the *world-line* of an object in Minkowski space-time is the time-like curve marked out by the object over the course of its existence. The *proper time* along an interval of such a world-line just is the absolute value of the length of that interval in the Minkowski metric given above. Finally, we say that a clock just is a system that reports the proper time along its world-line as the elapsed time.[4] Now the twin effect simply drops out. For any two otherwise identical physical systems such that one of them is at rest in some inertial frame and one is not, the one that is not will age less rapidly than the one that is. This is simply because one of them is following a time-like geodesic with maximum proper time and one is not.

Finally, this provides the opportunity to offer a more rigorous formulation of the results of Putnam and Rietdijk discussed above. In 1991, Howard Stein provided a detailed discussion of those results, echoing an earlier one from 1969. In the 1991 version, Stein considered what the relation constitutive of pastness must be like given the structure of Minkowski space-time. Before we can do this, we need some way to represent the time order, that is, the B-series, in Minkowski space-time. The geometry of Minkowski space-time itself is perfectly symmetric. In order to distinguish the past light-cone on which a given point depends from the future light-cone that depends on that point, we need to determine a *time orientation* for the space-time. We say that a space-time with a time orientation is time-oriented Minkowski space-time.

Once we consider time-oriented Minkowski space-time, it is clear that we should be able to define a relation between place-times, that is, the events of Minkowski's world or points in Minkowski space-time, "place-time *x* is present with or to the past of place-time *y*," or equivalently, "event *x* has become determinate as of event *y*." Call this relation **R**. **R** must satisfy certain conditions. First, it must be reflexive: every event becomes past as of its own occurrence. Second, it must be transitive: a past event remains past. Third, at least some of the events in the past light-cone of a given event must be determinate, that is, those on which it has actual causal dependence.

Finally, if we are to consider **R** as both objective and as purely spatiotemporal, then it must be definable in terms of the structure of Minkowski space-time. What might that mean? Intuitively, we can see that the basic structure of Minkowski space-time is captured by the light-cone structure sketched in Figure 6.10. Whether **R** holds between two events should depend only on their relative "location" in the light-cone structure. For example, given that **R** holds between a given point *p* and at least one point past time-like separated from *p*, it should hold for all of the events in the interior of the past light-cone of *p*.

What about space-like separated events and future time-like separated events? Consider space-like separated events first. Figure 6.11 shows three

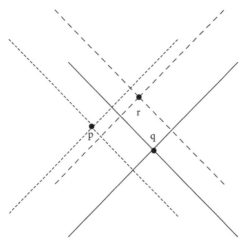

Figure 6.11 Space-time diagram illustrating Stein's theorem.

events, p, q, and r, where p and q are space-like separated from each other. Let's assume that $p\mathbf{R}q$, p is to the past of q. But then, from the requirement of Lorentz invariance, both q and r are to the past of p, since they are both space-like separated from p. But then, from transitivity, r is "to the past of" or if you prefer "determinate as of" p! Stein proves, more generally than we will here, that for a given space-time location p, if $\mathbf{R}$ holds for at least one event past time-like separated from p, then the only relations that satisfy these conditions are: past time-like separation, past causal separation, or the universal relation.

In other words, either everything is determinate in precisely the same sense as the past light-cone is or nothing is determinate outside the past light-cone. But, if nothing outside the past light-cone is determinate or real, then presentists or growing block theorists have a serious problem. That seems to require them to commit to an odd solipsism in which nothing becomes real until signals from it reach us, or at least could reach us. This takes us directly back to the worries articulated by Putnam in the previous section.

Therefore, the standard interpretation of special relativity as the claim that space-time has the structure of Einstein-Minkowski space-time seems to require an eternalist metaphysics for multiple reasons. First, it simply takes the complete set of events distributed throughout space-time as the basic ontology of physics. Second, it confirms, in a way even more difficult to avoid than that derived from the treatment of inertial frames, that any objective "passage of time" must be a property of existing things within the space-time, in particular, a property of their paths, and not of space-time itself. Finally, Stein's theorem confirms that, except for the causal past contained within the light-cone of an event, there cannot be division of the *universe* into past and future with any physical significance. And, since every event has a different past light-cone from every other event, no two observers could agree on the determinate contents of the universe.

Philosophical consequences of special relativity

So what are the philosophical consequences of Einstein's revolution? On the one hand, special relativity transforms the subject of the absolute versus relational debate, while failing to resolve it. This was not always obvious. Einstein and others, especially the philosopher Hans Reichenbach, originally saw special relativity as the culmination of a relationalist program in the physics and philosophy of space and time. Given the apparent frame dependence of all spatial and temporal quantities in special relativity, it seemed plausible that in the absence of a frame of reference, defined in terms of a reference object/observer and mechanisms of measurement, events do not bear spatiotemporal relationships to each other.

This is further supported by Hans Reichenbach's argument that simultaneity, the central concept of special relativity, is not merely relative but arbitrary and conventional. Reichenbach recognized that while the Michelson-Morley experiment demonstrates the frame independence of the round-trip speed of light, no experiment can directly measure the one-way speed of light in any frame.

To see why, consider Einstein's rule for clock synchronization again. Remember that I have two clocks, $clock_A$ and $clock_B$. I send a signal from $clock_A$ which is returned from $clock_B$ with a report of the time of its arrival at $clock_B$ according to $clock_B$. The two clocks are synchronized just in case the time at $clock_B$, t_B, is precisely halfway between the departure and arrival times, t_A and t'_A at $clock_A$.

But how do I know that the two halves of the round-trip each take the same amount of time? It would seem that I cannot; in order to measure the speed from A to B independently of the speed from B to A, I require pre-synchronized clocks at A and at B. We just saw that any such system of synchronized clocks depends on a choice as to the one-way speed of light. Reichenbach and others argued persuasively that in fact there are an infinite number of synchronization conditions all empirically equivalent to Einstein's standard one. To use Reichenbach's terminology, we say that a system of clocks are ε-synchronized just in case $t_B = t_A + \varepsilon(t'_A - t_A) = t_A - \varepsilon\Delta t_A$ where the standard Einstein condition is $\varepsilon = 1/2$. Since there can be no distinctively empirical reason to favor $\varepsilon = 1/2$, it must function as a pure definition or convention, much like a choice of units of measurement.

More recent work has demonstrated that this conclusion was arrived at too hastily. If Einstein's original formulation of special relativity as a theory of reference frames and measurement emphasizes its relational character, Minkowski's space-time formulation, adopted by Einstein in his own later search for a theory of gravity, a.k.a., general relativity, emphasizes the remaining absolute elements of spatiotemporal structure. In Minkowski space-time, the interval, as well as the distinction between inertial and accelerated motion, remains just as absolute as any aspect of classical

Newtonian physics. And the question of whether such remaining absolute structure can be eliminated in favor of a more parsimonious metaphysics remains just as much a philosophical problem in the Einsteinian universe as in the Newtonian.

On the other hand, the absence of a distinctive role for time separately from space in any formulation of special relativity creates serious problems for any metaphysics of becoming. The absence of any unique global division of the universe into past and future seems to make things untenable for any version of presentism or a growing block. The Putnam-Stein results discussed in this chapter seem to force any defender of such a view into a truly bizarre solipsism. In order to resist the block universe ontology, defenders of such a view seem to be required to claim that only the immediately present, both temporally and spatially, are real now. The view that nothing is real until a signal reaches me seems rather self-defeating. Everything was real, but nothing is real. The only alternative to this seems to be to deny that contrary to all experimental appearances there really is such a thing as absolute simultaneity. One might hope that simply being contrary to 100 years of scientific progress would be sufficient to reject such options. However, several philosophers have recently tried to rejuvenate absolute simultaneity.

To wrap up. While contrary to early hopes, special relativity does not immediately resolve the absolute versus relational debate, it does radically change the terms of that debate. In addition, it makes life difficult, to say the least, for any modern Heraclitus.

Further reading

Other basic introductions to some of the philosophical issues in this chapter include:

Grünbaum, A. (1963), *Philosophical Problems of Space and Time*, New York: Alfred A. Knopf.

This magisterial treatment includes a discussion of many related issues, but always from a perspective that takes the physics of time as the primary "data point."

Reichenbach, H. (1958), *The Philosophy of Space and Time*, New York: Dover Publications, Inc.

Earman, J. (1989), *World Enough and Space-Time: Absolute Versus Relational Theories of Space and Time*, Cambridge, MA, London, England: A Bradford Book, The MIT Press.

Sklar, L. (1974), *Space, Time and Space-time*, Berkeley, CA: University of California Press.

These useful introductions to the physics of space-time do presuppose a substantial math and physics background.

Some of the primary sources for these debates:

Leibniz, G. W., Clarke, S., and Alexander, H. G. (1998), *The Leibniz-Clarke Correspondence*, New York: Manchester University Press.

Lorentz, H. A., Einstein, A., Minkowski, H., and Weyl, H. (1923), *The Principle of Relativity: A Collection of Original Memoirs on the Special and General Theory of Relativity*, New York: Dover Publications, Inc.

Contains translations of Einstein's and Minkowski's original papers as well as others.

Putnam, H. (1967), "Time and physical geometry," *The Journal of Philosophy*, LXIV (8): 240–7.

Sellars, W. (1963), *Science, Perception, and Reality*, New York: Humanities Press.

Contains "Philosophy and the Scientific Image of Man"

Shoemaker, S. (1969), "Time without change," *The Journal of Philosophy*, 66 (12): 363–81.

Stein, H. (1968), "On Einstein-Minkowski spacetime," *The Journal of Philosophy*, LXV (1): 5–23.

Stein, H. (1991), "On relativity theory and openness of the future," *Philosophy of Science*, 58: 147–67.

Some basic introductions to the theory of relativity:

Bohm, D. (1996), *The Special Theory of Relativity*, London, New York: Routledge.

Einstein, A. (1961), *Relativity: The Special and the General Theory; A Popular Exposition*, New York: Crown Publishers.

Geroch, R. (1978), *General Relativity from A to B*, Chicago: The University of Chicago Press.

The first part of this introductory text offers a series of thought experiments designed to develop the basic physical intuitions that make space-time seem plausible.

McGlinn, W. D. (2003), *Introduction to Relativity*, Baltimore: Johns Hopkins University Press.

Mook, D. E. and Vargish, T. (1987), *Inside Relativity*, Princeton: Princeton University Press.

These two standard modern accounts of the philosophical foundations of relativity theory require a substantial physics background:

Friedman, M. (1983), *Foundations of Space-Time Theories: Relativistic Physics and the Philosophy of Science*, Princeton: Princeton University Press.

Torretti, R. (1996), *Relativity and Geometry*, New York: Dover Publications, Inc., (unabridged, corrected edition).

There are some attempts to avoid the consequences of the relativity of simultaneity by claiming that absolute simultaneity is real, but undetectable. Among such neo-Lorentzians, *see:*

Chapter 11 of Michael Tooley's Time, Tense and Causation.

A collection of papers is available in:

Craig, W. L. and Smith, Q. (2008), *Einstein, Relativity and Absolute Simultaneity*, London: Routledge.

What this author sees as a devastating criticism of the whole neo-Lorentzian project can be found in:

Balashov, Y. and Janssen, M. (2003), "Presentism and relativity," *British Journal for the Philosophy of Science*, 54 (2): 327–46.

Discussion questions

1   Can you name three differences between the scientific image of time and the manifest image of time?

2   Why does the Copernican revolution, according to which most of the heavenly motions are the result of the motion of the Earth, create the need for absolute time in Newtonian physics? How does Newton's third law of motion allow us to distinguish absolute from merely relative motion?

3 Can you explain Leibniz's stretching and shifting argument against absolute time? Can you explain the role of the principle of sufficient reason in Leibniz's argument?

4 Can you explain why the possible existence of a Shoemaker freeze-verse seems to imply the existence of absolute time in the real world? On the other hand, can you explain why only modal forms of relationalism seem plausible?

5 Can you identify two physical quantities that are Galilean invariant but not Lorentz invariant? Two that are Lorentz invariant but not Galileo invariant? For each of them, explain in ordinary language why they are invariant in the appropriate theories.

6 Can you explain two experimental tests or practical consequences of relativistic time dilation? Explain three possible philosophical responses to this fact.

7 Can you explain why the failure of absolute simultaneity in special relativity seems to imply the block universe?

8 *Food for Thought*: Do the consequences of special relativity discussed in this chapter imply that the philosophical problems of time in the manifest image from previous chapters are misguided in some way? Why or why not?

Notes

1. Most importantly, it's the time difference predicted by *general relativity*. The slightly reduced gravitational field at altitude of the traveling clocks cancels a small amount of the special relativistic time lag.

2. Of course, the "home" twin, at rest on the surface of the Earth, is not in a strictly inertial rest frame either. Fortunately, this doesn't matter for our purposes. The difference in elapsed proper time only depends on the relative difference between the frames.

3. Note for mathematically sophisticated readers: Yes, I recognize that being a differentiable manifold first requires being a topological manifold and that some manifolds such as S_2, the surface of a sphere, require multiple charts obeying the proper overlap conditions. But, none of these are particularly relevant here.

4. If necessary, we can simply define a family of "good clocks" such that the difference in their reported elapsed time when they are compared is proportional to difference in the proper time along their world-lines. Obviously, in an experimental setting we move in the opposite direction. We have a physical system that we believe is reliably periodic, and we compare copies that have followed world-lines of different lengths.

7

The Direction of Time

What distinguishes earlier events or times from later ones? This is really three distinct questions. How do we *tell* the difference between earlier and later events; what differences between events serve as markers for the arrow of time? Second, what are the relations between the various markers, especially the three most distinctive groups of them–the psychological, the causal, and physical arrows? Finally, can we identify some fundamental physical law or other fact as the master arrow? The second law of thermodynamics—that entropy never decreases—is the most commonly suggested such law; unfortunately, the status of the second law is somewhat enigmatic.

We have previously characterized the difference between time and space in terms of the intrinsic directionality of time and the lack of any such directionality in space. Remember our example of a train journey in Chapter 3; we considered the difference between the spatial ordering and the temporal ordering of two events, the departure of a train from Chicago and its arrival in New York City. The arrival is both later than and to the east of the departure.

As we saw, there is a crucial difference between those two facts. The spatial ordering of the trip seems fundamentally irrelevant in the following sense. Every path from Chicago to New York is also a path from New York to Chicago. The distinction between them is, in our familiar language, merely verbal. The same is not true of the temporal order of the trip. No trip originating in Chicago can be the same trip, through time, as one originating in New York. We simply never see the time reverse of a process in the way that we see their spatial reversals.

This fundamental temporal asymmetry seems to demand an explanation. Why is there no spatial equivalent of the B-series? Once we ask the question this way, we can see that there are really two questions hidden within it. There are many apparently distinct differences between events that depend on their temporal relations. For example, there are a variety of psychological asymmetries of which our ability to remember earlier but not later events seems to be the most obvious. Intuitively, there are also causal asymmetries; we ordinarily accept that only earlier and never later events can be part of the cause of some event. Finally, there are thermodynamic asymmetries; objects warmer than their environment cool spontaneously, losing energy, but not the reverse. What is the relationship between these various "arrows of time"?

Let's call this the problem of too many arrows of time. This is a problem that afflicts all theories of the nature of time in one form or another. Even radical Heracliteans who take pure becoming as the essential feature of time need to explain how the mechanism of pure becoming generates all of these apparently distinct asymmetrical structures within time. Even if we accept that the direction of becoming determines the relations of earlier and later, we need to explain how that generates something like the thermodynamic asymmetry. That my coffee cup always becomes doesn't seem to give me any a priori reason to expect that it can only spontaneously cool, never warm.

There is a second problem that particularly afflicts block universe or B-theories of time. We began by distinguishing time from space based on the intrinsic directionality of time. Unfortunately, there does not seem to be any role for such intrinsic directionality in the laws of physics. If physical time were intrinsically directional, we would expect the laws of physics to reflect that fact. The most obvious way they could do so is by prohibiting the time reverse of certain permitted processes. For example, when I drop a rock from my hand, the time reverse of that would be a rock spontaneously flying up from the floor into my hand. Such events do not happen, but we will see that certain fundamental physical principles seem to require that they *could* happen.

If that's correct, then it seems as though the direction of time is an extrinsic or accidental fact, and not an intrinsic one. The distinction between earlier and later events becomes like the difference between up and down near the surface of the Earth. Down is merely the direction toward the center of the Earth wherever it happens to be. In this account of the direction of time, the earlier/later distinction also depends on such an accidental arrangement of the stuff of the universe. There are two standard suggestions.

The later-direction might be defined as that direction in time in which entropy increases in accordance with the second law of thermodynamics (see p. 198), or the earlier-direction might be defined as that in which we find the big bang (see p. 212).

The suggestion that the direction of time might be extrinsic and accidental seems deeply implausible to many people. Hopefully the remainder of this chapter will persuade you that it's at least a suggestion worth taking seriously.

Three classical markers of the arrow of time

Let us begin by taking a closer look at those phenomena characteristic of the direction of time. I'm not claiming, at least yet, that any of these phenomena are responsible for our belief in the direction of time. Rather this collection of asymmetrical phenomena should be considered "markers" for the underlying reality of the earlier/later distinction. Even a radical Eleatic elimination of the direction of time must account for these phenomena. It is not merely an illusion that I remember yesterday, but not tomorrow.

These are the fundamental data that any theory of the direction of time must account for. Even idealists who claim that the world merely seems to have this structure must account for why it seems to have the structure. These markers belong to three basic categories: there are facts about our psychological makeup, about the apparent causal structure of the world, and about the asymmetrical appearances of certain physical processes, especially those involving heat.

The psychological arrow of time

The psychological markers for the arrow of time are basically just the distinctively temporal elements of experience revisited with a focus on their directedness. The most important of these are memory and our experience of ourselves as agents. Since we've discussed each of these in some detail elsewhere, we revisit them only to emphasize their directed nature.

We discussed the complicated interplay between temporal experience, memory, and flow in Chapter 5. Here we should notice the following important fact: at any time, I can remember only events earlier than that time. More precisely, I can only remember events that have previously been the subject of experience. That experience must precede memory seems to be nearly part of the definition of memory. For now though let's assume that it is not. That alternative seems to make the problem too easy. If we insist that memory is later than the relevant experience *by definition,* then we seem forced to make that the master arrow.

Instead, let us presume that there is a purely phenomenological difference between a memory and an experience of the same object. We can tell by introspection, by the mere inner feel, when we are having an experience and when we are remembering. This allows us to consider the mental life of a time-reversed person. There seem to be two possible such descriptions. In the first model, they experience themselves as having entered life as an old man or woman at some point in the future continuously accumulating memories of the future as they "age" into a young child, like Merlyn in T. H. White's *The Once and Future King.* Alternatively, they may come into existence in the future with all of the memories of an elderly person who has lived through the events objectively earlier within their life-line. Such a person would have the odd experience of remembering their life before they experience it, with their memory shrinking as they approach their "birth."

Given the problem that such people pose for our self-conception, it's probably a good thing that they don't seem to exist. If I regularly met people who remember what I am going to do tomorrow, it would be difficult to think of myself as an agent. Similarly, people who remember the outcomes of their actions, and the actions themselves, subjectively before the actions, would have a hard time thinking of themselves as agents. As we saw in Chapter 4, our conception of human agency seems to depend on some notion of the openness of the future. Here we should also notice that agency is also directed oppositely to memory. Just as I can remember only those events earlier than the given time, I routinely plan and act only relative to events later than those times.

This linkage between the various psychological arrows might lead us to see them as the manifestation of some master arrow, perhaps that of causation. On a causal account, I remember earlier experiences because memories are the effects of earlier experiences, and I only plan for and affect the future because my actions only have later rather than earlier effects. The strength of such an explanation depends on our reasons for accepting an independent arrow of causation, a question to which we now turn.

The causal arrow of time

Before we can discuss the markers for the causal arrow of time, the facts that point toward a fundamental causal asymmetry, we need to consider what we mean by cause and effect. Nonphilosophers don't seem to have too much trouble with causation. In particular, the ordinary application of causal ascriptions tends to be fairly neutral on the distinction between *substance causation* and *event causation* important to philosophers. Substance causation involves one substance or thing bringing another one into existence. For example, my father and mother are (parts of) the cause of my existence. Event causation involves events bringing it about that other events occur. For example, the impact of a cue ball with an object ball on a billiard table causes the object ball to move and hit the cushion. Although contemporary philosophers tend to treat event causation as more fundamental, both common sense and the philosophical tradition are ambiguous on this point. For example, Aristotle and those influenced by his analysis of causation generally take substance causation as paradigmatic. Fortunately, nothing in this chapter depends on settling this debate.

According to either account of causation, the problems that concern us arise when we attempt to explain "bringing into existence" or "bringing about" and the difference between that and merely "being around" when something happens. Philosophical theories of causation can generally be divided into two broad families: *regularity theories* and *power theories*. Regularity theories are based on the claim, generally attributed to the great Scottish Enlightenment philosopher David Hume, that, at best, all we ever experience are patterns of events. I cannot actually see one thing bringing about a second thing; I only see that certain similar kinds of things are always or generally preceded by other things similar to each other. In this Humean account of causation, I can never see a father directly bringing about the existence of their child. Instead, I know from experience that human beings are preceded by certain kinds of biological processes, and in a particular case a particular father appears in the appropriate role within that general process.

Causal power theorists claim that there is more to being a cause of something than merely appearing in its history in the appropriate way. Instead, that thing appears in that particular history in that particular way because it has the power to bring about that particular effect. According to causal power theorists, the regularities in nature are merely the manifestation of the underlying stability of the kinds of things that occur in the world and their powers to bring about other things.

The nature of cause and effect is a major metaphysical puzzle and, as with so many we've already met, is introduced really only to sketch its connection to the problems of time. Here, it is important to make sure that an implicit commitment to a particular kind of regularity theory does not blind us to the problem. Regularity theories face an obvious objection. Causes and effects seem to always come in matched pairs. Every image projected on a movie screen is associated with the light hitting the film in the projector. However, the opposite is also the case. Every operation of the projector is associated with an image. Why say that the image on the film causes the one on the screen and not *vice versa*?

There seems to be a general temptation among regularity theorists to respond by making temporal precedence part of the definition of a causal relation. Thus, in Book I, Part 3, §xiv of *A Treatise Of Human Nature*, David Hume defines a cause as "an object precedent and contiguous to another, and where all the objects resembling the former are placed in like relations of precedency and contiguity to those objects that resemble the latter."

Modern versions of Hume's definition are certainly more sophisticated than his, but they face the same problem of accounting for the intuitive asymmetries between cause and effect within an essentially symmetrical notion of regularity. They often solve the problem in the same way—determining by fiat that the direction of causation and the direction of time must run together. In Chapter 9, we will examine the possibility of backward causation, causal relations that run opposite to the ordinary direction of time, but it seems wrong to rule out the possibility of time travel simply by definition. If backward causation is impossible, then it should be the result of what causation there is, not of how it is defined.

Even if backward causation is possible, it certainly seems to be rare. Thus, we can now consider what evidence there is for a general causal asymmetry other than the mere absence of time travelers. Three of these markers seem to be particularly crucial. First, almost all causal forks seem to be open in the same direction. Second, there seem to be many true future-directed counterfactual conditionals and very few past-directed ones. Finally, there is the so-called record or trace asymmetry; there are many current records of earlier events, which are effects of those events, but very few if any current records of later events. Let's consider these in order.

There are many events in the world that are correlated with each other but that do not seem to have any direct causal connection between them. For example, getting a good grade in calculus shouldn't have any effect one way or the other on your grade in philosophy. However, it seems clear that getting a good grade in one class probably means that you are more likely to have got good grades in other classes as well. That is, one's grades tend to be correlated without being the causes of each other.

In such cases we tend to look for a common cause: something, like spending a lot of time studying, that is the cause of each of the good grades independently. When we find such an event we say that it *screens off* the two otherwise correlated events from each other. The likelihood of getting a good grade in philosophy given that one studies hard and that one got a good grade in calculus is, on this hypothesis, the same as the odds of getting a good grade in philosophy given that one studies hard. Such situations are often called causal forks because we can imagine arrows pointing from the common cause to each of the effects.

It turns out that in our universe such common causes, when they can be identified, tend to always be in the same temporal direction. We often find common causes that are earlier than the pairs of correlated events, but we rarely find single events later than the correlated events which screen them off from each other. It is not impossible that there can be later common causes—remember we're not yet ruling out backward causation—but it certainly seems to be rare. This is a distinctive bit of evidence that there is a temporally directed arrow of causation. In fact, the philosopher Hans Reichenbach argued that the predominant direction in which causal forks are open just is the later direction in time. We'll consider that suggestion in the next section.

Next, consider the fact that we tend to endorse many more future-directed counterfactuals than past ones. A counterfactual or subjunctive conditional is one where the antecedent, the "if" clause, is not true but could be. Thus, for example, if I were to strike the match, then it would light. Under normal circumstances this seems to be true, but only later than the present. We don't generally accept that if the match were burning now, then I would have struck it thirty seconds ago. What could be true now doesn't make it possible for the past to be different from what it actually is. We can easily multiply the examples in which we believe that if the present were different, the future but not the past would also be. We might ultimately be wrong about this at a metaphysical level, but our effectiveness at ordinary counterfactual reasoning is another marker in favor of a temporally directed order of causation.

Third, consider the record asymmetry. We routinely find consistent records of earlier events, but rarely if ever of future events. In fact, anything that could qualify as a record of the future is so rare that it's tempting to build the temporal asymmetry right into our definition of a record. However, that seems wrong. The record is a causal effect of an event that carries information about that event, and there does not seem to be any intrinsic reason why I could not have records of later events. For example, there was an American television program *Early Edition* where the lead character received the next day's newspaper at the beginning of each episode. There's lots of reasons to think that our world does not work like that. I don't see any obvious reason to think that it couldn't.

As a final note, it is plausible that the fork asymmetry is actually the fundamental one here. Consider that we might accept future-directed counterfactuals precisely because we expect present events only to screen off later ones, not earlier ones. Similarly, records of past events are considered such because they are the effects of a common cause. The consistent correlations between what we take to be records of the Roman Empire are explained by the existence of a common cause, the Roman Empire. It thus seems plausible that the fork asymmetry is the fundamental marker of the causal arrow of time.

The physical arrows of time

Our final set of markers for the arrow of time can be found in the many physical processes that seem to occur with a preferred direction in time. The time reverse of a physical process can be thought of as the temporal analog of the spatial mirror image of an object. Since a mirror image leaves all of the internal relations of an object intact, we fully expect that such a spatially inverted object is also a possible physical object. Thus the image of a left hand is still a hand, merely a right hand.

What would be the temporal analog of this? Consider our train trip from the introduction to this chapter. Now imagine that just as my train arrives in New York City, there's another train leaving New York City moving in exactly the same speed but in the opposite direction. It then mirrors the trip that I've just finished always moving exactly the same way that I did, just in the opposite direction. This comes very close to giving us the temporal mirror image of the original trip; it's much like watching a video of the first trip run in reverse.

Not quite, because it doesn't really account for all of the interactions between the train and the environment. We need to reverse all of those interactions as well; when the train loses energy to the tracks via friction, the mirror train absorbs energy. The more I control for these environmental interactions, more plausible it becomes that the time reverse of a given process can be found in the world. Many of the toy problems that we consider in basic physics have this characteristic. If the billiard ball can roll from right to left and I can completely ignore the interaction between the ball and the environment, then it can reverse itself and go back from left to right.

Once we leave the realm of idealized toy problems, things get much messier. In the real world there are many processes whose temporal mirror image seems to never occur. Probably the most obvious of these are those involving heat. The hot cup of coffee on my desk will always, at least within our experience, lose heat to the environment until it is the same temperature as the air in my office. Even though there is some heat in that air, that heat never gets spontaneously absorbed to warm my stale cup of coffee. This *seems* to be a general truth.

The universe seems to abhor concentrations of energy. Any time we find a structure that sticks out from the background, we seem to be able to infer that it took work to get it into that situation. That's true, whether that work was the energy required to heat my coffee or to raise the materials for a building against the pull of gravity. Left to their own devices, such structures always decay back into their environment—coffee cools and buildings collapse. The backward film of a train is just a train moving backward, but the backward film of a building spontaneously assembling from its rubble is just silly.

There's one final related asymmetry that seems to be related to these. Consider a moving electric charge that emits radiation as it moves; for example, consider the current in the antenna of a radio transmitter sending out a radio signal. Just as I never see the cup of coffee spontaneously absorb heat from its environment, I never see the antenna spontaneously absorbing radiation from its environment. The antenna can, of course, interact with radiation previously emitted from another source. What I don't see is the time reverse of the antenna's own emissions—an apparently source-less wavefront converging on the antenna from every direction.

What these processes have in common is that they all involve an increase in *entropy*. The concept of entropy was formulated in the nineteenth century as a measure of the efficiency or inefficiency of steam engines. The first law of thermodynamics tells us that the total amount of work that can be done by such an engine is equivalent to the total amount of heat that it contains. However, our ability to extract that heat depends on the existence of temperature differences within the system. No matter how hot I make the steam in the boiler of the steam engine, if the atmosphere around the engine is just as hot, the piston of the engine isn't going to move. The entropy of the engine is simply a measure of how concentrated and usable the heat within the system is; the lower the entropy, the more efficient the engine.

The second law of thermodynamics says that after doing work the entropy of the system is never less than that of the initial state. In real engines, the entropy always increases; as the steam in the boiler expands to move the piston, it also cools and moves closer to equilibrium with the surrounding environment. Because the entropy has increased, we can't just reheat the steam in the boiler by pushing the piston back down.

All of the thermodynamic examples above involve precisely this kind of evolution from a highly structured state to an unstructured state. The hot coffee in my cup is a concentration of heat energy within the liquid. Given the conservation of energy, all of that energy still exists within the larger environment after the coffee has cooled. However, that energy is not available to do work anymore; it's too spread out. Similarly, the radiation case involves the concentrated energy pumped into the antenna being dissolved into the distributed bath of the radiation.

Thus, this fundamental physical asymmetry can be understood as the tendency of the universe to dissolve structure into unstructured systems. This is expressed in the second law of thermodynamics as the tendency of entropy to increase but never to decrease.

Problem #1: Too many arrows of time

This collection of arrows poses two fundamental problems. First, we need to understand the logical and metaphysical relationships among the various arrows. Ideally, this should allow us to identify a single master arrow responsible for the rest of them. As we'll see in this section, that's easier said than done. Second, since we would expect any such master arrow to be a fundamental fact about our universe, we would expect it to manifest itself in the fundamental laws of nature. In the next section, we will see that despite the role of the second law of thermodynamics, the laws of physics accepted today do not seem to allow for any such fundamental asymmetry.

In attempting to unite the arrows of time, we have two choices. Either there is a further uniquely temporal arrow of time which must be responsible in some sense for the directionality discussed above, or it must be possible to show that all of the various arrows above are really one of them appearing under different guises.

Let us begin by considering the possibility of a separate intrinsic direction for time. Heraclitean A-theorists have an obvious built-in advantage here. Times later than a given time are obviously just those that have yet to become, whatever that might mean for a given metaphysical theory. Unfortunately, they come with all the implausible metaphysical baggage of the various A-theories. The most obvious of those problems being the incompatibility of the A-theory with other things that we know about the world, especially it's incompatibility with Einstein's theory of relativity (see the discussion of Stein's theorem in Chapter 6)

Clearly the problem of the direction of time is a more serious problem for B-theorists than for defenders of radical becoming. Although A-theorists are left with the problem of explaining why the thermodynamic arrow lines up with the direction of becoming, B-theorists do not seem to have an in-built mechanism for selecting one of the two directions in time as privileged. Some B-theorists treat the arrows discussed above as mere markers for some autonomous, intrinsic directionality of time itself. For example, Nathan Oaklander suggests that there is a primitive relation of "later than" between moments of time. The proposal for a "time field," by for example Robert Weingard or Tim Maudlin, seems to be a slightly more sophisticated version of the same proposal. Such a "time field" would be a new physical field existing at each point/event in space-time that indicates which of the two lobes of the light-cone at that event is the future or outgoing light-cone.

In principle, such an intrinsic directionality of time has the advantage of explaining all of the particular asymmetrical features we've already noted. Intuitively, there is a real appeal to postulating a single hidden structure as responsible for all of the apparently coincidental similarities we remarked on in the previous section. Unfortunately, it's not clear how such a metaphysically or physically primitive time order could explain those coincidences. Remember these are supposed to be pure primitive temporal relations; how could they be responsible for the fact that the open ends of causal forks are later than the closed ends or that high entropy states are generally later than low entropy states? It's hard not to see such primitive temporal structures as a third wheel unless they have the causal power to make things happen in a particular way. In that case, though, they're just another version of the causal arrow. So let's take a look at whether any of the arrows above could function as the master arrow.

In the philosophical literature on the direction of time, one often finds "dependency charts" that attempt to track the collection of relationships between these various arrows. Perhaps the best known of these is Paul Horwich's attempt to trace all of these back to the fork asymmetry which, in turn, results from the state of the early universe. Unfortunately, there is no general agreement on such a dependency chart. Rather than construct our own chart, we are simply going to look at the issues raised by any attempt to construct such relationships. Let's consider each of the arrows from the previous section in order, and let's see what problems are raised by taking them as fundamental.

Could directionality of experience and memory explain the direction of causation and the directionality of thermodynamic processes? That seems implausible on two counts. Suppose that I propose a purely psychological analysis of causation. Perhaps we should follow David Hume who suggests that our belief in causation is simply the result of habitually forming the idea of the object we call the effect when we have an experience of the cause. Even if, unlike Hume, we could formulate an account that wasn't subject to obvious failures, we face a serious problem with circularity. Isn't the idea of the effect caused by the idea of the cause? And don't we form the habit because of prior experiences of conjunction?

This problem doesn't even address any of the other costs associated with such an account. Once we endorse such a skeptical account of causation, we seem to be committed to a full-blown skeptical idealism or Humean skepticism. This isn't the Eleatic idealism we've already met according to which the world is radically different from our ideas about it. This skepticism requires that we accept that reality is always and essentially beyond our knowledge. That's a high philosophical price to pay.

This price seems particularly heavy since such Humean proposals don't seem to address the thermodynamic arrow at all. Just because my mental life has a certain asymmetrical structure and I organize my belief in the causal connections between things in the world to accord with that, I do not seem to have any obvious reason for believing that coffee cups always cool and never spontaneously warm.

What about the causal arrow? At first glance, that seems more promising. There are obvious explanations for the psychological arrow. Experiences precede memories because they are causes of them. I act for the future because my acts only have consequences later than their occurrence. Similarly, it seems plausible to treat low entropy states as the outputs of causal interactions which then decay into high entropy states. This seems to

Historical Note 19: Hans Reichenbach and the Logical Positivist Tradition

Hans Reichenbach (1891–1953) was a representative of the logical empiricism that became extremely influential in the United States after many of its German and Austrian adherents relocated there to avoid the Nazis. Reichenbach was trained in physics, mathematics, and philosophy in his native Germany where he was later a professor at the University of Berlin, thanks to the influence of Albert Einstein. After the Nazi rise to power, both Reichenbach's socialism and his Jewish ancestry made it wise for him to relocate, first to Istanbul, Turkey, and later to the University of California at Los Angeles, UCLA.

Following his attendance at Einstein's first Berlin lectures on relativity theory, Reichenbach focused on providing a philosophically and epistemologically acceptable account of relativity within the bounds of his own strict empiricism. Among the several important works he produced on these issues, *The Philosophy of Space and Time* (1928), in which he promotes a causal-conventionalist account of space and time, is probably the most influential (cf. Chapter 6). His posthumously published book, *The Direction of Time* (1956), provides the first thoroughgoing account of the entropic theory of the direction of time and remains a touchstone for all later work.

Adolf Grünbaum (b. 1923), born in Germany but largely educated in the United States, has spent his professional career at the University of Pittsburgh. Although not directly a student of Reichenbach, the influence is both obvious and acknowledged. Grünbaum's *Philosophical Problems of Space and Time* remains a standard text and probably the most fully developed empiricist account of these issues. His account of the sophistical nature of Zeno's paradox remains deeply influential; the mathematical resolution offered in Chapter 2 is largely that defended by him in *Modern Science and Zeno's Paradoxes*.

Out of the logical empiricist tradition of Reichenbach and Grünbaum has developed a substantial literature on the philosophy of time as beginning in the philosophy of science. The modern versions of the absolute versus relational debate focus on the metaphysical status of space-time as represented in relativity. See the Further Reading section of Chapter 6 for an introduction to this literature. There is also an extensive literature, with some of the major contributions listed at the end of Chapter 7, on the relationship between the direction of causation, the second law of thermodynamics, and the direction of time.

be what led the philosopher Hans Reichenbach to define the direction of time as the arrow of causation.

As plausible as it seems at first glance, Reichenbach's definition faces serious obstacles. In different ways, it seems to be both too strong and too weak. Too strong, in that it seems to rule out as impossible some things that seem to be possible and to do so for the wrong reasons. Consider a person or other system that demonstrated reliable precognition. They form beliefs and make statements about the future that turn out to be just as reliable as our memories of the past. The obvious conclusion would be that those future events were causing them to have those beliefs just as past events cause ordinary memories.

The problem is that if the arrow of causation is the direction of time and these events are having "earlier" consequences, then they're not actually later. If backward causation is impossible, then precognition seems to be impossible. But that also seems to be a substantive matter of investigation. It seems odd to say that precognition is impossible on the grounds that its occurrence makes the precognitively experienced events earlier rather than later than the precognitive experiences. Here we seem to be ruling out precognition on the grounds that the occurrence of precognition means that it wouldn't be "pre-" anymore.

A causal theorist might try to avoid this by appealing to the predominance of causation in a particular order. That is, we would still treat instances of precognition because most of the causal influences connecting the present to the future event run in the "ordinary" direction. But, this seems to get the order of explanation wrong for a causal theory of time direction. Wasn't the intrinsic direction of causation just supposed to be the direction of time? Precognition provides an example where B could cause A despite being later than A. Taking into account the basic principle of identity, the indiscernibility of identicals, this divergence makes it clear that they cannot be the same thing. It may well be that we believe that time moves in a particular direction because that's the predominant direction of causation, but this seems to illustrate that this connection between time and causation can be, at the most, another marker for the direction of time.

Consider the similar problem posed by the possibility of time-reversed regions of the universe. From our region of the universe, and assuming that we can interact with it, such regions are like a video running backward— fires reassemble themselves from their ashes until they concentrate themselves in the match that lit them and people appear in their graves, and are then removed from the ground and brought to the hospital where they come to life. It seems plausible that within such a region we should treat the causal arrow as reversed. The fire is still caused by the match, not the ashes, even if the match is applied after the ashes form. A sentient being trapped in such a region, might even find their psychological processes operating in reverse as well, leading them to mistakenly believe that the direction of time is from the future to the past.

The point here is not that such reversals are possible, although they do seem to be allowed by the physical laws with which we are familiar, but that the equation of the direction of causation with the direction of time forces us to misdescribe them. We seem to be required to say that time itself has changed direction in such regions. Processes are not running backward within that region, they're just running forward in a different direction. But if that's the case then the problem of the direction of time itself seems to be left entirely up in the air.

One further problem is that it's not clear that we can formulate the arrow of causation independently of a preexisting arrow of time. Some form of correlation seems to be a minimal condition for causal connections. The golf ball landing in the hole correlates, more or less, with the swing of the club. Then why say that the club causes the ball to move and not vice versa. Remember that since the direction of causation is supposed to pick out the direction of time, we must specify the difference between cause and effect without reference to temporal precedence. It's not at all clear that we can do so.

The one remaining alternative might be to associate this causal arrow with the thermodynamic one. If every causal interaction between physical systems involves an exchange of energy between them such that the total entropy of the two systems taken together always increases, then we get a link between the causal and thermodynamic arrows. In fact, the second law of thermodynamics seems to be a pretty good candidate to explain all of the arrows of time. Memories and records can be understood as low entropy products of even lower entropy events.

Although as usual there are problems about the details, this seems to be the most plausible proposal for a master arrow. Unfortunately it seems to get the nature of the direction of time wrong in at least two ways. First, imagine that there is a region toward what we ordinarily think of as the future with extraordinarily low entropy, much lower than the average entropy of the universe today. Perhaps the universe re-contracts into a low entropy big crunch or perhaps there's an act of divine intervention or science-fictional cosmic engineering. Whatever the cause there's a period toward what we ordinarily call the future in which the entropy decreases rather than increases.

Does that mean the time runs in reverse in that region? Some philosophers have suggested that it would. Lawrence Sklar suggests that we treat the difference between earlier and later like the difference between up and down. Down is just the direction of the biggest thing around; more precisely, the direction of the average gravitational potential in the immediate vicinity. Just as down on Earth is toward the Earth and down on Mars is toward Mars, later around us is the direction of entropy increase around us and later in the entropy reversed region is the direction of entropy increase then.

How one feels about this proposal seems to largely, but not universally, depend on one's exposure to physics. Those who become used to the fact that science shows us a world radically different from common sense tend to become a bit numb to such surprising consequences as the contingent nature of the direction of time. Others find it plainly absurd that anything as fundamental as the earlier/later distinction could be accidental in the way that the up/down distinction is.

The problem is made worse when we realize that according to modern physics the second law of thermodynamics isn't even really a law. Instead, it's merely a statistical regularity resulting from the apparently random behavior of the molecules that make up the relevant systems. Worse there are reasons to suspect that the fundamental laws governing interactions don't even allow for the application of the concept of entropy and of the second law of thermodynamics except under very special boundary conditions. That's where we turn in the next section.

Problem #2: Not enough arrows

Even if we could explain all of the temporal asymmetries in the world in terms of a master arrow, whether causal or thermodynamic, we're left with a further problem. We need to explain in what sense that master arrow is fundamental. The problem is that the fundamental physical laws, as far as we've identified them, are *time-reversal invariant*. Intuitively, we can think of the time reverse of a given process as the process that would create the same appearance as a video of the original process running backward. We say that a set of natural laws is time-reversal invariant just in case both versions of a process are always compatible with them.

To see what this means let's start with an example. Consider a system of point particles of varying masses interacting only by gravity. Given the initial positions and velocities of all the particles, I can use Newton's laws of motion and the law of gravity to determine their positions and velocities at any later time.[1] Gravity is a time-reversal invariant law of physics. To see this, consider the positions and velocities of the particles at some later time, t_f. If I simply reverse the velocities of each particle, the system will evolve back into the initial positions with reversed velocities.

Since these laws of physics are normally expressed in systems of differential equations, the time-reversal invariance is expressed as a kind of transformation such that when applied to a solution it always also generates a solution. Here's a slightly different way to make a similar point. Let's say that two possible worlds are *nomologically identical* just in case they obey the same laws of nature. To say that our fundamental physical laws are time-reversal invariant is just to claim that the temporally backward image of our world is nomologically identical to our world. If all I knew about *this* world is that it obeys the laws of physics, I cannot tell which version of it I occupy.

This seems to indicate first that there can be no intrinsic distinction between cause and effect. For any configuration that I take as the cause of some "later" configuration, it's just as possible that "effect" could have been the "cause"; there is simply nothing in the fundamental laws of physics that rules it out. From this perspective, the distinction between cause and effect seems to be a matter of accident. It seems to result either from the accidental boundary conditions such that in this universe the "cause" happened to come first, or from the accident of our perspective on the process. This seems to make any attempt to explain the direction of time in such terms seriously problematic.

We've already seen that the second law of thermodynamics seems to offer a way out here; here is a law which is clearly not time-reversal invariant. Unfortunately, it is also not a law in the relevant sense. In classical thermodynamics, as originally formulated by Clausius and others, both heat and entropy were taken as fundamental physical features of a system whose behavior was described by the laws. In modern physics, thermodynamics is taken as a mere approximation to statistical mechanics in which heat, temperature, entropy, and other thermodynamic quantities are merely statistical averages characterizing the collective behaviors of the fundamental atomic or molecular components of a system. Thus, the heat contained in a system is merely the total kinetic energy of the atoms that make up the system. The temperature is, roughly, the average kinetic energy

Historical Note 20: The Birth of Thermodynamics

Modern thermodynamics originates as the attempt to understand and improve the operation of steam engines in the late eighteenth and early nineteenth centuries. The first two crucial theoretical advances were the introduction of the concept of the "motive power" of an engine, which refers roughly to the height to which the engine can lift a given weight, by Sadi Carnot (1796–1832) in 1824, and the equivalence of heat and energy demonstrated by James Joules (1818–1889) in 1843. With these two concepts it became clear that there was a fundamental irreversability characterisic of heat engines; there was always less work done by the engine than there was heat lost from the engine.

Rudolf Clausius (1822–1888) introduced the concept of *"entropy"* as a measure of the waste heat lost in such processes and gave the first modern formulation of the second law of thermodynamics. Following the clue in Joule's concept of the equivalence of heat and energy, James Clerk Maxwell developed the kinetic theory of gases in the 1860s. According to the kinetic theory of gases the heat contained in a gas just is the energy of the motion of the particles that make it up. Maxwell and later Ludwig Boltzmann (1844–1906) were able to identify statistical properties of the mixtures of molecules that "mirrored" the classical thermodynamic quantities such as temperature and entropy, leading ultimately to the contemporary discipline of statistical mechanics.

Most importantly, Maxwell and Boltzmann were able to identify the entropy of a gas as the range of possible states available to a particular molecule of the gas given the overall thermodynamic state, for example, temperature and pressure, of the gas as a whole. This leads to the modern conception of entropy as the level of disorder in the system and the statement of the second law of thermodynamics as the tendency of disorder to increase.

of the micro-components, while the pressure is the average force exerted by all of the component's impacts on the container.

Entropy is more complicated, but it can be thought of as a measure of the disorder remaining in the system given our knowledge of the thermodynamic quantities of the system. Technically, it is a measure of the number of possible ways that the micro-components of a system, molecules of a gas for example, can be arranged while leaving the thermodynamic quantities such as the total heat, temperature, etc. unchanged. To see how this works, let's look at a couple of examples.

First, a completely "toy" example consisting of six coins. Let's say that we know that three of the coins are heads up, and nothing else. There are twenty possible arrangements, leaving the order of the coins fixed, that have this property. Now suppose that you discover that the heads aren't distributed evenly; two of the first three coins are heads. There are eight combinations with two heads in the first three coins. We therefore say that the first configuration has *higher entropy* than the second one because there are more possible instantiations of it than of the second one.

Obviously, this notion of entropy isn't particularly useful when I'm dealing with six coins and two possible states per coin. In such a case, it's much easier to just count. But what about a container of gas with one mole of gas in it consisting of about 6×10^{23} atoms, where all we know is the estimate of the total heat and the temperature. When the container is at the same temperature throughout, what we're saying is that the average kinetic energy in any particular volume of the container is the same as that throughout the whole container. Now suppose that there was a temperature difference between two sides of the container. (See Figure 7.1.) This means that most of the molecules that happen to be moving faster than the average for the whole container are concentrated in one part of the box, just like the heads of the coins were concentrated in the first few in our previous example. Just as with our coins, there are far fewer ways to arrange the atoms so that the speedy ones are concentrated at one end, rather than spread throughout the container. We say that the smooth distribution, which corresponds to thermodynamic equilibrium, has much higher entropy than the concentrated one.

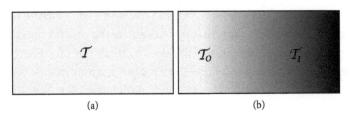

Figure 7.1 Gas contained in a box. (a) Gas in equilibrium at temperature T (b) Gas in nonequilibrium state, $T_0 < T_1$.

When things get this complicated, the notion of entropy becomes useful because I can apparently infer the following fact. Assume that each possible microscopic atomic distribution compatible with the thermodynamic state is equally possible. Also suppose that I have a box of gas in state 7.1(b). In the absence of some system working to keep it there, I'm much more likely to find a box of gas in the state of 7.1(a) than that of 7.1(b) when I examine it later. Apparently, we have just "derived" the second law of thermodynamics. Just based on the probabilities, any system in an unlikely, that is, low entropy state, will tend at any other times to be found in a high entropy state.

That's not quite right, however. First, there's the problem that however we characterize this tendency to move toward more probable states, it doesn't seem to be law-like. It is at best a statistical tendency that might explain why we accept the second law of thermodynamics. Here are two illustrations of that. The first is due to James Clerk Maxwell, the first man to work out the kinetic theory of gases in any detail. He proposed a thought experiment now commonly referred to as Maxwell's Demon. Imagine a box like that in Figure 7.1, but with a barrier down the middle. In the barrier is a shutter that can be opened whenever doing so would allow a molecule moving faster than average to pass from left to right. Similarly, for slower moving molecules moving from right to left. Over time and without doing any work on the gas, not changing the total heat, we would end up with 7.1(b). Whether or not such a system could actually be built, it illustrates the merely statistical nature of the second law.

Second, consider the symmetrical nature of the reasoning above. The low probability associated with low entropy states implies that we should find the system in a higher entropy state at any other time. That is, every low entropy system should have been in a high entropy state at earlier times, as well as at later times. It must have demonstrated anti-thermodynamic behavior to get into the low entropy state. As with Maxwell's Demon, we don't see this behavior at macroscopic scales. The thermodynamic version of the second law does not merely imply that nonequilibrium systems move toward equilibrium, but that equilibrium systems remain in that state. Both of these systems seem to show that that cannot be the case for the statistical version of the second law. Even if the statistical version of the second law can explain our tendency to believe the stronger thermodynamic version, it does not seem to make for a good foundation for the direction of time.

It is not even clear that it can do the first of those. We have reasons to suspect that the universal increase of entropy is incompatible with the time-reversible fundamental physics that governs the micro-components of the system. It should not be possible to derive any temporally asymmetric behavior from fundamental physical principles that are time-reversal invariant. Consider the following fact: for every microstate of the system that evolves into a higher entropy state, the time reverse of that initial state must also be a possible state of the physical system. But that time-reversed state must lead to a lower entropy situation. Think about a gas. If its molecules are all tending to spread out, and then I turn them around, what happens? They must tend to concentrate, a classic low entropy state. This objection, called the Loschmidt reversibility objection, seems to prove that there must be exactly as many possible transitions from high entropy to low entropy as there are from low entropy to high entropy.

The reversibility objection and other related results in classical mechanics such as the recurrence theorem seem to demonstrate that the irreversibility of irreversible processes cannot be the result of fundamental natural laws.[2] The apparent irreversibility of thermodynamic and chemical processes must be a product of special boundary conditions on what is allowed in the universe combined with the relatively large scale of human beings. These processes appear irreversible to us only because our universe just happens to contain one version of them rather than another, and because we are too big and clumsy to manipulate their individual components the way we do with macroscopic reversible processes.

The difficulty we have identifying any *fundamental* arrow of time brings out, once again, how difficult it is to make room for ordinary common-sense ideas of time in a modern physical universe. As with the arguments against becoming, perhaps we are better off seeing these attempts to explain the direction of time in causal or thermodynamic terms as explaining it away. As Huw Price puts it, we must be willing to adopt "the Archimedean standpoint" of the view from no-when, and accept that it is the asymmetry of our ordinary temporal perspective which is the source of the difficulty, so that the task of unraveling the anthropocentric products of this perspective goes hand-in-hand with that of deciding how much of temporal asymmetry is really objective, and therefore in need of explanation by physics.

The one alternative to this seems to be that the boundary conditions while not themselves laws are not quite as arbitrary as they seem. Perhaps there is something about the universe that explains these asymmetries even though they are not law-like. The best bet seems to be some fact about the beginning or evolution of the universe, a cosmological arrow.

The cosmological arrow of time

There is one further irreversible process that we haven't yet discussed; the evolution of the universe itself. There is extraordinarily persuasive evidence that the universe began in a big bang approximately fourteen billion years ago and has been expanding ever since. It has also been cooling as it expands—its average temperature now is approximately 2.7 Kelvin. Thus, on the one hand, the arrow of cosmological expansion and cooling seems to be independent of the other arrows, although aligned with them (More detail about cosmology can be found in Chapter 8.). On the other hand, the universe clearly contains regions of high temperature and low entropy. The surface of the Earth is clearly not a mere 2.7 Kelvin. Modern cosmology explains this structure as the result of irregularities in the early universe manifesting at cosmological scales as the universe expands. That is, the universe itself seems to have begun in a low entropy state. These slightly higher density and lower entropy regions within the early universe evolved into all of the structures we see today, from stars to galaxies and even larger structures. These cosmological seeds, as it were, became the source of low entropy, high-quality energy that drove the formation of lower-level structures. For example, the radiation from the concentrated energy of the sun provides the energy to drive ecosystems on Earth.

This past hypothesis, as David Albert has called it, seems to be the best available physical explanation of the direction of time. It also seems to many people to be an extremely implausible one. On the one hand, many people still think it gets the order of explanation wrong. The universe is expanding to the future because that's the direction of the future. If the future is defined as the direction in which the universe is expanding from the big bang, what happens if it starts to contract again? Since a big crunch seems to be indistinguishable from the big bang in reverse, would the arrow of time flip at the moment of contraction? That seems profoundly implausible to many people.

In the end, we are largely left where we started the chapter. There are many strikingly temporally asymmetric processes in the universe—psychological, causal, thermodynamic and chemical, radiation and even the expansion of the universe. Except that all of those processes seem to be almost accidental; they do not follow from any distinctive asymmetry of time itself or of the laws of nature. We are left still with too many arrows not to believe that there is something fundamental that they are pointing at, but with no ability to identify that one fundamental asymmetry. This leaves the direction of time as one of the most puzzling mysteries in the foundations of physics, the philosophy of science, and the metaphysics of time.

Further Reading

For other perspectives on the basic problem of the arrow of time, see the relevant chapters in:

Davies, *About Time,* Hawking's *A Brief History of Time,* Le Poidevin *Travels in Four Dimensions* and Dainton's *Time and Space* and Sklar's *Space, Time and Space-time.*

The following philosophical monographs are all fairly heavy going:

Albert, D. Z. (2000), *Time and Chance*, Cambridge, MA: Harvard University Press.

Horwich, P. (1987), *Asymmetries in Time: Problems in the Philosophy of Science*, Cambridge, MA: MIT Press, Number A Bradford Book.

Price, H. (1996), *Time's Arrow and Archimedes' Point: New Directions for the Physics of Time* Oxford, New York: Oxford University Press.

Reichenbach, H. (1991), *The Direction of Time*, Berkeley: University of California Press.

Chapter 4 of the following is the closest thing to a definitive statement of the "time field" alternative to entropic accounts of the direction of time:

Maudlin, T. (2009), *The Metaphysics within Physics*, Oxford: Oxford University Press.

For David Hume's regularity account of causation, the most straightforward account can be found in his *Enquiry Concerning Human Understanding.* For the contemporary debates about causation and causal order, see:

Sosa, E. and M. Tooley, eds (1993), *Causation* (Oxford Readings in Philosophy), Oxford: Oxford University Press.

These essays cover a wide range of topics, but also vary widely in their accessibility.

Discussion questions

1 Can you describe three aspects of your mental life that seem to be temporally asymmetric? Can you identify three natural processes that seem to be temporally asymmetric?

2 Can you explain any one of the psychological asymmetries above in terms of a nonpsychological asymmetry? Can you explain one of the natural asymmetries in terms of a psychological one?

3 In merely conceptual terms, can you explain why the conservation of energy seems to imply the reversibility of physical processes?

4 Why are concentrations of heat associated with lower entropy? Why is randomness another measure of entropy? Conceptually, rather than mathematically, explain the connection between the two understandings of entropy?

5 What is the second law of thermodynamics? How is it connected to the two conceptions of entropy above? What does Maxwell's Demon tell us about the nature of the second law?

6 Based on our current understanding of thermodynamics, how does the past hypothesis seem to explain the direction of time?

7 *Food for Thought:* In the absence of a time asymmetric universal law of physics, do you expect the primary explanation of the arrow of time to result from some more fundamental metaphysical truth or from merely contingent arrangements of matter? Why?

Notes

1. Just to head off picky physics students, there's a slight ambiguity here. I cannot necessarily solve the relevant equations for *all* later times. But, the existence and uniqueness theorem for ordinary partial differential equations guarantees that there is such a solution at *each* time.

2. The recurrence theorem is a result in classical mechanics that proves that any system governed by laws obeying certain conditions and having a certain state must eventually return to exactly that state. The detailed conditions are rather technical in nature, but are roughly equivalent to conservation of energy, and this condition is roughly equivalent to the conditions for time-reversal invariance. See the Further Reading section.

8

The Shape of Time

Could time have a beginning or ending? Could there be a first or last time? Need time be linear rather than cyclical? We examine these questions from philosophical, physical, and religious perspectives in this chapter; this takes us through discussions of big bang physics and the possibility of a multiverse, whether modern physics provides support for theories of divine creation, and the problem of infinite pasts or repeating presents.

Could time have a beginning or ending? Could there be a first time or last time? If time could have a beginning (respectively, ending), does it? Need time be linear rather than cyclical? Could precisely the same time reoccur?

All of these questions are manifestations of our central conflict between Parmenidean and Heraclitean conceptions of the world. So far we have focused on the status of entities within the world. We have asked, "Does anything in the world truly become, or is all becoming merely an appearance presented by being?" In this chapter we shift our focus to the world considered as whole. Does the world *become*? Does it have history and is it *produced*? Or has it always been in something like the same state in which we find it today?

These questions have been asked since the beginning of philosophy; both Plato and Aristotle considered them in some detail. Unfortunately, the classical debates about beginnings and endings generally fail to make certain crucial distinctions. There is a general failure to carefully distinguish questions about the origin of time from questions about the origin of the material things that make up the universe, the material universe. However, it seems clear that these are logically distinct questions. There does not seem to be any obvious contradiction involved in the claim that some period of time passed before the first material object came into existence. We therefore need to understand the relationship between cosmological questions regarding the structure of the universe and questions about the structure of time *per se.*

There's a second problem that infects the classical debates. Questions about whether time could have had a beginning are often formulated in terms of how much time could have passed. As we saw in Chapter 2, questions about the size of intervals for continuous structures like time are more subtle than they seem at first glance. As we might expect, so are questions about the nature of boundaries of such structures.

Our first task in this chapter is to characterize the various models of time *per se.* We saw in Chapter 2 that we have solid reasons for taking time as continuous, and that this notion of continuity can be made quite rigorous by appealing to the structure of the real numbers. However, nothing in that chapter or since gives us any basis on which to determine whether time has a beginning or an ending. In the next section, we will examine the possible structures of time compatible with its continuity and attempt to determine whether there are any logical or mathematical grounds for choosing one over the other.

Our principal conclusion from that section will be that there is not, or at least not independently of questions about the origin and fate of the material universe. We therefore turn our attention to two lines of evidence that the universe itself becomes or is brought into existence. All of the Abrahamic religious traditions—Jewish, Christian, and Islamic in all their varieties—teach that the world is created by God. How this alleged fact, taken by believers to have been revealed directly by God, fits with philosophical models of and arguments regarding the structure of time and the world is a central question at the intersection of philosophy and religion. We will consider various responses to these concerns beginning on p. 229.

Even for those who are not religious believers, these questions are of more than merely historical interest. These debates form a crucial context for the interpretation of modern cosmology. Beginning in the 1920s, with the discovery that all of the light from distant galaxies was more red than would have been expected (the cosmic redshift), several intersecting lines of evidence, both observational and theoretical, led to the creation of modern physical cosmology. Physical cosmology treats the universe as a whole as an object of physical research and theory, an object with its own distinctive history and structural laws. Most strikingly, converging lines of evidence seem to indicate that the universe originated approximately fourteen billion years ago when it "exploded" out of the physical anomaly popularly known as the big bang. Beginning on p. 224, we will examine some of the evidence for the reality of the big bang and consider the philosophical consequences, if any, that result from modern physical cosmology.[1]

In the final section of this chapter, we will turn our attention to a slightly different debate about the shape of time. Could time be cyclic, more like a circle than a straight line? On the one hand, there are various traditional cyclic cosmologies according to which the current universe is merely a stage in a cyclic process of growth and "re-birth." On the other hand, models according to which the same moment of time becomes present more than once are deeply problematic. There might be a version of these related to time travel universes, but we will reserve discussion of those for Chapter 9.

Can time have a beginning or an end?

Our discussion of Zeno's paradoxes seemed to suggest that time must be continuous in a way strongly analogous to the continuity of the real numbers. Since that point, we've largely taken it for granted that time has roughly the structure of the real line. Yes, in Chapter 4, we considered the suggestion that time might be branching; that from each time there might be a collection of distinct lines marking off distinct futures. And in Chapter 6, we considered that there might be many such timelines associated with distinct objects or frames of reference, as suggested by Einstein's theory of relativity. Nothing so far has depended on whether we treat time as a line or as a line segment of some kind.

For now, we are going to continue to assume that time has the form of some interval of the real numbers, or equivalently that it can be modeled by some segment of the real line where the whole line is also considered a segment.[2] We will consider whether time might be more like a circle or some other cyclic structure later in this chapter. Setting aside that case for now, there are actually three rather than two options regarding endpoints of the segment. In each direction, time might be unbounded, closed, or bounded but open.

The first two options are fairly straightforward. They correspond almost exactly to the traditional division in the metaphysics of time between eternalists and creationists. The first thing to note is a terminological oddity here; eternalists in this sense can be presentists in the sense intended in Chapter 4. It's not that eternalists in this sense believe that each thing always has, does, and will exist. Rather they believe that the world has always been becoming—that it is unbounded to the past. No matter how far backward we look in time, there was more time, in fact infinitely more time, that had already passed at that point. Creationists, of course, believe that time and the material universe are closed to the past. There is some first time at which time and everything else begins.

This characterization points directly toward the obvious arguments against eternalism. As we saw in Chapter 2, there is a long-standing suspicion of actual or completed infinities in philosophy. Eternalism seems to violate deep intuitions regarding *the impassibility of the infinite*. If time is unbounded to the past, it seems as though each time is preceded by an infinitely long time interval. This seems to be equivalent to beginning infinitely far away in space and arriving at Earth. It seems to involve us in a manifest impossibility.

A version of this argument seems to have first been offered by John Philiponus (490–570 C.E.) in his commentary on Aristotle and was later widely adopted in medieval Jewish, Christian, and Islamic philosophy. Its clearest statement is probably that offered by Immanuel Kant. As part of his transcendental idealism, Kant attempted to show that certain metaphysical questions, including those about the origin of the world, are fundamentally unanswerable. With these arguments, Kant hoped to inculcate what he saw as a needed humility about human beings' ability to understand the world as it is, rather than merely as it appears to us.

In the thesis of the first antinomy of his *Critique of Pure Reason*, Kant writes:

> If we assume that the world has no beginning in time, then up to every given moment an eternity has elapsed, and there has passed away in the world an

infinite series of successive states of things. Now the infinity of a series consists in the fact that it can never be completed through successive synthesis. It thus follows that it is impossible for an infinite world-series to have passed away, and that a beginning of the world is therefore a necessary condition of the world's existence.

Notice that, here, Kant seems to be treating the beginning of time and the beginning of material existence as interchangeable. The argument seems to apply equally to the possibility of an infinitely distant first moment of time or an infinitely distant moment of creation of the first thing.

There are various objections to this argument. The obvious one is simply that the modern mathematical theory of infinite sets demonstrates the logical coherence of completed infinities. Even if we cannot imagine such an infinite time, that's not a basis for believing that it's logically or mathematically incoherent. Second, even if the basic reasoning is sound, it's not clear that it proves that there must be a first time, as opposed to a first event. On a related note, even if Kant can prove that there can be no infinitely old things in the universe, that does not seem to be the same as proving that the universe cannot be infinitely old. Why is it not possible for the universe to have consisted of a sequence of things all of which have earlier causes, but none of which have always existed?

All of these, roughly, point out that the classical argument against an infinite past seem to depend on the same family of mistakes that we saw was so tempting in the case of Zeno's paradoxes—imposing our finitary intuitions on infinite quantities. The argument presumes that the infinite past is like a particular time from which we start and then move toward the present.

However, completing an infinite process is not a matter of starting at a particular time that just happens to be infinitely far to the past and then stopping in the present. It's to have always been doing something and then stopping. This point is illustrated by a possibly apocryphal story attributed to the philosopher Ludwig Wittgenstein. Imagine meeting a woman in the street who says, "Five, one, four, one, dot, three! Finally finished!" When we ask what is finished, she tells us that she has just finished counting down the infinite digits of *pi* backward. When we ask when she started, she tells us that she never started, she has always been doing it. The point of the story seems to be that the impossibility of completing such an infinite process is an illusion created by our insistence that every process has a beginning.

Historical Note 21: Rationalism, Empiricism, and the Philosophy of Immanuel Kant

The abandonment of long-standing scientific principles by the new science forced its practitioners to confront the nature of its basic principles. Rationalists such as Baruch Spinoza (1632–1677) and Gottfried Friedrich Wilhelm Leibniz (1646–1716) argued that it must be possible to derive them from a fundamental metaphysics of being. Empiricists such as John Locke (1632–1704) and David Hume (1711–1776) argued that, to varying degrees, these principles must be revealed within experience.

Perhaps unsurprisingly rationalism tends to be associated with versions of idealism reminiscent of the Eleatics. Baruch Spinoza, the son of a moderately well-off family of Portuguese-Jewish traders in Amsterdam who was excommunicated from the Jewish community for his radical views, defended a version of monism more radical than anything since the original Eleatics. He denies that there is any God distinct from the world, denies the immortality of the soul, and treats all appearance of change and human freedom as illusions resulting from unclear thinking.

Leibniz's mature metaphysical view is a variety of idealism, although not as extreme as Spinoza's. In *The Monadology* and elsewhere Leibniz claims that the only real things that can exist in the world are absolutely simple substances or "monads." These monads have the character of minds rather than corporeal beings and are also absolutely isolated from all other monads; no monad can be affected by any other. This is Leibniz's famous doctrine that "monads have no windows." As such, monads are not located in time or space. Time can be, at most, an aspect of the way that these souls represent themselves to themselves.

He vacillates over the course of his long career on the status of ordinary material objects. At times he seems to treat them as products or aggregates of monads in a more Platonic mode; at other times he treats them as mistaken representations of monads in a more purely Eleatic mode.

The empiricist strand tends to be more Heraclitean in its approach. This is most clearly true in the case of David Hume. Hume's skepticism amounts to a rejection of any claim to knowledge of ultimate reality and a suspicion of any metaphysical knowledge. As such Hume opens the door to all of those later philosophers and scientists who treat claims about the structure of time as contingent and fallible scientific hypothesis rather than pieces of a priori metaphysics. For this see especially Chapter 7 but this attitude is also central to the debates about closed time-like curves in general relativity in Chapter 9.

These two strands converge in the "transcendental idealism" of Immanuel Kant (1724–1804). Kant, the sage of Königsberg, is probably the most important philosopher since ancient Greece, and his philosophical system is extraordinarily intricate and far ranging, touching on everything from metaphysics and religion to moral theory and politics. Kant's treatment of time rests at the heart of his system.

His basic doctrine of time treats it as "the form of inner intuition"; time is the formal organizing principle of our own experience of ourselves as thinking. Of course, since our experiences of external objects are part of that thinking, time is also one of the formal principles of experience of external objects as well, cf. Chapter 3, p. 68 ff. for a brief discussion. This aspect of Kant's philosophy is deeply influential on Husserl's treatment of time discussed in Chapter 5.

Kant appears at two other crucial junctions in the debates here. Part of the point of transcendental idealism is to provide an absolutist account of the physical role of time as independent of the particular material objects in the world without having to commit to its ultimate metaphysical reality (cf. Chapter 6). Finally, Kant's first antinomy presents us with an important move in the debate over the eternity of the world (Chapter 8).

Even if we remain concerned about such past infinities, Kant himself recognized that the major objection to his thesis is that its antithesis is no more plausible a priori.

> For let us assume that it has a beginning. Since the beginning is an existence which is preceded by a time in which the thing is not, there must have been a preceding time in which the world was not, i.e. an empty time.

Unfortunately, at this point the ambiguity between the temporal and the cosmological question becomes pressing. Kant's formulation of the antithesis of first antinomy seems to presuppose the unboundedness of time. The "it" of the first sentence must be something like "the first thing." But then Kant's formulation of this antithesis seems to presuppose the unboundedness of time. Otherwise, how could it be a problem that there is empty time before the universe comes into existence? This seems to be confirmed by Kant's description of time earlier in the same work, where he tells us:

> To say that time is infinite means nothing more than that any determinate magnitude of time is possible only through the limitations of a single underlying time. Hence the original representation *time* must be given as unlimited. [A32/B47–48]

The first point here is how crucial it is to maintain the distinction between these two questions. Once we do so, we can recognize that, contrary to Kant, his thesis and his antithesis do not exhaust the possibilities. Whereas in the thesis Kant seems to argue equally that neither material existence nor time itself can be unbounded, in the antithesis he seems to argue *from* the unboundedness of time to the unboundedness of material existence. Unlike the thesis, the antithesis is not an argument that boundedness is, in itself, incoherent; it is, at most, an argument that a creationist about the material world must also postulate a first time. We'll move on at this point; as is usually the case, any consideration of Kant risks leading us down a rabbit hole of interpretive and philosophical puzzles.

Instead of deeply engaging with Kant, simply note that the third quotation above points to a slightly different family of arguments against temporal beginnings. The arguments go back to our old friend Aristotle and his attempt to demonstrate that being at a time logically requires the existence of both earlier and later times. As Aristotle puts it:

> Now since time cannot exist and is unthinkable apart from the now, and the now is a kind of middle-point, uniting as it does in itself both a beginning and an end, a beginning of future time and an end of past time, it follows that there must always be time; for the extremity of the last period of time that we take must be found in some now, since in time we can take nothing but now. [Physics VIII: 251b20]

Although Aristotle's argument obviously depends on his problematic definition of moments of time as boundaries between the past and the future, Richard Swinburne offers an apparently related argument in his book *Space and Time*. The following seems to be a logical truth that holds at every time:

Example 8.1 Either there were swans or there were not swans.

On either branch of this sentence, it seems that there must be some past time. Obviously, if there were swans, then there was some earlier time occupied by swans. However, if there weren't swans, it equally appears that there must be some earlier time unoccupied by swans.

As William Newton-Smith points out, this is not a valid argument, despite first appearances. The claim that "There were no swans." is, as Newton-Smith puts it, "Janus-faced." It might be interpreted as:

Example 8.2 In the past, it is not the case that there are any swans.

This obviously implies that there are past times, but it just as obviously begs the question against the creationist. Someone who wishes to defend the existence of a first time would simply accept that example 8.2 is false at that first time. The alternative is to claim:

Example 8.3 It is not the case that in the past there are swans.

This claim is obviously true at the first time simply because there are no past times that could be occupied by swans.

It therefore seems to be the case that we have no purely philosophical reason to either affirm or deny the existence of a beginning of time. This is particularly the case since there is an important third case according to which time is finite without having a first moment; this occurs if time is isomorphic to a bounded, but open or half-open interval of the real line.[3] This would mean that relative to each moment of time t there is some interval of time Δt_{max} such that no moment of time is more than Δt_{max} earlier than t. It would also be the case that *every* time t has some times earlier than it.

This is the result of the crucial fact, discussed in Chapter 2, that for continuous sets the metric structure governing the size of intervals and the order structure are independent. This seems profoundly implausible to us because we imagine ourselves moving toward the boundary in a series of fixed finite steps and it seems difficult to imagine how we could fail to cover all of the finite intervals in a finite sequence of steps. However, this failure is precisely what we would see in reverse, watching a clock fall into a black hole! The event horizon of the black hole, the boundary of the region from which nothing can escape and which gives black holes their names, is the future boundary of the clocks' lifetime or world-line. But, because of time dilation, it will take the clock an infinite amount of time as measured in the rest frame of an observer a long distance from the black hole to actually reach the horizon.

This model turns out to be particularly important because modern cosmology seems to indicate that it is precisely the correct model, absent quantum effects, implied by the big bang model of the universe. Thus, we now turn from purely temporal questions to cosmological ones.

The big bang and the beginning of time

In the 1920s, a collection of theoretical innovations and observational discoveries converged to trigger a revolution in the physical conception of the temporal structure of the universe. Until the advent of modern physical cosmology, even creationists had seen the world as basically homogenous in time. The world might have been created by God or some other force, but it had been created in the same fundamental condition in which we find it today. The discovery that the universe has a history is one of the great stories in the history of science.

Although the cosmological revolution represented by modern big bang cosmology cannot really be understood except as the continuation of the nineteenth-century revolutions in geology and biology represented by the theory of evolution, we can at least sketch the crucial components of the revolution.

The first component of the cosmological revolution comes from Einstein's theory of general relativity. On the one hand, general relativity is merely the reformulation of Newton's theory of gravitation to make it compatible with Einstein's theory of special relativity. Most readers should be familiar with Isaac Newton's law of universal gravitation according to which the gravitational force between objects at a time depends on their instantaneous spatial separation at that time. As we saw in Chapter 6, since spatial separation becomes a merely frame-relative quantity in special relativity, the gravitational "force" between objects cannot depend on that quantity and be invariant. Einstein's theory is more than merely a reformulation of Newton's, however. By taking the equivalence between inertial mass and gravitational mass ("the equivalence principle") as a fundamental postulate of his theory, Einstein demonstrated that gravity can be represented as a geometrical feature of the appropriate four-dimensional space-time.

Very roughly speaking, the gravitational field due to the presence of a massive object can be thought of as the difference between the geometry of space-time in the vicinity of the object and the Minkowski space-time described in Chapter 6. We'll look at some of the more bizarre possibilities for the geometrical structures that seem to be permitted by general relativity in Chapter 9. Here, we need only recognize that Einstein's theory makes questions about the structure of space-time, and therefore apparently questions about the structure of space, time, and the universe as a whole, legitimate objects of physical and empirical inquiry.

It is this fact about the field equations of general relativity that seems to have led Einstein into what he later, allegedly, called his greatest mistake—the introduction of the cosmological constant. In their simplest formulation, that most closely resembling Newton's theory of universal gravitation, the Einstein field equations seem to predict a fundamentally unstable universe. One that is either expanding or collapsing on a timescale that should be detectable. Since no such expansion or contraction had been detected, Einstein introduced a "counter term," a repulsive force between matter that would serve to weaken the gravitational field and allow for a stable, static universe.

Two further discoveries of the 1920s can be seen as crucial steps toward the modern conception of the universe expanding from an initial big bang. Russian mathematician Alexander Friedman and others discovered a collection of exact solutions to Einstein's field equations without the cosmological constant. Among these solutions are both expanding and contracting solutions with what we might call "a long middle-age." In these Friedman-Robertson-Walker models (FRW), the universe, while still expanding, does so slowly enough for enough of its history to allow the formation of what are, from the human perspective, quite large-scale structures such as galaxies.

During the same decade, Edwin Hubble was making two crucial observational discoveries. Using the 100-inch reflecting telescope at the Mount Wilson Observatory in California, Hubble demonstrated in 1923–4 that the Andromeda nebula was in fact another galaxy located outside of ours. Many other galaxies were quickly identified leading to a massive expansion in the estimated size of the visible universe. Second, Hubble was able to use his observations of galaxies to identify the redshift characteristic of an expanding universe. In an expanding universe, the atomic spectra of, for example, hydrogen contained in the stars of distant galaxies should be closer to the reddish end of the spectrum, with a longer wavelength/lower frequency than the spectra of the same substances measured in the laboratory.

Most significantly, using both new measurements by his own team and earlier measurements by the astronomer Vesto Slipher, Hubble was able to show a relationship between the distance to a receding galaxy and the degree of redshift that correlates with the speed of recession. The greater the distance, the faster the galaxy is receding from us. Remember that the further away a galaxy appears to us, the older the light which we are currently detecting. Since looking out further in space is equivalent to looking further backward in time, the increasing redshift with distance implies that the expansion of the universe is slowing down.

The various clues seem to have first been assembled by the Belgian priest and physicist George Lemaître. In 1927 he seems to have independently rediscovered Friedman's solution to the Einstein field equations. He also, unlike Friedman, recognized that something like a linear relationship between redshift and distance would be characteristic of a universe satisfying that model. Lemaitre seems to have recognized early that such a universe could be described as evolving from an initial highly compact extremely hot "atom" or "cosmic egg." He developed this model in a series of talks and papers throughout the early thirties leading to the first versions of what we now know as the big bang theory.

Despite theoretically viable steady-state models of the universe proposed by Fred Hoyle and others, the conception of the universe as originating in a primordial explosion and the associated Friedman-Lemaitre-Robertson-Walker (FLRW) models of general relativity quickly came to be recognized as the standard model. The final nail in the coffin of steady-state models was the discovery, in 1965, of the cosmic microwave background radiation by Penzias and Wilson. This radiation which seems to be almost perfectly homogenous and isotropic, the same everywhere and in every direction, has precisely the spectrum of radiation emitted by a body at 2.7 Kelvin. It is the radiation left behind by that initial cosmic atom that cooled as the universe expanded.

It is now pretty much universally agreed that the universe as we see it today evolved from such an initial explosive mixture. There are ongoing debates about the precise mechanism and processes that drove that early evolution and especially about how to explain the detailed structures in the early universe, before 10^{-36} seconds (0.0...01 with thirty-six zeros), that evolved into today's galaxies and other large-scale structures.

So what does big bang cosmology tell us about time? The obvious conclusion to draw is that there must have been a first time coincident with the beginning of the universe. If there has been a finite time of approximately 14,000,000,000 years since the big bang, then the same amount of time must have passed since the first time. Big bang cosmology seems to straightforwardly resolve Kant's first antinomy in favor of the creationist branch although for reasons inconceivable to Kant himself.

Unfortunately and unsurprisingly, things aren't quite that simple. There are both physical and logical/metaphysical reasons to suspect that the big bang need not be considered the beginning of everything in a philosophically significant sense. Let's consider the physical reasons first. The FLRW space-times are singular; at the "moment of creation" all of the matter in the universe is located at a single geometrical point creating infinite density. Technically, such space-times lack the property of *geodesic completeness*. Consider the path of a fundamental particle emerging from the big bang. From our perspective, that particle simply appears from the big bang with no particular antecedents. Looking backward from the present, the path of such a particle can be traced more and more closely toward the big bang singularity, but not *to* the singularity. In the language introduced earlier in this chapter, the histories of all of the matter in the universe are bounded but open. If the universe begins in an initial singularity, then there is a precise sense in which it begins without having a beginning. The universe originates from the initial singularity, but the singularity itself does not belong to the universe.

Physicists profoundly dislike singularities, especially those that cannot be hidden behind event horizons in the way that black holes can. Singularities represent the absolute breakdown of our ability to do physics. In the case of the initial singularity, it seems as though all of our physics actually ends up depending on something which is not itself subject to physical description. There are two basic strategies in modern cosmology to avoid this unpalatable conclusion. In quantum cosmology, the initial singularities are treated not as the absolute breakdown of physics but as the manifestation of the breakdown in classical general relativity. At the length and energy scales present around the big bang, quantum mechanical effects become extremely important. The other strategy, sometimes linked with the first one, is to invoke some form of a multiverse theory.

All of the programs in quantum gravity and quantum cosmology treat Einstein's general relativity as an approximate or effective theory of gravity that needs to be replaced by a quantum mechanical theory of gravity. The hope is that the initial singularity will turn out to be a mathematical anomaly of the approximating theory rather than a real breakdown in the structure of reality. I suspect that the only metaphysically interesting conclusion that can be drawn from quantum cosmology at this point is that extreme care is needed in drawing metaphysical conclusions. If physicists end up describing the fundamental structure of reality in terms of string theory, M-theory, or loop quantum gravity, it's not even clear how many of the questions about time that we have been asking are even well formulated. For further information about this fascinating realm of speculative physics, see the suggested readings for both this chapter and Chapter 9.

The second strategy to "discipline" the initial singularity is to embed the big bang into a larger cosmological context, one according to which the big bang is the beginning of our universe but not of the wider cosmos considered as a whole. The first attempts to "discipline" the big bang, sometimes called "big bounce" universes, construe our universe as one of the expansion phases of a sequence of infinite phases of expansion and contraction of the universe properly described. Hawking-Hartle no-boundary models provide one rigorous development of this conception. Stephen Hawking and James Hartle proposed a cosmological model that treats our universe as a bubble-like fluctuation in a quantum vacuum; a bubble that appears, grows, and then collapses in on itself. However, the best available current measurements of the expansion of the universe indicate that it is expanding too fast to ever re-contract to a big crunch. So, although these models are less ontologically profligate than multiverse theories discussed below, they also seem have a substantial empirical strike against them. It's possible that the future expansion of the universe could slow sufficiently to allow recollapse, but we don't currently have any evidence that we live in such a universe.

This leaves us with what we might call true multiverse theories: according to such theories, our universe is only one aspect of a greater reality consisting of many more or less similar copies of ours. There are many different versions of such a multiverse theory, but we can get the flavor of them by considering one that has received significant attention. In his 1997 book *The Life of the Cosmos*, physicist Lee Smolin suggested that our universe might be the "inside" or "opposite side" of a black hole that occurred in another universe. Black holes result from the collapse of a star or other supermassive object so large that no other force can overcome the internal gravitational attraction of the object's own mass. Such objects would collapse to a single geometrical point and create singularities that are the mirror image of the initial singularity of FLRW space-times. On such a view, our universe can be understood as merely a stage in the ongoing evolution of the cosmos as a whole, which should be understood as consisting of the whole set of produced and productive universes.

Smolin's black hole multiverse is simply the version easiest to describe in relatively concrete terms. The hypothesis that all of the components of the landscape associated with string theory or M-theory exist is another. All of these hypotheses have the advantage of making this universe merely one aspect of a radically Parmenidean greater reality. The initial singularity becomes physically tractable and, loosely speaking, the time associated with the evolution of this universe becomes a mere parameter placing this universe within its wider context.

However, one is forced to wonder what about such "hypotheses" could make them physical hypotheses. Smolin does suggest certain indirect tests for his theory of cosmological natural selection; however, in general, such hypotheses certainly seem more like the kind of desperate metaphysical speculation that Kant hoped to cut off at the knees with the first antinomy. What other than a metaphysical conviction that the whole of reality *must* be physically accessible to us could motivate such speculations? At least some defenders of the multiverse do so in order to block any connection between the big bang cosmology and religious conceptions of the creation of the world. So should religious believers take any solace from big bang cosmology? That's the question we now turn to.

The creation of the world and the structure of time

As we turn our attention back from physics to traditional metaphysical questions, the tensions between Parmenidean and Heraclitean metaphysics return to the forefront. On what can be easily recognized as basically Parmenidean grounds, some form of eternalism has been the default position in metaphysics and natural philosophy/science. Whether we consider the natural philosophy of Aristotle or the classical physics of Newton, creationism seems to make the world fundamentally mysterious rather than intelligible. Whether we see it as a presupposition or consequence of natural philosophy, the very practice of scientific inquiry rests on the intelligibility of the universe.

Unfortunately, a created universe seems to be a fundamentally unintelligible one. In the universe revealed to us by scientific inquiry, everything fits together with everything else. Each thing flows from and is determined by prior causes. Whether these are understood formally and genealogically as classical Aristotelian philosophy does or as the mechanical interplay between the purely corporeal objects of classical physics, each thing or event in the universe has its place. Except for any hypothetical first thing or event. By definition, it has no cause within the material universe. If that's correct, then in an important sense neither does anything else.

Certainly, this Eleatic intuition is too simple. Plenty of natural philosophers and scientists, of both Aristotelian and modern stripes, have belonged to religious traditions that explicitly state that the world is created. To pick just the most obvious, all of the Abrahamic traditions—roughly Judaism, Christianity, and Islam in all of their internal variety—agree that,

> In the beginning God created the heavens and the earth.

The general question of natural theology lies beyond the scope of this book. Here we are really focused just on the connection between the problem of the beginning of time and the status of the world as either metaphysically self-subsistent or divinely created. I suggest that there is much less of a connection than there is often taken to be. On the one hand, plenty of theists including St. Thomas Aquinas have held that God could have created an eternal world. On the other hand, the best argument to connect the beginning of the world to God—the Kalam cosmological argument discussed below—is deeply problematic at best.

The standard reaction of theists is to turn the Eleatic obsession with intelligibility back upon itself. Unless the cosmos is the created product of intelligence, the creationists argue, its very intelligibility remains inexplicable. If the world merely is and always has been, then there seems to be no reason to expect any unifying structure to be present within it.

It is this intuition that informs all of the cosmological arguments for the existence of God and the creation of the world. The general history and structure of cosmological arguments lies well outside the scope of this book. (See the Suggested Reading at the end of this chapter.) When placed into proper historical perspective, it is far from obvious that there is such a connection. Thus, Aristotle, whom we saw above is the quintessential eternalist, endorses and perhaps invents the crucial cosmological arguments from motion and causation. Aristotle claims that the presence of motion and causal order in the universe requires the presence of uncaused causes and unmoved movers respectively. Aristotle clearly understands these claims, endorsed by such religious thinkers as Maimonides and St. Thomas Aquinas, as entirely compatible with the eternality of change and motion.

This eternalism can be combined with the religious doctrine of the creation of the world as revealed in Genesis if we understand creation as a kind of ongoing dependence of the world on God. Instead of conceiving of the creation of the world as a singular divine act taking place at some particular time, we conceive of the world exhibiting an essential dependence on some deeper level of creative being. This isn't an unfamiliar strategy at this point; it's a version of the standard attempt to split the difference between Eleatic being and Heraclitean becoming that we've seen before. The fundamental structure of being serves an explanatory function within our metaphysical theories, but is not a replacement for our independent study of the natural world.

There is one traditional argument for the existence of God that cannot be given this gloss. In recent years, William Lane Craig, whom we have already met as a contemporary A-theorist and who is also a prominent Christian philosopher of religion, along with some other Christian philosophers has

---

KALAM   The universe has a nonphysical cause.

KALAM 1   Everything that begins to exist has a cause.
KALAM 2   The universe has a beginning.
KALAM 3   Everything physical is contained in the universe.

---

endorsed what they call the "kalam cosmological argument." The basic form of this argument is straightforward. It is given in the box above.
This is a slightly different version of this argument than one sometimes finds in the literature; KALAM 3 is not usually stated as a separate premise.

However, since much of the debate over this argument comes to grief over this issue, it's worth being explicit. The literature on both historical and contemporary versions of the argument is vast. We won't even attempt a survey here. Instead of adding to the debate over its soundness, we will see that the crucial "take-away" from that literature is that the argument is fragile.

There might well be interpretations of the crucial terms and claims in the premises that both make the argument valid and are plausibly true. However, there are equally plausible interpretations of the crucial terms and claims such that the argument is unsound, either because a crucial premise is falsified or because it is invalid. Put this in slightly different terms. Let's say that a "defeater" of the Kalam cosmological argument is an interpretation of one of its premises, plus a reason to find that interpretation plausible such that the argument is unsound, on that interpretation. I am not endorsing any particular defeater. Instead, I want to suggest that the ease with which critics generate such defeaters shows that there's something wrong with the whole debate.

There is an old carnival game called "whack-a-mole" that consists of a table with holes in it. Under the holes are spring loaded stuffed animals and when they pop up, you hit them with a mallet. Ultimately, the game is unwinnable; the moles come faster and faster until no one is able to keep up. When a philosophical debate begins to feel like a game of intellectual whack-a-mole, perhaps we should be suspicious that something is mistaken in the original problem situation. That's what seems to have happened here.

Begin with KALAM 2. First note that as with the other premises KALAM 2 can be given both a priori and a posteriori justifications. We have already seen that the a priori arguments for KALAM 2 are deeply problematic. They are all versions of the arguments against completed infinity, and we have already seen plenty of reasons to think that the simple incredulous stares which traditionally greet assertions of a completed infinity need to be replaced by arguments in our post-Cantorian age. Simply given the immense variety to be found in contemporary theories of infinite quantities, it seems unlikely that there is any simple logical error at their heart.

What about a posteriori arguments? It is probably not an accident that the first significant proponent of the big bang was a Catholic priest. However, I know of no evidence that Lemaître ever connected his physical theory directly to his religious beliefs. As we saw above the evidence for the big bang is at least equivocal as evidence that the universe, in a sense relevant to this argument, has a beginning. To put it another way, the applicability of KALAM 1 and KALAM 3 in this circumstance depend crucially on the details of what one means by the "beginning" of the "universe."

Consider a simple FLRW universe. As we saw, the singularity itself does not belong to the universe; it does not seem to be an event of anything like the kind on which we generally base our belief in KALAM 1. That the universe begins in a mystery might very well provide solace to religious believers; it seems to indicate that the world revealed by modern physical cosmology is not incompatible with their belief in a creator God. That is a long way from thinking that the existence of such a bizarre physical entity provides evidence, even defeasible evidence, for the existence of a personal Creator.

What about KALAM 3? Despite the fact that our universe is probably not a Hawking-Hartle no-boundary universe, it provides an interesting test of how crucial that premise is to these arguments. Those models seem to provide a cause of the beginning of the universe that is not God. This does seem to be a bit misleading; despite its name, the quantum vacuum is not *nothing*. It possesses energy that manifests as particles. William Lane Craig suggests that as such it is not an alternative to the explanation of the universe as created ex nihilo by God. However, we must then treat the quantum vacuum as a part of the physical universe, and we have no reason to think that *it* has a beginning.

In fact, all of the multiverse models of reality create similar problems for KALAM. What they demonstrate is that the connection between the big bang as the source of all matter and energy that we can detect is only equivocally connected to the origin of reality itself. It may well be that physical reality came into existence with the big bang and consists entirely of the matter and energy produced by it and spatiotemporally connected to us. This universe may also be an aspect of some larger reality whose structure is less congenial to the argument.

It is not my intention to defend either atheism or theism here, or even to claim that this is a definitive refutation of the Kalam cosmological argument—whatever that would amount to. Instead, I just want to indicate that this argument is much more unstable than some of its defenders seem to believe. Its persuasiveness depends on extremely fine-tuned interpretations of its premises; all of which are at least problematic. In addition, the historical evidence that the crucial religious questions are separable from claims regarding the beginning of time suggests theists might be well advised to proceed with caution and look for alternatives.

Cyclical time and repeating universes

All of the Abrahamic religions portray the working out of God's plan for the world according to a single linear progression. The world begins in an act of creation and eventually concludes once its purpose is fulfilled. This linear cosmology is far from the only or even the most common possibility. Cyclical cosmologies according to which the universe moves constantly through cycles of growth and decay have been at least as common in human history. Both the ancient Egyptians and Mayans seem to have had a fundamentally cyclical conception of the universe. Perhaps the most familiar cyclical cosmology today is that presented in the Vedas, the fundamental texts of the Hindu religions of India.

The cosmological timekeeping system of the Vedas consists of a complex system of nested cycles called *yuga*. The longest of these, the *kalpa* or day of

Brahma, is traditionally estimated to be approximately 4,000,000 years and is a period of growth, expansion, and life. This is followed by another period of the same length without life. As with the Christian cosmology discussed above, defenders of a cyclical universe have also found support from modern cosmology. The analogies between the Vedic cycles of the universe and the big bounce cosmologies have not gone unremarked.

There's not really much hope that I can settle the traditional religious/ philosophical disputes about linear versus cyclical cosmological systems. However, the analogy between traditional Vedic cosmology and modern physical models seems even weaker than that driving the connection between Judeo-Christian conceptions of creation and the big bang. If I'm right, then perhaps the best lesson to take from all of this is that the religious, philosophical, and physical debates each need to be settled on their own home grounds. Once again, there's no magic bullet in the philosophy of time.

We can clear up one bit of confusion. Cyclical cosmologies are often taken to point toward a cyclical conception of time itself. In a cyclical conception of time, precisely the same event occurring at the same time repeats itself. Even the notion of repetition is problematic here. When I repeat something, I create another of the same kind. In a truly cyclical temporal structure, it would be better to say that the same events become present more than once with an intervening period of time in which it is not present.

While such circular time may be possible, it also seems clear that it is not what traditional cyclical cosmology intends. Instead of the cosmological metaphor of life that drives the Judeo-Christian conception—the universe is born lives and dies much like a single organism—the cyclical cosmologies take the yearly cycle of the seasons as their dominant metaphor. Thus, the universe consists of a cycle of cosmic seasons much as the terrestrial year consists of a repeating cycle of terrestrial seasons of spring, summer, fall, and winter. To say that such a cosmic cycle repeats no more commits us to circular time than our belief that summer will return. Circular time might be possible, but the traditional cyclical cosmologies don't seem to offer any support for it.

Any such circular time would have to have some extremely odd properties. Consider the three events—A, B, and C—in Figure 8.1. Notice that event A is both earlier and later that events B and C. Depending on one's attitude toward the direction of time, this is either odd or incoherent. These prior occurrences, if they exist, don't seem to leave any traces for us to detect. At the very least, this implies that the circle of time is huge. We can currently detect light from objects about 10,000,000,000 light years away, which means

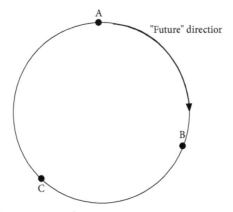

Figure 8.1 Three events in circular time.

that the light was emitted approximately 10,000,000,000 years ago. And there's no hint of such repetition in the available data.

There shouldn't be, though. In order for it to be the very same event it has to include us being in the very same state of not having prior experience of the event. What does it even mean to say that an event becomes present more than once, but does so exactly as if it had never become present before? How is that any different from the event merely becoming present once?

In addition, circular time seems to require that each event be past, present, and future *relative to itself*. This is a particularly striking example of McTaggart's paradox. In such a universe, the apparent directedness of time must be understood as a kind of illusion, in an even stronger sense than that suggested by entropic theories in Chapter 7. Instead of the creative Heraclitean flow into the future, we have a stagnating closed loop where the present creates only itself; we have a universe probably better described as not temporal at all. This seems to have been the fundamental point of the most famous defender of circular time. Friedrich Nietzsche's doctrine of eternal return seems to be less a metaphysical doctrine than a practical reminder. Nietzsche seems to be principally interested in getting us to abandon what he takes to be the illusion that we are creating the present by convincing us to embrace the belief that the present has and always will be what it is.

Whatever Nietzsche's, or Parmenides's, original intentions it is striking how much of contemporary physics pulls us toward a metaphysical picture in which human agency has at most an equivocal role to play. We have already seen that Einstein's theory of relativity seems to be incompatible with an ontological interpretation of the distinction between the past and the future and that the physical basis for the direction of time seems to be radically contingent. In our final chapter, we examine the evidence that Einstein's general relativity might allow for time travel and the complete breakdown of the past-future distinction on anything but a personal level.

Further reading

Basic background:

Immanuel Kant's most important works in metaphysics are *The Critique of Pure Reason* (1781/1787), commonly referred to as the first *Critique*, and *The Prolegomena to Any Future Metaphysics (1783)*. The first antinomy mentioned here is discussed in detail in the *transcendental dialectic* of the first *Critique* and in slightly more accessible form in §50–54 of *Prolegomena* dealing with the cosmological idea.

In addition to passages from *Physics* discussed above, Aristotle considers arguments for and against the eternity of the world in *On the Heavens*.

Toulmin, S. E. and Goodfield, J. (1965), *The Discovery of Time*, London: Hutchinson.

The best book examining all of the ways in which we have discovered that the universe itself has a history, in geology, biology, and in physics.

Munitz, M. K. (1981), *Space, Time, and Creation: Philosophical Aspects of Scientific Cosmology*, 2nd edn, New York: Dover Publications.

Some of the original sources for arguments considered in this chapter:

Swinburne, R. (1968), *Space and Time*, London, Melbourne: Macmillan; New York: St. Martin's Press.

Richard Swinburne's argument that time must be unbounded, including his "swans" example appear in Chapter 10.

Newton-Smith, W. (1980), *The Structure of Time*, London, Boston: Routledge & Kegan Paul.

Newton-Smith's criticism of Swinburne appears in chapter V, and is reprinted in Le Poidevin and MacBeath.

There are many introductions to modern cosmology.

Greene, B. (1999), *The Elegant Universe: Superstrings, Hidden Dimensions, and the Quest for the Ultimate Theory*, New York: W. W. Norton.

Greene, B. (2004), *The Fabric of the Cosmos: Space, Time, and the Texture of Reality*, New York: Alfred A. Knopf.

Greene, B. (2011), *The Hidden Reality: Parallel Universes and the Deep Laws of the Cosmos*, New York: Alfred A. Knopf.

These books are based on leading string theorist Brian Greene's popular television programs of the same names. They remain the best entirely nontechnical introductions to contemporary physics.

Guth, A. H. (1997), *The Inflationary Universe: The Quest for a New Theory of Cosmic Origins*, Boston, MA: Addison-Wesley Publishing, Reading.

Introduction to the post–big bang inflationary cosmologies by one of the initial discoverers of inflation.

The next stage of physics seems to require some reconciliation of quantum mechanics with general relativity in a theory of quantum gravity. Two useful resources are:

Callender, C. and N. Huggett, eds (2001), *Physics Meets Philosophy at the Planck Scale: Contemporary Theories in Quantum Gravity*, Cambridge, UK, New York: Cambridge University Press.

The papers in this volume generally presume substantial background knowledge in both physics and philosophy of science.

Smolin, L. (2001), *Three Roads to Quantum Gravity*, New York: Basic Books.

The article from The Stanford Encyclopedia on "Cosmology and Theology" by Hans Halvorson and Helge Kragh provides a somewhat more detailed account of the relationship between modern physical cosmology and religion, as well many useful references.

Kellenberger, J. (2007), *Introduction to Philosophy of Religion*, 1st edn, Upper Saddle River, NJ: Pearson/Prentice Hall.

Any standard introduction to the philosophy of religion has at least a chapter on cosmological arguments for the existence of God.

Friedrich Nietzsche introduces the doctrine of eternal recurrence in The Gay Science (1882/1887). It plays a major role in Thus Spoke Zarathustra (1883–1885), arguably Nietszche's most important work.

Discussion questions

1 Can you explain the distinction between the claim that the universe has a beginning and that time has a beginning? How might one's opinion on this dispute depend on one's position on the absolute versus relational debate of Chapter 6?

2 Can you explain, in conceptual terms, how it is possible for a finite amount of time to have passed without the existence of a first time?

3 Why does the fact that light from more distant stars and galaxies has a greater redshift imply that the universe is expanding? Can you visualize and explain how it is possible for the universe to appear to be expanding from every location? (Hint: In two dimensions, try to visualize yourself standing on the surface of an inflating balloon.)

4 Can you explain why the existence of the initial singularity might seem to vindicate religious traditions that believe in divine creation? Why does the possibility of a physical multiverse create problems for such intuitions?

5 What is the difference between circular time and cyclical cosmology? What are two reasons to suspect that even in a cyclical universe time itself must be linear?

Notes

1. We are largely going to ignore the more esoteric cousins of the big bang such as inflation. Among other problems, inflation seems to solve the "horizon problem"; widely separated regions of the universe are so similar that it seems that they must have interacted with each other at some point in the distant past. In the 1980s Alan Guth, Andrei Linde, and others proposed that, instead of expanding continuously from the initial singularity, the universe had a brief 10^{-36} seconds period of stability after the singularity followed by a period of exponential expansion lasting until between 10^{-32} and 10^{-33} seconds after the initial singularity. It then stabilized into the relatively slow period of nearly linear expansion in which we find ourselves today. Neither inflation nor its even more exotic cousins have much effect on the general questions about the beginning of time or of the cosmos that concern us in this chapter.

2. Technically, we are continuing to assume that time is a one-dimensional, connected, real manifold.

3. An open interval of the real numbers contains all of the numbers between two numbers, but not those numbers themselves. Closed intervals contain the endpoints.

9

Time Travel

What is *time travel* and what would it take for it to be possible? This chapter introduces both purely imaginary mechanisms, such as those in *Dr. Who*, and speculative physical mechanisms like worm holes. The chapter argues that all time travel requires an Eleatic eternalist metaphysics. In addition, while Einstein's general relativity might, in principle, allow for events that resemble time travel, such physical *causality violations* probably require kinds of matter and energy that have not yet been detected.

Introduction: Time travel in science fiction

H. G. Wells's *The Time Machine*; fifty years of *Dr. Who*; every version and variety of *Star Trek*; the *Terminator* movies; *Back to the Future* I, II, and III. These are just a few of the most famous examples of *time travel* in popular culture. Time travel, the ability to visit and perhaps alter one's own past or future, has become an important narrative device in all forms of science fiction, whether literary, televised, or cinematic.

The ubiquitous presence of time travel in popular consciousness is particularly puzzling because of a near universal agreement among philosophers that time travel is impossible and probably incoherent. Although there are examples of time travel that predate his work, H. G. Wells's *The Time Machine* provides the primary source and inspiration for the later proliferation of time travel stories. Yet Wells tells us essentially nothing about how the machine is supposed to work. Time travel probably represents the only example in which a literary device, introduced largely in order to sharpen certain social commentaries, comes to be treated as a metaphysical problem.

Wells's traveler tells us, without explanation, that time is a fourth dimension of space through which it is possible to move in a way precisely analogous to the ordinary spatial dimensions. For reasons we've explored throughout this book, that can't possibly be accurate. Even in modern physics, where time is treated mathematically as one of the four dimensions of space-time, it is not a fourth dimension of space. Two events separated from each other along the temporal dimension of space-time, time-like separated as physicists say, have a very different relationship to each other than do space-like separated events. Most importantly, time-like separated events can be causally connected to each other in a way that space-like separated events are not; this is why physicists often call time travel-like events causality violations.

The immediate problem with such scenarios, whether fictional time travel or physical causality violations, is their internal consistency. The most obvious such concern involves the existence of current records of the traveler's visit to the past. Why do there seem to be no records, consequences, or other traces of his invention of the time machine at times later than those he visits? As an aside, it's worth noting that this is one of the few serious aspects of time travel that the new *Dr. Who* gets right. Pretty consistently, the Doctor and his companions show up in the appropriate historical records of later times following their interventions.

So, our first task is to determine whether there could be a consistent and coherent representation of time travel. Only then will we be able to determine whether and in what sense it might be possible in the actual world. In order to do this, we are going to look at one popular and relatively contained presentation of time travel, that in the movie *Back to the Future*. *Back to the Future*, especially if we restrict ourselves to the first film, has certain advantages over other time travel franchises such as *Terminator* and *Dr. Who*. Most importantly it illustrates most of the philosophical pitfalls of time travel while still maintaining a reasonably coherent internal timeline. Trying to assemble a coherent timeline of the Terminator universe or of *Dr. Who*'s life is almost certainly impossible.

By contrast, the basic plot of *Back to the Future* is pretty simple. In 1985 Marty McFly uses a DeLorean automobile converted into a time machine to travel thirty years into the past, to 1955. On arriving he accidentally prevents a car accident that would have led, ultimately, to his parents' marriage and his own existence. Marty and the 1955 version of his friend "Doc," who will later invent the time traveling technology in the DeLorean, discover this when they examine a photo of Marty's family and discover that it is fading away. Marty spends the remainder of the film (re-)igniting his parent's relationship and locating a power source that will allow him to return to 1985. Both of which he accomplishes and in true Hollywood fashion returns to a much improved version of his family in 1985.

This relatively simple story illustrates the three principal pitfalls to which time travel stories are vulnerable. First, they need a consistent metaphysics of time and almost certainly an Eleatic one. Second, they need consistency in the world they portray; how is it possible that Marty McFly both does exist in 1985 in order to return to 1955, and does not exist in 1985 because his parents never got married? Third, like most time travel stories, *Back to the Future* makes no attempt to explain how all of this is supposed to work. Let's consider these in order.

First, what theory of time is compatible with time travel? It would seem that only an Eleatic metaphysics according to which past and future events and objects have the same basic metaphysical status as present ones could possibly be consistent with time travel. Consider two issues for Heraclitean time travel. At the most basic level all Heracliteans agree that the universe is flux, in some sense. The passage of time is not some additional fact laid on top of an underlying metaphysics of being; it is the one and only way that things, including ourselves, constitute a world. Moving around in Heraclitean time in any way analogous to moving around in space is a straightforward category mistake. According to Heracliteans, where things are is just another fact about them like their mass; when they are is the fundamental condition for their possessing any of these other properties or relations.

To make this a bit more concrete, consider contemporary A-theoretic or tensed versions of Heraclitean time. Whether conceived as a shared property or as a shared metaphysical status, being present is not a relation according to any of these theories. It literally makes no sense to say that the flux capacitor in the DeLorean moves Marty through time in such a way that 1985 ceases to be present to him and 1955 becomes present to him. The DeLorean cannot move Marty in time; it alters the fundamental metaphysical status of everything else in the world so that those things in 1985 cease to be present and presentness comes to inhere, once again, in 1955. Once we think about the flux capacitor resetting the entire universe to 1955, not merely moving Marty around, things become a whole lot less plausible.

However, a mere block universe or Eleatic metaphysics is not sufficient to allow for time travel. We also need the arrow of time to be contingent, local, and manipulable. As Marty travels back and forth through time his personal arrow of time continues to point in the direction he's currently moving. Otherwise, as he moved back toward 1955 we would expect him to get younger and younger until he reached the point before he was born and simply vanished. Even as Marty travels backward relative to the general history of the world, he continues to age normally in his own personal timeline. This seems to be a general requirement for any coherent conception of time travel. As the philosopher David Lewis famously described in "The Paradoxes of Time Travel," we must have a distinction between personal and external time, where personal time is:

> That which occupies a certain role in the pattern of events that comprise the time traveler's life. If you take the stages of a common person, they manifest certain regularities with respect to external time. Properties change continuously as you go along, for the most part and in familiar ways. First, come infantile stages. Last come senile ones. Memories accumulate. Food digests. Hair grows. Wristwatch hands move. If you take the stages of a time traveler instead, they do not manifest the common regularities with respect to external time. But there is one way to assign coordinates to the time traveler's stages, and one way only (apart from the arbitrary choice of a zero point), so that the regularities that hold with respect to this assignment match those that commonly hold with respect to external time.

Lewis's explication is worth quoting in full because it brings out the extent to which any meaningful discussion of time travel depends on quite substantive metaphysical presuppositions, including at least: eternalism, some version of the B-theory of tense, the lack of a metaphysically basic arrow of time, and probably a four-dimensionalist theory of persistence. If we have any reason to deny any one of these, then we have good reason to suspect that time travel is impossible despite its apparent familiarity.

So let's assume that we've already been persuaded by the arguments for a tenseless, eternalist Eleatic universe with a contingent direction of time. Could Marty have gone back and accidentally prevented his own birth? Almost certainly not. The movie scenario requires that two incompatible versions of 1985 exist; one in which Marty gets in the DeLorean, and one in which he simply never existed. But that's not one way the world could be, not one possible world, but two. As far as I can tell the only way to make sense of this is that the DeLorean is not a time machine but a world jumping machine. It takes Marty to a world that is precisely similar to his world up until the time of his appearance in 1955, at which point it begins to diverge.

Alternatively, consider the status of the past in Marty's world before he gets into the DeLorean. There should already be a record, somewhere, of his appearance in 1955. For example, all of his parents' high school classmates should remember the odd performance by the kid who looks exactly like Marty at their high school prom. He should have been hearing about this all his life. If instead he's jumping not into his own actual past, but into another possible world with a situation very similar to his in 1955, then things start to make better sense.

This is not quite the classical "grandfather's paradox" in which the time traveler takes actions that would prevent him from engaging in time travel. The problem here is not that Marty prevents his own birth in particular, but that every moment after his arrival in 1955 seems to exist in two distinct versions. But that's just nuts! There might be many ways the world could be, but it can only actually be one of those ways. Notice that future branching from 1955 doesn't help us here, since all of these are in Marty's own personal past. Unless we're back to world jumping, branch jumping in this case, one and only one of these branches must be actual for Marty. Therefore, a world with time travelers in it must be strongly fatalistic since the ability to do something other than what one actually did can trigger the need for multiple actualities. These worlds actually do manifest the problems that so bother people about Eleatic metaphysics and that we discussed in Chapter 4.

Suppose that we are persuaded that the basic metaphysical structure of the world is compatible with time travel and that the consistency constraint can be satisfied leading to a single history. That still leaves us with the problem of how. How are these devices supposed to work? As far as we can tell, they are simply magic. They operate either according to Clarke's Law or the principle of narrative necessity. The Doctor's time machine, the TARDIS, operates on scientific principles which human beings not only do not but apparently cannot understand—a classic instance of Arthur C. Clarke's statement that any sufficiently advanced technology is indistinguishable from magic. The phrase "flux capacitor" in *Back to the Future* simply functions as the magic spell necessary to give the filmmakers a story to tell.

The philosopher John Earman has called this variety of fictional time travel Wellsian. As in *The Time Machine*, one simply sits on, enters into, or otherwise activates some device; one disappears from the time at which the device is activated and reappears, perhaps sometime later along one's personal timeline, at a time different from that which one would have occupied if the device had not been activated. As far as we can tell such devices are prohibited by the laws of nature as currently understood.

The one possible exception would be the discovery of some way to travel faster than the speed of light. Traveling faster than light from Earth to the Alpha Centauri star system requires that one arrive at one's destination in time to receive a signal emitted at the time of one's departure that moved at the speed of light. Since light and other electromagnetic radiation travel along the null cone of the space-time metric, it literally takes zero time for the light to reach its destination. It therefore must take any traveler moving at more than the speed of light less than zero time. Literally, faster than light travel (FTL) *is* time travel. Unfortunately, as far as we can tell, it takes literally an infinite amount of energy to accelerate any massive objects to the speed of light.

However, the laws of physics might allow for some "cheats." Basically, they allow one to move the departure and the destination closer together instead of making the traveler move more quickly. We will discuss some of these later in this chapter; absent such cheats, FTL seems to be physically impossible and thus so is Wellsian time travel.

Philosophical arguments against time travel and backward causation

Suppose that we cannot rule out time travel on general Heraclitean grounds and that we can rule out obvious absurdities such as the requirement that the universe contain multiple overlapping actualities. There remain some more subtle objections to time travel. First, time travel seems to prohibit certain actions that seem to be otherwise possible; this is the famous grandfather paradox. Second, time travel seems to permit certain occurrences that seem to be otherwise impossible; this is the problem of causal loops or causal anomalies. Let's consider the grandfather paradox first. The name comes from the suggestion that a time traveler might, whether deliberately or accidentally, kill their own grandfather prior to the birth of their parent. In such a case it seems clear that the time traveler would not come into existence, and therefore not eliminate their grandfather, leading them to come into existence. This leads to an apparently straightforward contradiction according to which the time traveler both does and does not kill their grandfather.

Historical Note 22: Michael Dummett, David Lewis, and Analytic Metaphysics

In Chapters 6 and 7, and especially in Chapter 9, we have been introduced to a version of analytic philosophy that takes philosophy of science as fundamental. There is another strand that takes logic and philosophy of language as fundamental. As represented by Michael Dummett (1925–2011), this strand has tended to be more sympathetic to Heraclitean or A-theoretic accounts of time. Compared to the versions of analytic philosophy more influenced by philosophy of science, the versions represented here, and their defenders, are more concerned with the structure and presuppositions of common sense or what was once called "ordinary language." Michael Dummett (1925–2011) was an influential English philosopher of language and metaphysician who wrote extensively on time. In addition to the debates on backward causation, Dummett's "A Defense of McTaggart's Proof of the Unreality of Time" in 1960 deserves substantial credit for the continuing attention that McTaggart's argument receives. A paradigm example of this approach might be identified in the 1950's debate about backward causation culminating in Dummett's own "Bringing About the Past."

Among other significant figures, Arthur Prior (1914–1969), a New Zealander who spent many of his most productive years in Britain, deserves particular mention for his unflinching defense of a Heraclitean metaphysics (cf. Chapter 3, p. 75), and his creation of formal tense logic in an attempt to provide logical expression of such views.

While Dummett's general metaphysical position is antirealist, the American philosopher David Lewis (1941–2001) is often given credit for rejuvenating realistic metaphysics within analytical philosophy. In his *On the Plurality of Worlds,* he articulated a sophisticated defense of B-theoretic metaphysics as part of his defense of the existence of merely possible worlds. In addition, his "The Paradoxes of Time Travel" remains essential reading in that area of study.

Obviously the basic problem applies to any action time travelers might take to prevent themselves from engaging in the original time travel. The basic solution is the same as well: the same, currently unknown, laws of nature that permit time travel prohibit paradox-generating time travel. Suppose that I actually had some reason to murder one of my grandfathers when he was a young man and that I had access to a time machine. What I would find is that no matter how many attempts I make, something always interferes—the gun jams, I slip on a banana peel, etc. As best as the time traveler can tell, the only thing that the various interferences have in common is that they prevent me from generating a paradox. There seems to be some form of chronology protection law operating.

The existence of chronology protection doesn't quite solve the problem. It prevents the situation when I both do and do not travel in time, but does not seem to eliminate the fact that I both can and cannot carry out the actions that would prevent me from traveling in time. Consider the original grandfather paradox variant. I'm standing there in front of my grandfather with the loaded gun and every intention of pulling the trigger. If anyone else was there in the same circumstances and carried out the same actions, my grandfather would be toast. Because I happen to be the time traveler, some apparently otherwise random event occurs, and I fail.

It therefore seems to be the case that I both can and cannot kill my grandfather. This, while a bit more subtle, is just as much a contradiction as actually killing and not killing. The standard solution to this is that offered by David Lewis. The apparent contradiction is actually a fallacy of equivocation. What I can or cannot do is always defined relative to some background presuppositions, and the presuppositions at work in the two branches of the conjunction are different. I can carry out the assassination in the sense that any arbitrary person could do so, but I cannot in the sense that none of his grandchildren could.

Now this makes for a really odd universe given our ordinary conceptions of the natural world; the chronology protection agency seems to be a very bizarre law of nature. Somehow the universe knows and cares who is carrying out a particular action. It permits it for some and denies it for others. Why are there special rules for time travelers? Unfortunately, odd and impossible turn out to be two different things. The world presented to us in contemporary science is strange enough by the standards of common sense that additional oddities are difficult to rule out.

So if I can't kill my grandfather, could I become my own parent? This is the question posed by Robert Heinlein in his classic short story "'—All You Zombies—'." In the story the time traveling protagonist is both his own father and mother. The problem is: where did the original genetic information for this person, or these people, come from? He seems to be truly and entirely self caused, a power normally reserved to God. Again this seems to be a general problem posed by time travel. Another example might be someone stealing a time machine from a museum which they use to go back in time and place the time machine in the museum. Where does the time machine come from originally? It seems to simply appear as an uncaused component of the world locked into a loop.

One's reaction to such causal loops seems to depend on the depth of one's commitment to causality and the PSR. The classical PSR is precisely what it sounds like—a denial that anything just happens. In a universe where the principle holds, everything that occurs has an explanation, generally a causal one. Clearly a world with closed causal loops must violate the PSR as ordinarily understood.

What we make of this violation depends on what we believe about the status of the principle. If we agree with the traditional interpretation of the PSR as an a priori metaphysical principle, then this seems to rule out time travel involving causal loops. However, the current status of the PSR is problematic even absent time travel; both the big bang and radioactive decay seem to involve violations of the PSR. Why should we not interpret the existence of causal loops as another marker of the oddity of the universe compared to that of the classical representation of it?

There is one final philosophical dispute relevant to time travel debates: the problem of backward causation. The modern debate began with an exchange between Michael Dummett and Anthony Flew in 1954 and culminates, for our purposes, in Dummett's classic but difficult "Bringing about the Past." I'm not going to attempt to reconstruct the history of this debate here. Instead, we will examine two classic arguments that emphasize how fragile any purely philosophical conclusions regarding backward causation, including time travel, are.

The first argument is Max Black's "bilking argument." Consider two events A and B. Assume that the following two conditions both hold of A and B. B is later than A, and A is causally dependent on B. Now consider sometime between A and B. At any such time it seems to be possible to prevent B. Since it's now the case that A has already happened and B will not happen at all, B cannot be part of the cause of A.

At first glance, this seems like another version of the grandfather paradox, but that's not quite what's going on here. Suppose that I have an apparent time travel situation in which someone steps into a time machine in 2014 to prevent a murder in 1990. Suppose as well that the murder is successfully prevented in 1990. The bilking argument seems to show that my initial description of the situation must be mistaken. The "time traveler" does not prevent the murder by getting into her time machine in 2014; the prevention of the murder in 1990 causes her to get into the time machine in 2014.

However, notice that in setting up the bilking argument, we assumed that outside of the special cases the ordinary relationship between the past and the future holds good. Why should we assume that? What bilking arguments really seem to show is that a world with backward causation must be really weird! Once I have a world in which the global time order of events *can* be independent of the order of causal dependence, then they are always independent.

Let's consider one more of these, a variation on one from Dummett's "Bringing about the past." Imagine someone who believes that prayer can change the past. They believe, for example, that even if a loved one has already died in a car accident, praying for them to survive can be efficacious. In fact, assume that even in cases where one had been informed of the death, one followed up with prayer and in a significant proportion of cases the loved one later turned out to have survived.

What should we make of this? We might, at least initially, be tempted to explain this as coincidence. It might just be an accident that in the cases in which someone prays for the past the records or reports turn out to be mistaken. However, as Dummett points out we can complicate the situation so as to make this implausible. The alternative is just to accept that prayer does affect the past, and, therefore there are no reliable records of the past. Although Dummett does not put it this way, what he seems to be demonstrating is that the existence of backward causation requires us to deny the record asymmetry (cf. Chapter 7, p. 195 ff.) between the past and the future.

What all of these various arguments illustrate is just how bizarre a time travel universe must be. One cannot merely drop a time traveler into a universe which otherwise behaves in accord with our intuitions and end up with a consistent world. In any consistent time travel universe many things that seem impossible are possible and many other things that we expect to occur cannot. Our manifest image of time does not seem to allow for time travel or backward causation. The fact that the scientific image does allow for it, in a sense to be explored in the remainder of this chapter, emphasizes the ultimate conflict between these two approaches to understanding the world.

Technical interlude #4: Causality conditions in general relativity

There are two senses in which Einstein's theory of relativity seems to allow for the possibility of time travel. The first, which permits only time travel into the future, is the time dilation effect responsible for the twin paradox discussed in Chapter 6. In the space-time representation of special relativity, massive particles follow time-like trajectories through Minkowski space-time. Intuitively, this means that their world-lines are curves through space-time that are always directed within the future light-cone. The existence of multiple time-like curves connecting the same two events leads to the so-called "twin paradox."

Each of these distinct paths connecting the same two events has a different length as measured by the interval defined in Equation 6.8: the elapsed proper time for an object following one of those curves is the absolute value of that length. The proper time is largest for an object following an inertial path, one at rest in some inertial frame. It is reduced for objects which accelerate and decelerate relative to that frame. The closer that the average speed is to that of light, the closer the proper time comes to zero, which is the elapsed time of a light signal between the two events.

This means that it is possible for someone currently alive to examine the distant future of the human species using nothing more exotic than a sufficiently powerful spaceship. For example, in order to see what the solar system is like after 1,000 years of development by the people who stayed behind while only aging about ten years yourself, you would have to make a round-trip to an arbitrary point in space moving at an average speed of about 99.9975 percent of the speed of light. While the accelerations required for such a trip are probably unreachable and almost certainly unsurvivable, no exotic time machines are required.

In addition, general relativity also implies that gravity creates time dilation effects. Einstein's equivalence principle states that there is no physical difference between freely falling in a gravitational field and being at rest in an accelerating reference frame. As such, being at rest in a gravitational field also generates the kinds of time dilation effects that lead to the twin paradox, and another way to time travel into the far future would be to simply orbit a black hole sufficiently close to its event horizon.

To understand this the crucial thing to remember is that in *general relativity* space-time is curved by the presence of matter and energy as opposed to the flat geometry of Minkowski space-time. We define a flat space as one in which Euclid's classical parallel postulate holds for all points and all geodesics: for a given geodesic *l* and a point *p* not on *l*, there is exactly one geodesic through *p* that does not intersect *l*. However, in curved spaces there are either *no* parallel geodesics, such as on the surface of a sphere where all great circles intersect, or there are many, for example, in hyperbolic geometry.

I hope it is intuitively clear that there must be a sense in which the "straight" lines of such curved spaces must be curved when compared to an analogous flat space.[1] For example, the great circles on a sphere are the straightest curves along the surface, but they're still circles from the perspective of Euclidean space. One of Einstein's central insights was to extend the inertial principle in Minkowski space-time, according to which freely moving bodies follow time-like geodesics, to curved spaces via what he called "Mach's principle." As we've all seen in videos of astronauts, bodies in free fall, even those in orbit around a massive object such as the Earth, don't seem to be subject to any forces; they just float wherever they are placed. Mach's principle suggests that we must not treat these objects as being pulled out of an inertial path by the force of gravity. Instead they are simply following their natural path around a geodesic in a space whose shape is determined by the nearby mass of the Earth.

Finally, we generally assume that space-time is *asymptotically Minkowski*; a long way from any concentrations of matter or energy the geometry reverts to that of flat Minkowski space-time. But, this just means that free falling paths of objects near large masses are curved in a way analogous to the curved paths of the accelerated rocket ship of the traditional twin paradox.

Unfortunately, these are one-way trips into the future; there is no way to return to one's own past or send a signal back to the beginning of the trip. Neither the Minkowski space-time of special relativity nor the standard cosmological solutions of general relativity discussed in Chapter 8 allow for any *closed time-like curves* (CTCs). However, this is not true *in general* for the space-times of general relativity. Once it is possible for the structure of space-time to respond to the distribution of matter and energy, there are space-time structures allowed by the Einstein field equations much different from standard FLRW universes that do allow for CTCs.

The Einstein field equations that determine cosmological structure in general relativity are sixteen coupled nonlinear partial differential equations relating the distribution of mass and energy in the universe, *the stress-energy tensor,* to the geometry of space-time as represented by the curvature. These equations are extremely difficult to solve for arbitrary general cases. However, physicists have developed various mathematical techniques to allow them to identify the solutions. Two families of such techniques are relevant here.

First, one can look for symmetries in the matter-energy distribution that reduce the number of independent equations one must solve. For example, the FLRW space-times of standard big bang cosmology discussed in Chapter 8 as well as the Schwarzschild solution for the geometry surrounding a nonrotating massive point source were found by imposing very strong spherical and radial symmetry conditions. Some such cosmological solutions, to be discussed in the next section, have been found to permit CTCs.

Second, physicists attempt to classify various space-time structures in terms of general features of their causal geometry. As discussed in the "Technical Interlude" of Chapter 6, we can think of the geometry of a mathematical space as the description of various families of curves and the angles between them within that space. For example, the geometry of straight lines and their intersection forms the basic subject of classical geometry. Unfortunately, in curved spaces, and especially in the variably curved space-times of general relativity, the concepts of distance and direction become rather messy, to say the least.

In a flat space, I can just use a distance, or in Minkowski space-time the interval, to identify the geodesics through a point. I then apply the parallel postulate to identify families of parallel geodesics at each point in the space. These families of parallel lines then define all the directions in the space. Most importantly, I can use this classification to define whether a given curve at a point has a time-like, light-like, or space-like direction. Curvature breaks this connection between distance and direction: I can't directly infer a light-cone on the directions through a point from the distances to other points.

Instead, we go in the other direction. I begin with a classification of the directions of all possible curves through a given point in such a way that we can use it to derive the lengths of the curves and, thus, identify geodesics and a version of distance. Imagine that every curve through a point has a little arrow attached indicating how you need to "move" to continue the curve, its tangent vector. We then characterize the length or norm of each of these vectors by defining a metric, **g**. For those unfamiliar with vectors, all you need to know is that these metrics are analogous to the distance functions previously introduced on regular spaces. Just as with the Minkowski distance function, the Minkowski metric on the tangent spaces of a manifold partitions the tangent spaces at each point into cones of time-like, null (or light-like), and space-like components.

This lets us determine for every curve through a point whether it is time-like (light-like, space-like) directed based on its tangent vector. Events in space-time are time-like (light-like, space-like) separated depending on whether they can be connected by curves that are everywhere (time-like, light-like, space-like). Notice something odd about this definition: in principle the same two events could be both time-like and space-like separated from each other!

In this case we want to understand the relationships within and between classes of curves that can be characterized in terms of this light-cone structure of relativistic space-times. For example, we want to know whether any curve that always "points" in a future time-like direction can intersect itself, form a closed time-like curve. Physicists attempt to classify space-time structures according to certain requirements on the behavior of such curves by articulating various *causality conditions*. Physicists then attempt to understand what configurations of matter and energy, which stress-energy tensors, might lead to such geometries.

In a flat space-time such as Minkowski space-time the metric that determines the light-cone structure is the same everywhere, and so curves can't loop back on themselves while staying inside the light-cone, cf. Figure 9.1(a)

Minkowski space-time is:

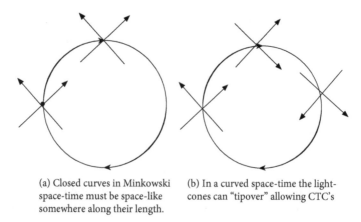

(a) Closed curves in Minkowski space-time must be space-like somewhere along their length.

(b) In a curved space-time the light-cones can "tipover" allowing CTC's

Figure 9.1 Closed curves in different space-times. (Arrowheads indicate future time-like direction.)

Chronological

There are no closed time-like curves.

However, there are other space-times, illustrated in Figure 9.1(b), where the light-cones "tip over" allowing material objects to loop around on themselves without ever having to move faster than the speed of light. Nonchronological space-times allow for something resembling time travel in a rather obvious sense. There is a path connecting certain events in the space-time with themselves. Such paths are not otherwise obviously different from other kinds of paths that objects can take through space-time. Other conditions that "well-behaved" space-times are sometimes required to obey include:

Causal

There are no closed nowhere space-like curves.

Strongly causal

For every point p in the space-time there is a neighborhood U of p such that no time-like curve intersects U more than once.

Some chronological, but acausal, space-times still allow for *causal* signals to be sent back to their own pasts. For example, suppose that we could send radio waves backward in time along the null cone.[2] Strong causality rules out "almost closed" paths. It means that no causal path comes arbitrarily close to any point in its own past.

There is a final standard condition, the one satisfied by the candidates for our actual universe.

Globally hyperbolic

A global time function for the space-time is definable.

There are various equivalent formulations of global hyperbolicity, but they all capture the sense that the actual world does seem to have a strong distinction between space and time. This seems also to be required if the Einstein field equations are to have a formulation as an initial value problem. Unless it is possible to make sense of the concept of the global distribution of matter and energy in the universe at a time, any hope of identifying the structure of the universe based on observational data seems lost. All of the standard big bang cosmologies are globally hyperbolic, although the same is not generally true for inflationary models.

Finally, it would be useful to identify some general rules about the kinds of matter-energy structures that appear in causality- or chronology-violating space-time structures. Unfortunately, the fact that the Einstein equations place essentially no constraints on the possible characteristics or distributions of matter makes this difficult. Instead, physicists attempt to characterize the behavior of "ordinary matter" in such a way that violations of these characteristics can be ruled out as "unphysical," or as not being candidates for the actual makeup of the world.

These conditions are called *energy conditions* and the hope is that properly characterizing the way that matter must be will allow us to rule out spatiotemporal pathologies such as causality violations. There are a variety of such conditions, many of them too technical to even be stated without advanced mathematics. However, *the weak energy condition* and *the dominant energy condition* are two of the most important, both in general and for purposes of the study of causality violations. Fortunately, they can also be given reasonably accurate formulations in ordinary language.

> **Dominant Energy Condition (DEC)** For every time-like observer, all apparent flows of mass-energy are causal, their velocity vector is within or on the light-cone.

> **Weak Energy Condition (WEC)** For every time-like observer, the mass-energy density of the universe everywhere is greater than or equal to zero.

> A time-like observer is just one whose world-line is a time-like curve.

Notice two facts about these conditions. First, notice that a violation of the dominant energy condition is equivalent to straightforward faster than light travel; therefore, it always allows for causality violations. Second, notice that matter that violates the weak energy condition would, among other oddities, manifest repulsive rather than attractive responses under gravity. This is what seems to involve it in most, but not all, known cases of causality violations that don't violate DEC. We'll examine a few of those in the next section.

Time travel and modern physics

One of the really surprising and odd things about Einstein's general relativity is that it turns out to be pretty easy to identify conditions that generate solutions to the field equations that contain causality and chronology violations. These solutions belong to two basic families: *Gödelian time travel universes* and *Thornian time machines*. (The terminology is based, once again, on that of John Earman.)

Gödelian universes are those that contain CTCs as a fundamental aspect of their geometrical structure. These are named after the most famous example, the solution to the field equations discovered by Kurt Gödel in 1948.The stress-energy tensor of the Gödel universe consists of a rotating dust cloud plus a negative cosmological constant, a universal repulsive force.

The geometry of the Gödel universe is extremely odd. For our purpose, the most significant consequence is that there are CTCs through every point in the space-time. These CTCs are not geodesics and would take significant power and acceleration to traverse. However, the costs have been calculated by the philosopher David Malament and while they're substantial, they're not absurd. For Gödel himself an even more significant feature is that there is no way to "slice" or *foliate* the space-time; there's a sense in which the passage of time in such a universe is truly illusory.

The Gödel universe and similar oddities are principally of intellectual interest. There are obvious observations that demonstrate that our universe does not have this structure. For example, in the Gödel universe, the entire universe is rotating around every point in the space-time. We rather obviously don't live in such a rotating universe.

Fortunately, there are various other "devices" or space-time structures that can exist in otherwise well-behaved space-times. As usual the details require more math and physics background than we are assuming in this book. Here, however, are three examples of a possible Thornian time machine, which is named after the physicist Kip Thorne, who provides us with our first example.

A wormhole is a path through space-time that has certain unusual properties. Let's consider two objects with time-like world-lines, for example, my apartment building and my office. In order to interact with the contents of my office from my apartment, I need to send a signal or influence along a causal path from one "spatial" location to the other.[3] The reception of the signals must be strictly later than the sending of the influence in all frames of reference.

Suppose that I could open up a hole which would be a time-like path connecting the two locations, but which connects events on their world-lines that would otherwise only have space-like separation. What this means is that I can reach through the hole and grab a book off my shelves before I could even send a radio signal to the office that I wanted it without using the wormhole. This is what I meant above about "cheats" to the ban on FTL. I connect events that would otherwise require FTL not by changing how fast I go, but by manipulating how "far" I have to travel. Here we have an example of events connected both by everywhere space-like paths and by time-like paths.

Now instead of using this as a library convenience, I open the wormhole between my apartment and a spaceship in orbit around the Earth. I now take advantage of ordinary time dilation effects and send the ship on a near light speed round-trip as above. I'm now connected to a period in the history of the Earth, an arbitrary time in my future; I can travel there and check it out. More significantly, my descendants can use it to come back and visit apparently allowing for the straightforward generation of CTCs.

So are such traversable wormholes possible? On the one hand, some arguments from quantum field theory seem to indicate that microscopic wormholes lasting tiny fractions of a second are constantly appearing and disappearing. However, converting such a wormhole into a stable traversable wormhole seems to require "exotic matter" that violates the weak energy condition. There are also some arguments from quantum field theories that macroscopic wormholes are fundamentally unstable. So perhaps the most interesting question raised by wormholes is philosophical rather than physical: what do we mean by possible and impossible?

There are two more typical examples of "Thorn-style" time machines. The physicist Frank Tipler proved that a rotating, infinitely long cylinder of ordinary matter can generate CTCs as the result of "frame-dragging" effects. Frame-dragging effects are an exotic consequence of general relativity, but basically they result from the requirement that the shape of space-time in the immediate vicinity of an odd structure like a Tipler cylinder must smoothly relax to ordinary Minkowski space-time a long way away from it. The other standard examples are "Kerr-Newman black holes." When a charged rotating star of sufficient mass collapses into a black hole, the "balance" between the electrical forces, the rotational energy, and the gravitational effects can cause it to collapse into a ring-like singularity instead of a point. There are a family of CTCs that loop around the ring-shaped event horizon of such black holes.

Finally, Stephen Hawking has argued that *all* space-times with CTC violate the weak energy condition. Hawking has claimed that this applies even in cases like Tipler cylinders, at least for non-idealized cases with finite cylinders. However, Hawking's theorems all involve quite strong assumptions in addition to the weak energy condition. Whether there are CTCs without violations of plausible energy conditions remains a matter of debate among mathematical physicists.

Philosophical consequences of the physics of CTCs

The fact that causality violations seem to be almost a generic feature of general relativistic space-times sets up two philosophical problems. First, why don't we see any evidence of causality violations to our past? Second, what does the possibility of closed time-like curves tell us about the relationship between the metaphysics of time and the physics of space-time? Let's begin by considering the nature of chronology protection hypotheses.

Chronology protection: What does the absence of causality violations tell us about the universe?

So, why isn't there any evidence of chronology violation? The first answer to this is simply that there just happens not to be any causality violations leaving traces within our past light-cone. That seems rather surprising given the range of phenomena that we can detect within our own past light-cone; we have at least partial data on a sphere about 10,000,000,000 light years in diameter which means signals going back equally far in time.

Instead, Stephen Hawking has postulated that there is a "chronology protection agency" at work in the universe. By this Hawking means not an actual agency, but some natural law that prohibits the formation of CTCs. The problem is to specify the conditions of chronology protection in a way that is not completely *ad hoc*. Let us assume that the conditions for the formation of CTCs are actually *generic*; there is no physical principle that always and only leads to the formation of CTCs. This is beginning to seem plausible; no one has yet managed to formulate a general condition on the kind of matter and energy that could lead to a CTC.

How then could the "universe" prohibit CTCs? It seems to require some actual agency in the universe that interferes as CTC-generating conditions form. Avoiding this is why Hawking and others have hoped that some version of the energy conditions could lead to a chronology protection theorem.

As mentioned above, Stephen Hawking once thought that the weak energy condition could serve this purpose. It does seem that most ordinary matter satisfies the weak energy condition. Unfortunately, it doesn't seem to work. The requirement that we respect the weak energy condition does place severe constraints on the generation of closed time-like curves, but the strong auxiliary assumptions required mean that it cannot prohibit them absolutely. Second, there do seem to be some effects in quantum field theory that violate the weak energy condition. For example, under certain conditions, the Casimir effect, involving two metallic plates a few nanometers apart in a vacuum, can lead to volumes of space with negative total energy.

This only seems to leave us with a few options to make sense of our observations. The first option is that something like the appropriate energy condition can be used to prove a chronology protection theorem. This is an active area of research in general relativity, but the prospects do not seem particularly bright. The second option is that the universe really is full of chronology violations, but that they are all hidden from us either in causally isolated regions of space-time, for example behind the event horizons of black holes, or to our future. This unfortunately seems to leave us with the same question: why?

It is possible, but unsatisfying, to think that we might just be unlucky. Perhaps, for no particular reason, our universe happens to be one where the initial conditions do not lead to causality violations.

The final option, intended only half seriously, is the existence of an actual chronology protection *agency*. I'm not sure that I've ever seen this discussed seriously in the physics or the philosophy literature, but Charles Stross explores it, to a certain extent, in his novels, *Singularity Sky* and *Iron Sunrise*. If we assume that causality violations are a routine aspect of space-time structure, then it seems likely that some time to our future some being will develop the ability to generate causality violations. It would be strongly in the interests of any such being to actively prohibit causality violations to its own past. Again, I intend this only half seriously, but it would solve the problem.

Finally, and most plausibly for those disturbed by the possibility of causality violations, this may simply be one of the places where general relativity breaks down. We know that at quantum mechanical length scales on the order of 10^{-32} meter and high energies, general relativity will need to be replaced by a quantum theory of gravity, whether string theory, loop quantum gravity, or one of the other esoteric alternatives. It may turn out that the true theory of gravity and space-time does not permit causality violations. Our experience with quantum theories of other domains should make us suspicious of such claims. This would be the only example of a quantum theory making things *less* weird.

Are closed time-like curves instances of time travel?

There are two reasons to suspect that the answer to the question in the title of this section is "no." The first is relatively restricted. We saw above that a clear definition of time travel seems to require a distinction between external time and personal time. Even space-times that are well behaved up to the operation of a Thornian time machine cannot be globally hyperbolic. There cannot be a universal definition of external time in any universe containing closed time-like curves.

In such a universe we simply have many distinct paths, some of which just happen to involve space-like or past-directed trajectories from the perspective of other observers. The simple fact is that in such a universe maintaining any commitment to the metaphysical significance of time would quickly come to seem foolish. When something occurred would become just as much a fact about its relationship to me as where it occurred.

Such a universe is likely to be a profoundly unfriendly place for human agents and in fact is likely to be largely incomprehensible. It's really not right to say that in such a universe one travels into either one's future or one's past. Because of the consistency constraints that would have to operate, it would be true from every when in my life that I have always been earlier and later in my lifetime. Here we have what seems to be the Eleatic dream realized. Neither my life nor the universe is the product of my agency or of change; it simply is tenselessly and timelessly. It's worth noting that demonstrating this Eleatic consequence of relativity theory seems to have been the primary motivation behind Kurt Gödel's original discovery of the first solution with CTCs.

This leads to the final reaction; something has gone horribly wrong. The possibility of closed time-like curves has seemed to many philosophers to confirm the suspicion with which Bergson greeted Einstein's theory of relativity. Bergson pointed to the twin paradox as evidence that whatever the theory of relativity is, it is not a theory of time. The possibility of closed time-like curves in general relativity seems to confirm this fact. Such philosophers need not deny the utility of general relativity as a physical theory of gravity. Instead they merely must remind us not to confuse such inadequate mathematical representation with the unrepresentable reality of becoming.

Further reading

Michael Dummett's "Bringing about the Past" and David Lewis's "The Paradoxes of Time Travel" are both reprinted in Le Poidevin and MacBeath.
The "bilking argument" originates in:

Black, M. (1956), "Why cannot an effect precede its cause?" *Analysis*, 16 (3): 49–58.

There are four directly relevant articles in The Stanford Encyclopedia of Philosophy. "Time Travel" by Nicholas J. J. Smith focuses on the classical philosophical debates sketched in the section "Philosophical Arguments against Time Travel and Backward Causation". "Time Travel and Modern Physics" by Frank Arntzenius and Time Maudlin addresses the general issues around CTCs in some detail. "Time Machines" by John Earman and Christian Wuthrich deals with how to characterize a time machine in a universe without a global time function. "Backward Causation" by Jan Faye focuses on exactly what it says it does. In addition, it's worth consulting,

Arntzenius, F. (2006), "Time travel: Double your fun," *PHC3 Philosophy Compass*, 1 (6): 599–616.
Another useful introduction with slightly different emphasis than this one.

Here are three attempts to "do" time travel fiction by physicists who actually know what they are talking about:
Baxter, S. (1994), *Ring*, New York: HarperPrism.
Benford, G. (1980), *Timescape*, New York: Simon and Schuster.
Forward, R. L. (1992), *Timemaster*, 1st edn, New York: TOR.

Finally, here are two general works on "weirdness" in general relativistic space-times:
Al-Khalili, J. (2012), *Black Holes, Wormholes, and Time Machines*, Boca Raton, FL: Taylor & Francis.

Earman, J. (1995), *Bangs, Crunches, Whimpers, and Shrieks: Singularities and Acausalities in Relativistic Spacetimes*, Oxford: Oxford University Press.

Parts of Earman's book are dauntingly technical, but his discussion of consistency constraints and Gödelian time travel is a classic.

Discussion questions

1   Can you explain two ways in which a Heraclitean metaphysics makes the consistent description of time travel even more problematic? After rereading David Lewis's distinction between external time and personal time, attempt to reformulate it in Heraclitean terms.

2   Why does the requirement that the world be a single way impose substantive constraints on time travel?

3   How does a version of the grandfather paradox arise even when a chronology protection law prevents me from killing my grandfather?

4   Why do causal loops seem to involve violations of the principle of sufficient reason? Do you believe that the violation of the PSR is sufficient grounds to rule out causal loops? Why or why not?

5   Energy conditions and causality violations:

   a   Explain the difference between ordinary matter and that which violates the dominant energy condition. What about the weak energy condition?

   b   What is the difference between chronology-violating and merely acausal space-times?

   c   Remembering that regions of high gravity involve time dilation, can you explain why it seems plausible that violations of the weak energy condition are involved in closed time-like curves?

6   Does the absence of chronology violations require explanation? Must any such explanation have independent motivation in order to be plausible?

Notes

1. This can be made precise, but not without a lot more math than we're going to mess with here.
2. See the novel *Timescape* by physicist Gregory Benford for an example of causality violations without chronology violation.
3. The concept of "spatial" location remains useful here because the various entities approximately share a rest frame.

10

Conclusions and Open Questions

So where are we? Way back in the introduction we set up the problem of time as the conflict between Eleatic partisans of being and Heraclitean advocates for radical flux. We saw that the most radical form of the Eleatic dream is idealism; in their purest forms the philosophies of being insist that the material world of change and becoming is an illusion. In Chapters 2 and 3, we saw that the two classic attempts to demonstrate the incoherence of becoming fail. Neither Zeno nor McTaggart manage to demonstrate the unreality of becoming, but they do both leave us with a much more clearly focused sense of the problems involved in explicating becoming.

Radical Heracliteans, who generally wish to promote the lived and felt experience of human life over theoretical understanding, can take little solace from that fact. The most plausible accounts of becoming resulting from those arguments explain becoming in terms of some more permanent underlying structures. In addition, Chapters 4 and 5 tried to show that the phenomenology of human life is not as resistant to explanation in terms of the structure of being as it might seem to be. We seem to be able to do better than silence or poetry.

Finally, in Chapters 6–9, we explored the transformation of time at the heart of the evolution of modern physics from Newton to Einstein and beyond. In doing so we uncovered many of the roughly Eleatic conclusions that flow from modern physics. The theory of relativity seems to make it almost impossible to explain becoming by appealing to changes in the total content of the universe; neither presentism nor the growing block even seems to have a coherent formulation in a relativistic universe. Similarly, investigation into the arrow of time at least suggests that it is contingent and not determined by any fundamental principle. Finally, our examination of time travel and physics also suggests that the appearance of objective time in our universe is the accidental product of living in a well-behaved universe.

Things are looking grim for Heracliteans, but perhaps not quite as bad as they seem at first glance. There are a few alternatives available. One might rely on the few clues that the Eleatic appearances of modern physics are merely appearances. For example, we saw in Chapter 8 that the universe itself, considered as an object of physical study, seems to be evolving. How is that possible? What is the source of the universe? This provides at least a hint of the kind of spontaneity characteristic of Heraclitean universes.

Things aren't quite as sanguine for the most radical Eleatic theories as they might seem either. The universe of modern physics is not a completely atemporal Parmenidean monad. Instead, it is an arrangement of matter and energy within a spatiotemporal manifold. Evolution in the time-like direction of space-time may not be metaphysically fundamental becoming, but it's not an illusion either. According to most interpretations of modern physics, our experience of the world is another model of the same world as that given a more adequate representation in physics. We don't abandon the world of the manifest image in favor of the scientific world; we use the scientific image to *explain* the manifest image.

Since our manifest image of the spatiotemporal world is not so much a matter of illusion as of incompleteness, physics actually points us at something more like what the introduction calls Platonic reductionism than Parmenidean idealism. Even Plato's version of the Platonic model seems to remove the fundamental physical principles too far from the world as experienced. Instead, a more Aristotelian perspective might better match up with our natural philosophy of time; these fundamental principles act within the world to produce the world, including beings like us who have a particular perspective on the world. However, part of that perspective is the ability to move beyond our limited position and begin to understand the fundamental principles on something like their own terms.

The philosopher Abner Shimony once claimed that the fundamental problem of philosophy of time was to "close the circle," to explain how the apparently atemporal principles of the physical world generate the world of appearance. We've already been introduced to some of the questions that need to be answered if we are going to close the circle. Among others, we

- need an adequate account of human agency and deliberation compatible with the eternalism of contemporary physics. Whether such an adequate philosophical anthropology is entirely naturalistic or not, it shouldn't contradict what physics tells us about the world.

- need an account of how time consciousness arises. This probably requires a general account of the mind-body relation in addition to everything else we saw was involved in Chapter 5.
- need to make sense of the possibility of acausal space-times and what that does or does not tell us about our place in the world.

There are other problems that we have only barely mentioned here. I leave you with two, each of which has the potential to radically transform the problems of time presented here. First, we have largely treated the manifest image of time as subject to introspection; we have followed Augustine in assuming that we "know" it even if it resists explanation. However, time is not merely personal, but social. Time is deeply embedded in our social relationships, and there is at least some evidence that different cultures have very different "times." How do these sociocultural questions about time fit into any kind of metaphysics of time? Do they require that we adopt a kind of cultural metaphysical relativism parallel to the cultural ethical relativism advocated by some anthropologists?

Second, at various points in Chapters 8 and 9, it was suggested that Einstein's general relativity needs to be replaced by an alternative theory of gravity compatible with quantum mechanics. Unfortunately, all of the currently legitimate competitors make the problem of closing the circle profoundly more difficult. The most popular alternative in mainstream physics is string theory which claims that the universe is the "product" of the behavior of strings in an eleven-dimensional space-time, ten space-like dimensions and one time-like. Other alternatives, such as loop quantum gravity, propose that the spatiotemporal universe is the emergent product of entirely non-spatiotemporal phenomena. For our purposes, what they have in common is that they make it ever more profoundly difficult to understand how to connect the world of OMDGs to that of fundamental physical theory. Perhaps, these theories herald the ultimate dissolution of our dichotomy; those of an Eleatic temperament can embrace the pure mathematical being of contemporary physics while Heracliteans can accept that the ordinary world of becoming cannot be explained in those terms.

I hope not! This kind of move combines the least attractive features of Heraclitean and Eleatic approaches to the world. But that's just me. If only because of my own temperament, I continue to hope that time will provide the key to see how the world as a whole fits together. You may, however, feel that the intractability of these problems points in a different direction. Like so much else in the philosophy of time, that too remains a matter of judgment.

Technical Terminology

A-determination The properties or relations that constitute the A-series. Past, present, and future are A-determinations, as are such properties as "being 10 years in the past." Chapter 3

A-series, B-series, and C-series McTaggart's A-series, B-series, and C-series are three distinct orderings of events and/or instants of time. The C-series simply associates a simple linear order with the set of events. The B-series adds a direction from earlier to later events to that ordering. An A-series ordering attributes presentness to a particular instant or set of simultaneous events. All other moments are located in the A-series a greater or less distance into the past or the future depending on their relationship to the present. Chapter 3

absolute theories of time Any theory according to which time is independent of the events in the world. Absolutists generally claim that time is not merely independent of the particular events in the world but of the occurrence of anything at all. In the purest form, an absolutist believes that time can pass even in a completely empty universe. Chapters 3 and 6

abstract An object that does not exist at any particular location in space or time and, generally, does not interact with OMDGs via causation. Chapter 4

block universe The most common contemporary version of eternalism according to which everything exists relative to all times, but is distributed along both the spatial and temporal dimensions. In this sense, rather than being a succession of three-dimensional arrangements of things in space, the universe is conceived as a four-dimensional block, but without boundaries. Chapter 4

cardinality The size of a set defined as the number of elements. Two sets are the same cardinality if and only if there is a one-to-one correspondence between the elements of the set. Chapter 2

causality violation Time travel. Any physical situation generating closed or almost closed causal (i.e., time-like and/or light-like) curves in a relativistic space-time. Chapter 9

chronology protection agency Any hypothetical mechanism that prevents the formation of causality violations. Chapter 9

closed time-like curve Just what it says—any curve through space-time which is both time-like, and thus traversable at less than the speed of light, and closed like a circle. Chapter 9

compatibilism A collection of theories according to which human beings possess free will and significant agency despite metaphysical determinism of the universe. Chapter 4

Eleatic 1. Originally, the name for a school of philosophers founded by Parmenides of Elea. 2. The general philosophical attitude characteristic of the original Eleatics according to which the apparent world of becoming is a mere illusion or mistaken impression of pure being. Chapter 2

eternalism The claim that everything that ever has or will be exists alongside those things that exist in the present. While there are and have been idealist versions of eternalism, such as Augustine's, according to which the truly real beings exist together outside of time, the most common contemporary versions are block universe theories. Chapter 4, *see* block universe

event horizon The boundary of a region of space or space-time from which it is not possible to send signals to the remainder of the universe. For example, the event horizon marks the edge of the region surrounding a singularity at the heart of a black hole from which not even light can escape. Chapter 9

four-dimensionalism Based on the conception of time as the fourth dimension, another synonym for block universe. Sometimes used in a more restrictive sense for theories of persistence of objects that conceive them as extended in time analogously to their extension in space. Chapter 4

Friedman-Lemaitre-Robertson-Walker cosmological models The family of expanding universe solutions to Albert Einstein's equations of general relativity. These are the theoretical basis for contemporary big bang theory and physical cosmology more generally. Chapters 8 and 9

future contingent For many, if not all, future events, it seems to be possible that they could either occur or not occur; that they are contingent as opposed to the necessity or impossibility of the past. This is sometimes applied to statements or propositions about the future whose truth-values are taken as either subject to change or indeterminate. Chapter 4

gauge transformation Any transformation of the physical laws such that the new version represents the same underlying physical reality. The name comes from the fact that the choice of measurement units, the gauge, should be arbitrary and independent of physical situation. Chapter 6

Gödelian time travel Cosmological models of general relativity, like that discovered by Kurt Gödel, containing closed time-like curves. Chapter 9

Hawking-Hartle no-boundary universe Stephen Hawking and James Hartle proposed an alternative cosmological model to standard big bang and inflation models according to which our universe is the result of a quantum fluctuation in a quantum vacuum. This is one example of various expanding universe models without a first time or moment of creation. Chapter 8

Heraclitean 1. Originally, the name of a school of philosophers founded by Heraclitus of Ephesus. 2. The general philosophical attitude characteristic of the original Heracliteans according to which the universe is pure flux and does not contain any permanent substances. Chapter 2

idealism What appears to be an independent feature of the world is actually merely a mental construct or idea. In its most general form idealism is the metaphysical theory that only minds and their ideas exist. Chapter 3

indeterminacy/determinacy An entity is indeterminate if it neither has nor lacks some property that it would ordinarily possess. Thus, a sentence or proposition is indeterminate with respect to truth-value just in case it is neither true nor false, and an ordinary middle-sized dry good is indeterminate with respect to color if it is no particular color. The future is often characterized as indeterminate in this sense, while the past is determinate. Chapter 4

indeterminism/determinism An event is determined just in case its own causal antecedents require that it, and no other event, occur. Determinism is the metaphysical position that everything that occurs is determined in this sense, especially including human decisions and actions. Indeterminism is the contrary of determinism so that an indeterministic event could be otherwise. Indeterminism must be distinguished from indeterminacy; many past events, for example, nuclear decay events, are indeterministic despite now being entirely determinate. Chapter 4

indexical A word or phrase whose reference depends on the context of use. For example, "I" refers to different people depending on who uses it, usually to the speaker. Tense markers for verbs as well as explicit references to the A-series function to give an indexical character to whole sentences. Sometimes called "token-reflexives" because an early theory suggested that the meaning of indexical types could be defined in terms of the reflexive self-reference of particular tokens. *see* type-token distinction

inertial frame of reference A frame of reference is a system for representing the spatiotemporal location of events and the path of objects through space and time. Such a frame of reference consists of a reference object serving as the origin point of a three-dimensional coordinate system for space and an associated reference clock or time standard. An inertial frame of reference is one in which the reference object only undergoes inertial motion in accordance with Newton's first law of motion. Chapter 6

intentionality "Aboutness"; the features of anything, especially thought or language, in virtue of which they represent something else. Chapter 5

logical fatalism The general name for a group of philosophical positions or arguments that attempt to demonstrate a strong version of determinism from the logical properties of sentences about the future. Aristotle's sea-battle argument is the most well-known example. Chapter 4

manifest image The world of ordinary experience as transformed by philosophical reflection and theorizing into a theory of the world. The passage of time is clearly a fundamental element of any manifest image of the world. Chapter 6

multiverse Any of a variety of physical theories that treat our universe as merely one part of some larger physical reality. Chapter 8

mysterianism Used as a general term for any philosophical position that treats some aspect of the world as not subject to rational explication. Originally proposed by contemporary philosopher Colin McGinn as a name for his position on the nature of consciousness. Chapter 1

null cone The set of all events with null separation is the surface of a four-dimensional cone in four-dimensional Minkowski space-time. Chapters 6 and 9

ontological commitment A philosophical term of art, from W. V. O. Quine, for the fact that certain beliefs or theories commit us to the existence of particular things in the world. Chapter 4

ontological dependence One entity, for example, my cup, is ontologically dependent on another, for example, the plastic that makes up the cup, just in case the first cannot exist without the second. One test of ontological dependence is to imagine a world in which the second one is destroyed, would the first continue to exist? I cannot destroy the plastic that makes up the cup without destroying the cup. Chapters 3 and 4

ordinary middle-sized dry good (OMDG) Used here as a general term for the ordinary stuff of the world, including human beings, animals, inanimate material objects, stuff like water, and artifacts. Chapter 3

particular An entity that exists exactly once, if it exists at all. Individual material objects are the paradigm example of particulars. Unlike universals, any two things that have any difference between them cannot be the same particular. Chapter 3

phenomenal The way something seems to us considered in itself. Used in Chapter 5 in contrast with the intentional features of an experience. Chapter 5

phenomenology Generically, the study of experience and of how things manifest themselves to us. More specifically, a particular method, associated with Edmund Husserl, dedicated to the description of experience. Chapter 5

possibilia Any hypothetical entity which could exist but does not. Chapter 6

presentism The claim that only those entities that are present exist. Contrast with eternalism and growing block. Chapter 4

principle of sufficient reason The general metaphysical principle that every occurrence in the universe must have happened in precisely that way and no other for some discoverable reason. Chapters 6 and 9

proposition The abstract object suggested as the meaning of indicative sentences. Two sentences can make the same statement when they express the same proposition, even when the sentences are in different languages. Chapter 3

realism The opposite of idealism. Realists believe that some or all of our beliefs about the world refer to entities that are ontologically independent of us. Chapter 3

relational theories of time The opposite of absolute; time depends on the occurrence of at least some events in the universe. Chapters 3 and 6

retention/protention Philosopher Edmund Husserl's terms for the influence of past events, via retention, and future events, via protention, on the constitution of present experiences. Chapter 5

scientific image The world as it is represented in modern scientific theory. The scientific image of the world clearly contains many things not present in the manifest image, for example, subatomic particles, and does not contain many things that feature in the manifest image, for example, colors and possibly time. Chapter 6

secondary quality Features, such as color, which seem to be properties of objects in the world but which actually depend on our ability to perceive them. Chapter 3

semantics The study of the way that language and other meaning-bearing entities "hook up" with the world. For example, the attempt to understand the reference of names and the truth-conditions of indicative sentences. Chapter 3

sophism A logical fallacy, but especially one that is rhetorically persuasive and gives the appearance of philosophical insight. Chapter 2

stress-energy tensor The measure of the total matter and energy contained in some volume of space-time used in general relativity. Chapter 9

substance Something ontologically independent of any other entities. Chapter 2

tense logic The general attempt to model the temporal properties of ordinary language by constructing formal languages analogous to those of modern symbolic logic. Chapter 4

tensed theory of time Any theory of time that takes McTaggart's A-series as a fundamental feature of reality. Also called A-theories. Chapter 3

tenseless theory of time Any theory that attempts to account for the appearance of becoming without treating the A-series as a fundamental aspect of reality. Also called B-theories. Chapter 3

Thornian time machine Some universes are well behaved, that is, they do not contain causality violations, for some "initial" region despite containing structures that act like time machines and generate closed time-like curves. Universes containing wormholes, Kerr black holes, or Tipler cylinders are examples. Chapter 9

time dilation The consequence of special relativity according to which moving clocks measure less time passing than do clocks at rest in a particular reference frame. This leads to the twin paradox. Chapters 6 and 9

time-like, space-like, and null separation between events Although special relativity demonstrates that neither spatial nor temporal separation between events can be a fundamental physical quantity, there is another quantity, the spatiotemporal interval, that is invariant in all inertial frames. Unlike ordinary distances, the *interval* can take any value—positive, negative, or zero. Relative to each event, those events with a positive interval are called space-like and are simultaneous with that event in some inertial frame. Events with null separation can be reached by a signal traveling at the speed of light. Events with a negative interval are time-like separated and can be reached by traveling at less than the speed of light. Chapters 6 and 9

type-token distinction In philosophy of language, a linguistic type is the set of all utterances or inscriptions in a particular language that have the same meaning. Tokens are particular utterances or inscriptions of a word, phrase, or sentence type. The distinction corresponds roughly to sense in which two

276 Technical Terminology

copies of the same book, the tokens, are also the same thing, that is, of the same type. Chapter 3

universal A universal is an entity that can exist, or be instantiated, more than once. For example, properties and relations. The contrast is with particulars. Chapter 3

Wellsian time travel Fictional time travel models, like that of H. G. Wells's *The Time Machine* in which some device allows one to appear at an arbitrary point in time. Chapter 9

wormhole Any path through space-time connecting events that would otherwise be "farther apart." Often used for time-like paths created between otherwise space-like separated events. Chapter 9

Index